★ ★ ★ ★ ★ ★ ★ ★ ★ ★ ★ ★ ★ ★ ★ ★ ★ ★

ADVANCE PRAISE FOR *E PLURIBUS ONE*:

"What a fantastic, straightforward, and honest book about what our founding fathers and mothers envisioned for us as one unified and proud nation."
—*Betsy Rothstein, Columnist,* The Daily Caller

"A must-read for anyone who wants to understand the beginnings and greatness of America."
—*Mayor Kevin L. Faulconer, San Diego, California*

"Sophia Nelson reviews and revives the unshakable values that bonded Americans from our founding— through the Civil War—to the present. It's nothing short of magnificent, serving as inspiration for every citizen who seeks our national healing."
—*Donna Brazile,* ABC This Week *Contributor*

"Sophia Nelson has done it again. *E Pluribus One* is more than just an American history book, it is a book of American inspiration and what has kept us one, united people for over 240 years."
—*Rebecca Lopez, WFAA Dallas News*

★ ★ ★ ★ ★ ★ ★ ★ ★ ★ ★ ★ ★ ★ ★ ★ ★ ★

★ ★ ★ ★ ★ ★ ★ ★ ★ ★ ★ ★ ★ ★ ★ ★ ★ ★

ADVANCE PRAISE FOR *E PLURIBUS ONE*:

"Sophia Nelson makes a compelling case
for a fractured America to realize that we are
still in this thing together. It may not feel like it,
but we are more united than divided."

—*Roland S. Martin*, Tom Joyner Morning Show
and News One Now Anchor

"In times of great turmoil, Sophia Nelson
reminds us that our nation is stronger when we
celebrate and respect our diversity, that our survival
depends upon an enlightened citizenry."

—*A'Lelia Bundles, Chairman, National Archives Foundation*

"As America looks for guidance and direction
this book provides a road map. Sophia Nelson brings
critical thinking to the nation's attempt to unify."

—*Ed Gordon*, The Steve Harvey Morning Show
and host of Ed Gordon *on Bounce TV*

★ ★ ★ ★ ★ ★ ★ ★ ★ ★ ★ ★ ★ ★ ★ ★ ★ ★

e Pluribus
ONE

e Pluribus

ONE

Reclaiming
Our Founders' Vision for a
United America

SOPHIA A. NELSON, Esq.

CENTER
STREET®

NEW YORK   BOSTON   NASHVILLE

* * * * * * * * * * * * * * * * * *

AUTHOR'S NOTE

The author wishes to acknowledge that she has used mostly secondary (and some primary sources where available) to compile the biographical sketches for the men and women profiled in each chapter of this book. This book is meant to be more current affairs, political science, and political inspiration as opposed to historical biography. Hence, the author was careful to provide sources in the endnotes section, indicating where she gathered her information for the book as well as how she adapted, analyzed, and/or interpreted secondary sources such as abstracts, articles, encyclopedias (online such as Wikipedia and *Encyclopaedia Britannica*), history and biography websites, as well as the Library of Congress, historical societies, and scholarly texts. Every possible effort has been made to properly credit every source used. If a source was left out in error, please bring it to the publisher's attention and we will gladly correct and update subsequent editions of the work.

* * * * * * * * * * * * * * * * * *

Center Street
Hachette Book Group
1290 Avenue of the Americas, New York, NY 10104
centerstreet.com
twitter.com/centerstreet

First Edition: January 2017

Center Street is a division of Hachette Book Group, Inc. The Center Street name
and logo are trademarks of Hachette Book Group, Inc.

The publisher is not responsible for websites (or their content)
that are not owned by the publisher.

The Hachette Speakers Bureau provides a wide range of authors for speaking events.
To find out more, go to www.HachetteSpeakersBureau.com or call (866) 376-6591.

U.S. Constitution image © iStock.com. The Great Seal image © shutterstock.com.

Book design by Timothy Shaner/nightanddaydesign.biz

ISBNs: 978-1-4555-6939-7 (hardcover), 978-1-4555-6937-3 (ebook)

Printed in the United States of America

LSC-C

★ ★ ★ ★ ★ ★ ★ ★ ★ ★ ★ ★ ★ ★ ★ ★ ★ ★ ★

To Alexandra and Mikaela Nelson

May the America you inherit from my generation
be as great as the one I have lived in and benefited
from so abundantly thanks to my parents' and
grandparents' generation.

America is the greatest land on the face of the earth.
Never forget it.

Please be good and engaged citizens. Help to make
America an even greater nation for the children and
grandchildren I pray you are blessed to have someday.

Love always,
Aunt Sophia

★ ★ ★ ★ ★ ★ ★ ★ ★ ★ ★ ★ ★ ★ ★ ★ ★ ★ ★

CONTENTS

★ ★ ★ ★ ★ ★ ★ ★ ★ ★ ★ ★ ★ ★ ★ ★ ★ ★ ★

SECTION I: THE CITIZENS' CODES

CONTENTS

★ ★ ★ ★ ★ ★ ★ ★ ★ ★ ★ ★ ★ ★ ★ ★

CONTENTS

★ ★ ★ ★ ★ ★ ★ ★ ★ ★ ★ ★ ★ ★ ★ ★ ★ ★

15 FUNDAMENTAL CODES OF OUR FOUNDING FATHERS*

1. The United States of America shall be a republic.

2. All men are created equal, and are endowed by their Creator with certain unalienable Rights, among them Life, Liberty, and the Pursuit of Happiness.

3. The unalienable rights of the people are most likely to be preserved if the principles of government are set forth in a written constitution.

4. A constitution should be structured to permanently protect the people from the human frailties of their rulers. Efficiency and dispatch require government to operate according to the will of the majority, but constitutional provisions must be made to protect the rights of the minority.

5. The proper role of government is to protect equal rights, not provide equal things.

6. A system of checks and balances should be adopted to prevent the abuse of power. The government should be separated into three branches: legislative, executive, and judicial.

7. Only limited and carefully defined powers should be delegated to government, all others being retained in the people. Strong local self-government is the keystone to preserving human freedom.

8. A free people should be governed by law and not by the whims of men. A free people cannot survive under a

★ ★ ★ ★ ★ ★ ★ ★ ★ ★ ★ ★ ★ ★ ★ ★ ★

republican constitution unless they remain virtuous and morally strong. The most promising method of securing a virtuous and morally stable people is to elect virtuous leaders.

9. The core unit that determines the strength of any society is the family; therefore, the government should foster and protect its integrity.

10. A free society cannot survive as a republic without a broad program of general education.

11. The majority of the people may alter or abolish a government that has become tyrannical.

12. Life and liberty are secure only so long as the right to property is secure.

13. The highest level of prosperity occurs when there is a free-market economy and minimal government regulations.

14. The burden of debt is as destructive to freedom as subjugation by conquest.

15. The United States has a manifest destiny to be an example and a blessing to the entire human race. Peace, commerce, and honest friendship with all nations—entangling alliances with none.

---

* These fifteen principles were adapted from the book *The 5000 Year Leap*, by W. Cleon Skousen. There are twenty-eight actual principles but I adapted fifteen of them that most closely fit the codes we wanted to discuss in the book.

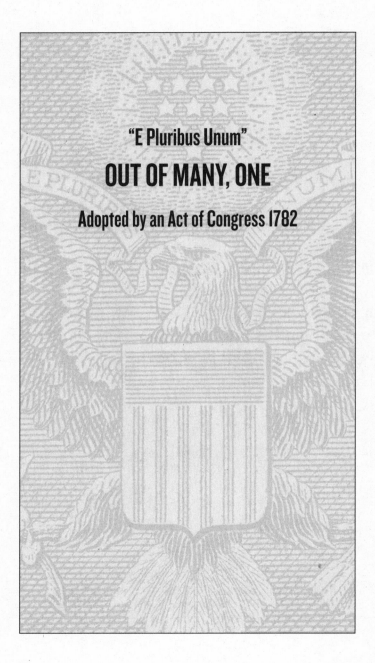

"E Pluribus Unum"

OUT OF MANY, ONE

Adopted by an Act of Congress 1782

PROLOGUE: *E PLURIBUS UNUM*

We the people. We. Us. Not them versus us. America is the story of us. And it is time for us to make America one. To make America whole. To bind up our wounds and go forward wiser. Stronger. And better, together.

Our nation has just come through one of the most difficult periods of political upheaval and divisive elections in our nation's history. We have never seen anything like it, ever: FBI investigations, classified emails, secret audio/videotapes, WikiLeaks, alleged victims coming forward to share their stories of assault, or of pay-for-play access, and on and on. Things got so bad that the two major party presidential candidates didn't even shake hands before or after the final presidential debate. We had members of Congress, governors, and even Supreme Court justices making inappropriate public statements, withdrawing their support of their party's nominee. Even the normally lighthearted and collegial annual Alfred E. Smith Charity Foundation Dinner in New York left us aghast at what we heard coming from both candidates about one another.

I decided to write this book because of the rancorous 2015 presidential primary cycle and, of course, the primary and general election cycle of 2016. The summer of 2015 was very troubling. Baltimore burned in race riots in what looked like a newsreel from 1968. Police shootings or beatings of unarmed black citizens seemed rampant. Police themselves were the targets of racial violence and vigilante acts in Dallas and Baton Rouge. Pastors and citizens across racial lines marched for peace as nine African-American Charleston citizens were murdered by an avowed white supremacist as they sat peacefully in Bible study on a Wednesday night. Candidates engaged in unprecedented name-calling and ethnic attacks on Muslims, Mexicans, and immigrants. Stunningly, during the primary debates candidates called each other names, demeaned and insulted one another. It was simply jaw-dropping and sad all at once. Reality TV had come to American politics. And we the people sat passively by, mumbling under our breaths as we watched on our devices and television sets.

The campaign of 2016 will go down in history as one of the most ugly, mean-spirited, and disappointing in our democracy. Yes, it is true that politics has never been for the faint of heart. Yes, it is true that campaigns have always been rough and tumble. And, yes, it is also true that presidential candidates have been attacked (and they have attacked their opponents) before. But something very different happened to America and to Americans during this election cycle, and *we the people* have been turned off in a way that calls for us to act.

As someone who believes deeply in America and in my fellow Americans, I am convinced that it is time for us to reclaim our Founding Fathers' (and Founding Mothers') vision for a strong, free, prosperous, God-fearing, citizen-run government and united America.

It has to start with us. And that means all of us. Not just some of us. We are in this together, after all. We always have been. And I pray that we always will be. Truth be told, the only way we will come out of the mess of the 2016 election is to begin to understand who we are and what we want as we continue into our fourth century as explorers who settled in America, and our second century (plus forty years) as a great and independent nation. We can no longer entrust our lives to the politicians, and to those who, instead of leading us, seek to divide us.

The election results tell a story. Beyond the fact that we elected Donald Trump president. A billionaire businessman with no political experience at all. There is anger among we the people. We are divided by race, region, and even religion. We are shouting at one another, but not listening to one another. What we experienced in this last campaign, regardless of race, region, or religion was frustration, fear, and a familiar contempt for Washington, D.C., and what it has failed to do for all of us. We are tired. We are, many of us, angry. Too many Americans feel left out and simply not heard. Some of us are white-collar workers. Or the long-term unemployed. Others are black inner-city youth. Some are women having to deal with the disdain and disrespect of men who still feel the need to harass or demean. Some of us are farmers who have no place to sell their goods. Our jobs are shipped overseas to developing nations whose citizens will work for lower wages. Our small-business owners are overburdened with too many regulations, too many taxes, and expensive healthcare premiums. Our nation is still great, my fellow Americans, but our nation has lost her compass. And only we can get America back on track.

It is time for we the people to experience a great awakening. A reclamation of who we are and why we were founded. The great promise of America and the great story of America is not what we get wrong, but that we strive to make right. And that we continue to perfect this union with each passing election, and with each passing generation.

We were founded because our forefathers tired of excessive taxes, no representation, and the heavy hand of a tyrannical king. America was never supposed to be like this: a place where Washington has all the power and the citizens feel they have none. We are at each other's throats, because we have forgotten what it is that we are supposed to be fighting for: **one another**. Our politics have become so divisive that we are now divided against each other. And as President Lincoln said in the Gettysburg address: "A House divided against itself cannot stand."[1]

Our Founders were visionaries, truth-seekers, and people of great faith. People of virtue. They were a brave and adventurous people who dared to dream of an *ideal* that had never been dreamed of or charted before: The American ideal of liberty, freedom, and equality for all. The ideal of land ownership. Prosperity. Family. Farms. And fortune. The ideal that made the world take notice of the small new nation that would one day become the envy of the world.

America is a story indeed. It is a promise. It is a decision that changed the history of mankind. I wrote this book because I believe that it is time that we the people come back together. That we reclaim our Founders' vision for a united America, a vision so strong and radical in its day that it brought the great

British Empire to its knees. Our oneness, our hunger for freedom and liberty still makes other nations and peoples around the world want to be like us, and live among us. They want to be Americans because they know America is unique.

Our Founders' vision was so strong that Thomas Jefferson wrote these powerful words in the Declaration of Independence:

> We hold these truths to be self-evident, that all men are created equal, that they are endowed by their Creator with certain unalienable Rights, that among these are Life, Liberty and the pursuit of Happiness.

Our Founders' vision inspired farmers, merchants, bankers, soldiers, saloon owners, and all colonists alike to stand against the greatest military power on earth at the time, and beat it back into surrender. So you see, America doesn't need to be made great again. America has never stopped being great. America doesn't need to be made whole again. America has always been predicated on the notion that we are "one" nation under God, with liberty and justice for all.

Nothing is wrong with America that can't be made right by us. Yes, we have our problems and, yes, we have our divisions, but we are not divided. We are big. We are diverse. We are wealthy. And we are strong. We are many different peoples from many different regions, religions, and experiences deeply devoted to one American ideal. The challenge is that we don't always see that ideal same way.

The past election is a wake-up call to us all, many different people seeking to live the ideals of one nation. We, like those in the original thirteen colonies, do not and will never always agree. Some of us are conservative. Some are liberal. Some are right smack in the middle. And that is okay. It is clear to me, at least, that we all love America, but we have failed to learn how to love our fellow Americans.

Let's start talking about the 800-pound elephant in the room: We are no longer a white, Anglo-Saxon Protestant nation. Our demographics have shifted dramatically since the 1970s and again in the 1990s. And that is where the big push-back came from in this past election. I get it. And I understand it, even as an African-American woman.

Author Robert Jones wrote a powerful article in *The Atlantic* entitled "The Eclipse of White Christian America,"[2] which was accompanied by an even more powerful video showing how the nation's demographics have changed since the 1990s, making us a nation more "of color" and less "Christian." The significance of the demographic shift is that, as a result, many white Americans feel disenfranchised and unheard in the political discourse. It should then come as no surprise that we see the rise of such groups as the "Tea Party" or even candidates like Donald Trump, because they speak to a group of Americans (still the majority) who feel their country changing from the one they have always known, thus the large rallies, the anger, even the fisticuffs between citizens of different races or views at political rallies in 2016. Jones said it best: *"People fight like that when they are losing a sense of place, a sense of belonging, and a sense of the country that they understand and love."* [Emphasis mine.] I agree with his assessment 100% and he summed it up perfectly below:

> These racial and ethnic changes are dramatic, but they only partially account for the sense of dislocation many whites feel. In order to understand the magnitude of the shift, it's important to also assess white Christian America's waning cultural influence. It's impossible to grasp the depth of many white Americans' anxieties and fears—or comprehend recent phenomena like the rise of the Tea Party or Donald Trump in American politics, the zealous tone of the final battles over gay rights, or the racial tensions that have spiked over the last few years—without understanding that, along with its population, America's religious and cultural landscape is being fundamentally altered.[3]

This is why we seem to be fighting each other, and sometimes, tragically, even shooting each other. We seem afraid of one another, disrespectful of one another. Worse, at times downright mean to one another. America needs citizen leaders who will engage one another, listen to one another, and talk together about where we must go from here. We cannot just pretend 2016 didn't happen. It did. And it put a dent in our cultural identity as well as how our friends and allies view us around the world. We have work to do. And, as in any dysfunctional relationship, we have to do the work or things will just get worse. Although the election is over now, the campaign has left both America and Americans badly bruised and cynical.

But take heart: Our Founders got it right. The reason America has endured is that we are always evolving. We are always moving toward becoming *a more perfect union*. We do not quit until we get it right. And it is time for us to make things right for we the people again. Divided we will fail and fall. United we can withstand any foe and bear any burden. And our oneness lights and leads the rest of the world. It is time for us to remember the vision of our founding: *E Pluribus Unum: Out of many, one.*

How We Began

"It always appeared a most iniquitous scheme to me to fight
ourselves for what we are daily robbing and plundering
from those who have as good a right to freedom as we have."
—*Abigail Adams, letter to her husband, September 22, 1774*

E Pluribus Unum was the motto suggested by the committee Congress appointed on July 4, 1776, to design a seal for the United States of America. The committee was adamant that the motto show "unity" and "oneness." *E Pluribus Unum* was the official motto selected by Charles Thomson in 1782, when he created the Great Seal, featuring the eagle with the scroll in its beak. Thomson explained that the motto alluded to the union between the states and federal government, as symbolized by the shield on the eagle's breast. The thirteen stripes "represent the several states all joined in one solid compact entire, supporting a Chief, which unites the whole and represents Congress."[4]

Yet, seven of our Founding Fathers (Washington, Jefferson, Madison, Lee, Pinckney, Rush, and Rutledge) owned slaves, fellow human beings transported in the hull of merchant ships, and sold at auction to the highest bidders once they arrived in America. We know that African slaves arrived in America as early as 1502. How many we'll never know, because our first official U.S. Census was taken in 1790 and there were 3,929,326 people living in the thirteen colonies—697,681 of whom were slaves in the South. *That's almost 18 percent.* What we do know is that during the peak years of the slave trade, between 1740 and 1810, Africa supplied 60,000 captives a year—outnumbering European immigrants by a ratio of 4 or 5 to 1. By the beginning of the eighteenth century, black slaves could be found in every New World area colonized by Europeans, from Nova Scotia to Buenos Aires.[5]

How does a nation founded on the principle "equality" start half-slave and half-free? Good question. And one that has confounded us for hundreds of years. The answer is complicated. In truth, several Founding Fathers acknowledged at the Constitutional Convention that slavery violated the core American ideal of liberty, yet their simultaneous commitment to private property rights, principles of limited government, and intersectional harmony prevented them from making a bold move against slavery. Couple that with the considerable investment of southern Founders in a slave-based staple agriculture, combined with their deep-seated racial prejudice, and that posed additional obstacles to the early abolition of slavery.[6]

It would take America almost one hundred years from her founding before we eradicated slavery, despite the fact that, as early as the Jamestown settlement in the early 1600s, free Africans played a critical role in shaping the development of the colonies. And so we started out of the gate as a new nation in 1776 with an "equality" and "liberty" *defect* that, frankly, haunts us to this very day. As former U.S. Secretary of State Condoleezza Rice put it in an interview with the *Washington Times* in 2008, a great "birth defect":

> Africans and Europeans came here and founded this country together—Europeans by choice and Africans in chains. That's not a very pretty reality of our founding. Descendants of slaves did not get much of a head start, and I think you continue to see some of the effects of that. That particular birth defect makes it hard for us to confront it, hard for us to talk about it, and hard for us to realize that it has continuing relevance for who we are today.[7]

Yes, we all know that women, enslaved Africans, and Native Americans were not considered part of our American nation when we declared our independence from Great Britain in 1776. But, as this book will show, American gradualism (my phrase) always moves us toward that more perfect union. I believe the Founders knew exactly what they were doing. And I believe they knew that it was wrong to enslave millions of Africans in order to build this nation. They made a choice, a choice that to this day still leaves scars and remnants of inequality and division. But, despite their wrongs, the documents they wrote, the vision they brought to life, has allowed each generation of Americans to move ever closer to that "more perfect union" with each passing decade and century that we celebrate as a nation.

However, despite the fact that slavery existed at the birth of our republic, my charge to those of us of African descent is to begin to see ourselves not just as the descendants of our slave mothers and fathers, but as stakeholders in America, the heirs of a great legacy of patriots, among them: Frederick Douglass (social reformer, abolitionist, orator, writer, statesman); James Armistead (a slave in Virginia, who, with the permission of his master, enlisted in the Revolutionary War under General Lafayette); Benjamin Banneker (a free African-American almanac author, surveyor, naturalist, and farmer, part of a group, led by Major Andrew Ellicott, that surveyed the borders of the original District of Columbia, the federal capital district of the United States). I could go on and on talking about the many African Americans who contributed to America in spite of slavery. My point is this: Slavery is not the only historical narrative of black Americans. Even in slavery, and after slavery ended, black men and women contributed to the building, prosperity, freedom, and patriotism of America.

Lessons from the 2016 Presidential Primaries and Campaign

Elections do not solve our problems in America. We the people do. We do so by electing leaders from among us to represent our interests. We have just done that, as we do every four years. The votes have been counted. We have a new president and our nation will go forward as it always does. We will rally around our new president, and we will pray for the best of America to come forward in service as a new administration begins.

As for younger Americans, known as Millennials, Gen Y, or Gen Next, they largely supported Senator Bernie Sanders. As their

Baby Boomer grandparents start to retire, and their Generation X parents settle into midlife, the Millennials are now the single largest block of citizens and workers, 80 million strong. As the *New York Post* opined, "Millennials support more gun control but oppose an assault-weapons ban. They're blazingly optimistic, but they're also terrified about how they're going to pay the bills. They love President Obama despite opposing his two main legislative achievements. They're the narcissist humanitarians. They tell marketers they care about sustainability and cruelty to animals, and yet their meat consumption is on a par with previous generations. They love socialism, so long as it doesn't mean government taking over the economy or anything weird like that. They're going to change the world, but they're in no hurry to move out of the room over Mom's garage. You could say the Millennials are nuanced, multifaceted and open to many modes of thought."[8]

Whatever the state of the different generations, it is now time for us to heal from the bluster and bitterness of the last campaign and begin a much-needed conversation about who we are, and what we want for future generations of Americans. Yes, our politics are deeply divided, but we Americans *are not* as divided as the media might portray us to be. In fact, we agree on a lot, and what we all seem to agree on, across race, gender, and religious lines, is that our politicians and our system of politics are badly broken. Just look at poll after poll taken over the past decade right up until the end of 2016 and you will see what I mean. I don't need to recite those polls here, because we all know what they say: *Americans distrust politicians. Americans believe the country is on the wrong track. Americans believe race relations are worse.*

Congress has had its lowest approval ratings in a generation over the past decade, sinking to 9 percent in 2013, and rising two points to 11 percent in 2015 in a Gallup poll.[9] Gallup has been tracking congressional approval ratings for over forty-one years and the ratings since 2011 have been among the worst ever recorded. Congress experienced a record-high 84 percent approval rating in October 2001, a month after the 9/11 terrorist attacks. In a 2015 Gallup poll, 8 percent of Republicans said they approved of Congress, while 13 percent of independents and 11 percent of Democrats said the same about lawmakers on Capitol Hill.

Here are some key takeaways from the last election cycle:

- Americans wanted an outsider in the presidential primaries, as proven by the candidacies of Donald Trump and Senator Sanders.
- Americans did not trust either major party candidate— both Hillary Clinton and Donald Trump had the highest negatives and untrustworthiness ratings on record.
- Americans overwhelmingly did not believe the country was on the right track.
- Americans felt powerless to change Washington, so they turned to a businessman on the GOP side and a self-described democratic socialist on the Democrat side to speak to their anger, frustration, and disenfranchisement with the current political process.

I challenge us Americans to take our body politic back from lobbyists and special interests—and even from people like me

SOPHIA A. NELSON, ESQ.
18

(journalists and pundits). We know that we still have the power to make changes: Look at what happened with the water crisis in Flint, Michigan, which exposed an outdated, unresponsive local and state government that had badly failed the people of that urban community. That is just one example of what we the people can do when we get mobilized and engaged in our own destiny. On the other hand, I will challenge us to take a long, hard look at ourselves and our culture and how it is that we can regain our footing as families, patriots, parents, role models, and leaders. How do we regain our love for each other, while respecting our differences? How can we demand that our leaders lead with a code of ethics, respect, and civility that calls forth the best among us who want to serve in political office? I think it has to start with an understanding of who we are called to be as Americans: *One nation. One people. Equal. Unified. Free. Under God.* That is how we began. That is our political Code in a nutshell.

What We Want from Our Leaders

In order to add some context to the book you are about to read, I have used data points from two studies, conducted in 2016 around the presidential primary season, that measure the attitudes of Americans on the efficacy and our trust of the government, as well as our outlook on where we are as a country. According to one study, the Gallup polling data from 1996 through 2014 demonstrates that there is extreme discontent among the American people with both the Republican and Democratic parties. The data also shows that Americans have grown more likely to see sharp differences between the major parties, and to perceive both parties as too ideological—either too conservative or too liberal, and dug into their party positions versus being champions for the issues facing the electorate. As for the party system, Americans express a high degree of ambivalence. On one hand, many believe that the major parties do not do an adequate job of representing the people, and that the country needs a third political party. On the other hand, there is skepticism that a third party would improve the quality of American democracy.[10]

I wanted to take a closer look, however, at attitudes around our current state of politics as we went through the primaries and the election from the summer of 2015 through the fall of 2016. A study, conducted by the Center for American Progress, the Brookings Institution, and the American Enterprise Institute (AEI), was taken in February 2016, and its focus was on how the changing demographics of America have and will continue to impact our politics, elected officials, and policy directions as a nation.[11] The core findings of this study are crucial if we are going to understand the critical importance of racial, regional, and even religious diversity in how Americans vote and choose their leaders at the highest levels. This study also informs both Democrats and Republicans of a coming demographic tsunami that will radically change how the parties reach out to voters and build new diversity coalitions. In 1976, 89 percent of voters in America were Caucasian. That dropped to 74 percent in 2008 and 72 percent in 2012. President Barack Obama won in 2008 with 43 percent of white voters and only 39 percent in 2012.[12]

- Racial diversity, particularly with African Americans and Latinos, put President Obama over the top in both the 2008 and 2012 elections.
- The youth (18–29) vote in 2008 gave President Obama a 10-point edge over his rival, Senator John McCain. And 60 percent voted for Obama in 2012.
- The female vote went 56 percent for Obama in 2008 and 55 percent in 2012.

Three core groups—racial minorities, young people, and women—are the future of American electoral politics. On the contrary, Baby Boomers are living longer and they make up a more reliable base of voters, especially in slower-growing states of elderly populations. To be clear, voting among racial and ethnic lines is not a new phenomenon. A majority of white voters have voted Republican in every single election since 1968, whereas a majority of black voters have voted Democratic since the second term of Franklin Roosevelt in 1936, with the 1960 election being the watershed for black voters, giving Democrat John F. Kennedy the decisive edge in that contest over Republican Richard Nixon.

The second study was conducted by Burson Marstellar, "Conversations with America Research Study," May 9, 2016.[13] For the purposes of this book, I am interested in the first set of findings, which addresses whether the country finds itself polarized by race and politics. I think we all intuitively know the answer is yes, but I want to provide a snapshot of the findings here:

- Roughly half of Americans say the country is more polarized around race relations and that it will stay that way for the next five years.
- Americans feel that the media and economics are the two driving forces that contribute most to racial and political divisions.
- 4 in 5 said that the 2016 presidential election worsened our divisions as a nation.
- About 46 percent believe that race relations are worse now than in their grandparents' generation.
- Americans are more likely to think "conservative" groups are more responsible for the political divide than are "liberal" groups.

These two different polls offer a snapshot in time. But they are also representative of many polls taken over the course of the past decade that tell us two distinct things:

1. Our union is becoming *more and more diverse. When we began in 1776, our "many" were thirteen colonies,* overwhelmingly European and Caucasian. Now our "many" is all of us, including women, African Americans, and Native Americans.

2. Our union *is more fractured and divided* because groups that did not have a voice at the founding of our nation (for example, women, blacks, etc.) now have that voice. We are no longer monolithic. Unlike at the turn of the twentieth

century, when we had a huge influx of legal immigrants coming to the United States, mostly from European nations, we now have illegal immigration and other issues that divide us deeply in ways that, perhaps, they did not before.

As an American citizen and journalist in the free press, I felt it was my duty to remind both myself and my fellow Americans of the core values upon which our great nation was built. And that it requires of each of us engagement, knowledge, and vigilant self-governance. If we are to remain the greatest political beacon of light on earth, then we must change. And we must get off our La-Z-Boy chairs and start chairing committees, fund-raisers, town halls, and meetings that keep us informed, engaged, and on top of our republic.

How to Use this Book

This book is intentionally being presented after a major presidential election cycle. It is intended to remind us as American citizens and as American leaders that every four years we get a new start as a nation, with a new leader, or with one whom we have reelected to a second term as president. In that vein, it is the time-honored tradition of our founding to equip and refresh the citizenry with examples of good morals, character, integrity, civility, activism, inspiration, revolution—if needed—and community. The fact is, there are *dos* and *don'ts* in life. Good leaders and good citizens are developed from explicit instruction, examples, exhortations, and training. There are many things that we Americans agree on, among them the timeless and trusted virtues of faith, honesty, integrity, and civility in our public discourse. Yet we seem to have lost our connection with those virtues and ideals.

These ideals and virtues don't just apply to our civic life, they apply to our everyday life as citizens of a nation founded on a standard of unity and respect for differences. We have become a culture of rude, entitled people. Too many of our children engage in unthinkable conduct. They, too, are disconnected, angry. In April 2016, a young high school girl was beaten to death by classmates while they videotaped the attack and cheered on her assailants. Who have we become? And how did we get here?

My hope is that by exploring how we became the "United" States of America, and by reminding us of our Founders, our American heroes and heroines, we will reclaim the traits and Codes that we Americans recognize as essentials for both citizens and leaders. We say we want to leave our children with a better America (and world), but in order for that to happen we have to offer them examples of good and bad, right and wrong.

This book calls us to be a model for the next generations, as past generations have modeled for us. It is a "how to" for political and civic responsibility and civility. More than that, however, I hope it will help us all to understand that people of good character and good intentions are not always going to come down on the same side of political, moral, religious, or social issues. And that is okay! We need to reclaim a simple truth: Good people can be conservative, they can be liberal, they can be moderate, and they can be libertarian. We must reclaim the timeless virtue of respecting one another's different points of view, and respecting one another's patriotism when we disagree. We must not permit our disputes or our disagreements to divide us as Americans.

Regardless of his or her age, every American should know about the men and women in this book who embodied the character, courage, ingenuity, bravery, wisdom, sacrifice, and insight to use their individual gifts in order to challenge, change, defy, protect, preserve, and defend the Constitution of the United States of America. To the young people (including my two Millennial nieces) in this country: Both our leaders and citizenry have failed you in failing to lead by example. Instead we have shown you anger, vitriol, disrespect, rancor, division, hatred, incivility, prejudice, and intolerance. We have not honored the timeless virtue of our forefathers by teaching your generation about the value of hard work, family, integrity, character, and community. We have shamed public service, and instead shown you how mean, nasty, and base political campaigns can be. We have allowed you to "tune out" on your devices. To text instead of talk. We owe you better than that, and I pray that we as your elders wake up and rise to the occasion that is before us and find a way to connect with you that truly lifts and builds a greater America than the one we experienced in the last campaign cycle.

In the pages that follow I will take you on that journey of American character, courage, bravery, ingenuity, civility, integrity, humanity, rebellion, revolution, civil disobedience, and consistency. It is my profound hope that this book will be read by grade school children and high school and college students and that it will reengage, reinvigorate, and familiarize them with the greatness of the American journey.

It will call you (and me) as fellow Americans to something greater. To rise to the challenges of this tumultuous time. I hope this book will lift us. Inspire us. It will ask us to take care of one another, and not focus on what divides us, but instead on what unites us.

I believe that America needs to return to our core Code. Our center. Our values. And our most enduring precept: *E Pluribus Unum: Out of many, one.* One nation under God. One nation founded in liberty. One nation that self-checks and self-corrects. One nation that uses diversity as a great strength. One nation that tolerates and protects peaceful protest. One nation that honors the voice of her people, differences of religion, differences of ethnic group. One nation that is indivisible with liberty and justice for all.

I have pulled principles from our history and from our present day to inspire we the people and our leaders to become merchants of character, hope, integrity, and action. This book will challenge us to demand of ourselves, and our leaders, a politics of integrity, inclusion, humility, nobility, and service to the people. And it will challenge our leaders in Washington and in statehouses throughout America to lead with courage, selflessness, sacrifice, and an undying dedication to the people before super PACs, money, influence, and power. Where do we go to find such examples?

The heart and soul of this book is to help us reclaim our lost political Codes. There is no better way to do that than through the power of illustration and example. We have a wealth of examples, starting with our Founding Fathers (and Mothers), to great presidents, abolitionists, activists, scientists, journalists, clergy, inventors, astronauts, educators, and athletes, as we learn together about the exciting adventure of America.

The book is broken into two sections:

- **Section I: The Citizens' Codes:** What are we the people called upon to do as citizens of the greatest democratic republic in the world? Freedom is never free. We have become lazy, disengaged, entitled. We used to believe in offering a helping hand, or offering a hand up. Now we have a hand out. These Codes give us our civic responsibilities as citizens, and remind us of our duty and responsibility to our founding principles.

- **Section II: The Leadership Codes:** America is a republic, and that means we elect the men and women who do our bidding and voting and who serve as our voice in Washington. We chose a representative form of government from the beginning, because we put our faith in our fellow Americans whom we elect to high office to do what is best for America. Yet, as we all just witnessed in the 2016 presidential campaign, our leaders are less than stellar. They are influenced by big money, corporations, book deals, lucrative lobbying jobs, reality TV shows, celebrity, and worse—their egos. Enormous egos.

In the final analysis, we are still a fractured people striving to become one nation. We are, in fact, still trying to find our way as to how we can all come together, yet retain our own individuality. The great thing about America is that, despite our differences, despite our disputes, and even despite our diversity, we always stand together as one nation when it counts. The great challenge we face now is not an external one. The challenge we face now is very much an internal one. At this dawn of the twenty-first century, we find ourselves facing global terrorism, low wages, lack of good jobs here at home, increasing poverty, poor educational systems for far too many of our people, a broken immigration system, too much government regulation, too much corporate largesse, and on and on.

We the people fell asleep somewhere along the way, and we broke some of the fundamental Codes of our Founding Fathers. It is time for us to become engaged citizens once again. It is time for us to take back our liberties and freedom. It is time for us to hold our leaders to account. It is time for us to model the kind of government we expect from those we elect to serve us in this great nation. In other words, it is time for us to get up and act like the citizens our Founding Fathers envisioned for us to be.

I believe that the way we get there is not through more government intervention or regulations. Our Founders fought vehemently against a tyrannical king and a form of British government that took more and more of their freedoms, and allowed for fewer and fewer liberties. This is a time for American heroes.

The great strength of America is our people. Americans are risk-takers. We are fixers. We are generous. We have a natural resistance to big government and being ruled as subjects. That is how we were born. And I believe that the way we can get back there is through dialogue, listening, engaging, lifting one another, inspiring one another, and in returning to the core Codes of our founding: Oneness. Unity. Liberty. Freedom. Faith. And Fidelity to our Equality and Humanity before Almighty God.

Yours in Freedom,

Sophia A. Nelson

SECTION I

THE CITIZENS' CODES

* * * * * * * * * * * * * * * *

We the People. These words are ingrained in us from the time that we are school-aged children. We are taught to love America. To love our symbols. But we can all agree that our great republic is in trouble. We have steered off course. We have become disconnected, disengaged, desensitized, and in many ways entitled. We used to believe as a collective people (one American people) in offering a helping hand, or offering a hand up. Now too many of us look for a hand out. These Codes give us our civic responsibilities as citizens, and remind us of our duty and responsibility to our founding principles. These Codes are meant to reignite a spark in us through example, and the actions of citizens who changed and refreshed the tree of liberty from our beginnings as a nation to our own time today. Every leader and every citizen lives by a Code whether they realize it or not. An American Code.

* * * * * * * * * * * * * * * *

"An enlightened citizenry is indispensable for the proper functioning of a republic. Self-government is not possible unless the citizens are educated sufficiently to enable them to exercise oversight."

—Thomas Jefferson

CODE

1

BE INFORMED, ENGAGED, AND SELF-GOVERNING

America was clearly intended to be a unified citizen government. Plain and simple. Yet we the people look very different today than we did in 1776. We are no longer a nation of a ruling-class, wealthy, white male landowners and merchants. Women are now able to vote and raise their voices. And be nominated for president of the United States. There are no slaves being held as property. In fact, President Obama is half-African and half-American. We are a nation of "many." We are more diverse than our Founding Fathers could have ever imagined. But are we more divided now than perhaps ever before. Our diversity, once viewed as a great strength—"Out of many we are one"—is now seen by some as a weakness. Those who have enjoyed privilege and entitlement unfettered for centuries now resent that a new class of women, blacks, Hispanics, and every group imaginable now demands a seat at the table. America has ironically fulfilled the call of her founding, yet we still wrestle with that "oneness," when we are so very different by region, religion, and race.

But when we understand our history, we will begin to understand that being different is not what matters. It's what unites us that matters. The one core value where we are not different as Americans is in our responsibility to be engaged, informed, and self-governing.

There are many obligations in life, but none more important than the obligation of citizenship. We the people are obligated to be informed, engaged, and committed to the vision our Founding Fathers had for this great ideal called America.

To be informed is to be limitless.

To be engaged is to be relevant.

To be self-governing is to be free.

America is a dream. And the only way to realize that dream is to show up every day with the knowledge and the information that help to further secure and perpetuate that dream for generations to come. But liberty comes at a price, and our Founding Fathers understood this all too well. They charted this great nation from the blood and ashes of Lexington, Boston Harbor, Yorktown, and Bunker Hill. America was birthed in revolution and risk, and we should never, ever forget that beginning. It is our beginning that tells the story of who we are, and I pray forever will be.

From our beginning we established a great and bold political Code. A Code like the world had never seen. A Code of the power of the people. A Code of being accountable for what we value. A Code of being informed about what we want, and what we need. A Code of being engaged in our communities, in gathering information about people, places, or things that threaten our liberty, and a Code of self-governance that is the core principle upon which we are founded.

We all pledge allegiance to a Code of liberty. A Code of individualism, coupled with a heart for community. A Code of freedom, paid for by the blood of our Founders, has stoked the fire of revolution in other great nations, and is still to this day the light of the world.

The great question we will explore in this book is this: Have we forgotten our beginnings? Have we turned from the founding virtues and Codes of our birth? And, if so, how do we the people get them back and put them into practice? And, more important, how do we hold our leaders accountable to us, and not to special interests or their own personal gain?

It would appear that, based on the presidential election of 2016, we have lost our way as an informed, engaged, self-governing citizenry. The Founding Fathers were strongly influenced by English philosopher John Locke, who advocated government as a social contract. The term "will of the governed" encapsulates this concept, which means that the people are the boss. The power of the people is declared in the first three words of the Constitution, "We the People . . ."

This principle is also the underlying basis for our Declaration of Independence: "governments are instituted among men, deriving their just powers from the consent of the governed. That whenever any form of government becomes destructive to these ends, it is the right of the people to alter or to abolish it, and to institute new government, laying its foundation on such principles and organizing its powers in such form, as to them shall seem most likely to affect their safety and happiness."[14]

There is one huge misconception that we must address at the outset about our form of government, and that is the notion that America is a democracy. *It is not.*

America is a republic. A republic is a representative government ruled by law (in our case the U.S. Constitution). A democracy, on the other hand, is ruled by the majority, or, as our Founders saw it, mob rule. Democracies focus on the needs of the good of the public, or, in other words, the majority. A republic recognizes the rights of individuals. In our form of government, we recognize the rights of the majority as well as the minority. We have a system of checks and balances. A judiciary, an executive, and a legislative body of government. Article IV, Section 4 of the Constitution states: "*The United States shall guarantee to every State in this Union a Republican Form of government, and shall protect each of them against Invasion.*" The word *democracy* is not mentioned in the Constitution at all. Along with more warnings from others, James Madison warned us of the dangers of democracies with this quote:

> Hence it is that democracies have ever been spectacles of turbulence and contention; have ever been found incompatible with personal security or the rights of property; and in general have been as short in their lives as they have been violent in their deaths. A republic, by which I mean a government in which a scheme of representation takes place, opens a different prospect and promises the cure for which we are seeking.[15]

Our nation, then, was born from men and women who understood that those who would be *governed best, must be governed least.*

In this Code we will look at three fundamental values that pushed two great Americans to rise up and model these core principles:

1. **Informed:** Being aware and knowledgeable; reading; writing; watching; in other words, researching what is going on around you by those who have been given responsibility to govern you.
2. **Engaged:** Taking action in your community, alerting other citizens, and being active in the goings-on of your nation, state, or community.
3. **Self-Governing:** Understanding that we the people have the final say-so on our form of government, and that we must be willing to pay any price, bear any burden, to protect our freedoms.

Informed. Engaged. Self-Governing.

Knowledge is power. Information is access. Engagement is influence. And the right to govern oneself is revolutionary. The rights that we enjoy today as twenty-first-century Americans were procured not just in the American Revolution, but in every century since. We Americans have remained Americans because we are hungry for information. We arm ourselves not just with weapons, but with knowledge. And we are prepared at a moment's notice to rally together as one nation when duty calls us to serve in the protection of our unique form of government.

One of the great things about our nation is that from the least influential to the most powerful, one person can make an impact and effect great change. The notions of self-governance and self-freedom have pushed men and women from every walk of life to fight to protect our unalienable rights, from Lexington to Seneca Falls, to the shores of Normandy, to the faraway desert fields of Afghanistan and Iraq. **Rights** and **duties** are two sides of a coin, absolutely inseparable. Whenever and wherever we have rights, we must have corresponding duties. Whether it be the home, the society, or the country, in every sphere of life, rights and duties go hand in hand. We have rights in the same measure as we have duties. Let us be very clear: There can be no rights without an equal measure of corresponding duties or responsibilities.

Engagement and self-governance have been the underlying formula for the success of any movement, any rebellion, and any progress ever made in America. This important Code is fundamental to who we are as Americans. If we have indeed lost our way as a nation, it is because we the people have stopped being informed about, and engaged in, our public and civic affairs, our politics, and the election of our political leaders.

A quote often attributed to Thomas Jefferson but cannot be verified in his writings is, "An informed citizenry is a vital requisite for our survival as a free people."[16] Jeffersonian attitudes toward the necessity of a free flow of information as a prerequisite for participatory democracy led to a fervent belief in freedom of speech and the power of a free press at the outset of our founding. The power to protect our freedom was placed squarely in the hands of the citizenry, and not those who would be elected to serve in government.

So what does it mean to be "informed" and "engaged" as a citizen? It means many things, but here are a few basic tenets of an informed, effective citizenry:

1. We help to inform and write the laws through our elected officials.
2. We stay knowledgeable about laws and make sure to protest those that are not in keeping with our core principles and founding Codes.
3. We read and stay informed about the news, including local, national, and international affairs impacting our form of government.
4. We obey the law and encourage others to do the same.
5. We stay connected to our fellow citizens, honor the Bill of Rights, and assemble ourselves as needed to stay vigilant about protecting our freedoms.
6. We vote in elections, and participate in jury duty.
7. We make sure that we have the use of libraries, and access to a free press that keeps us informed and educated.

What does it mean to practice self-governance? Again, it means many things. But fundamental to our core Codes of self-governance are these:

- Freedom to express yourself
- Freedom to worship as you wish
- Right to a prompt, fair trial by jury
- Right to vote in elections for public officials

- Right to apply for federal employment requiring U.S. citizenship
- Right to run for elected office
- Freedom to pursue "life, liberty, and the pursuit of happiness"

It is one thing to know these Codes, but it is another to see them played out by great Americans from our nation's past as well as in our present day. There are examples from our history of men and women who understood these three core principles of being informed, engaged, and vigilant about self-governance. In this Code we will look at the lives of one man and one woman who exemplify these principles and who, by their vigilance, helped to birth a new nation, and contribute to the essence of her founding.

Two Americans Informed, Engaged, and Devoted to Self-Governance

Two of America's best-known historical figures modeled this Code over seventy years apart. We can learn great lessons from their lives and from their undying commitment to ensuring that all men, and ultimately all women, would have the right to govern themselves.

PAUL REVERE[17]

> *"No matter what you do, you'll never run away from you."* —*Paul Revere*

Paul Revere is best known for his famous ride through the streets of Boston yelling, "The British are coming! The British are coming!" (However, some historians challenge whether or not he did so.)[18] But Revere was much more than a prosperous silversmith or a famous horseman. He participated in public affairs long before his famous ride. He was well informed. He was engaged. And he made the decision, when the time came, to protect the people's right of self-governance by putting his own life at risk.

Revere served as a second lieutenant in the French and Indian War. He became a Freemason in 1760 and soon joined two more overtly political groups, the Sons of Liberty and the North End Caucus.[19] Through them, he participated in Samuel Adams's gradually accelerating movement toward independence, serving primarily as a courier and an engraver of propaganda pictures, the two best-known examples of which are a "view" of British ships landing troops in 1768 and a wildly inaccurate cartoon depicting the Boston Massacre of 1770.

Revere effectively and diligently used the limited tools of his time at his disposal to not only stay informed himself, but to inform and engage other citizens living in the colonies. One of his most important contributions to the Revolutionary War was an "information highway" of sorts. Revere put himself at risk daily to help organize an intelligence network to keep watch on the British military. Working with his fellow colonist Samuel Adams, Revere was one of the leaders of the historic Boston Tea Party. Shortly after the Tea Party, Revere began a "spy network" by watching British movements and then riding to New York and Philadelphia to give information on the British and the unrest within Boston.

In April 1775, the British Army was set to start its attack

on the American militia as a way to quell the colonial rebellion. Initially Revere was sent to tell the people of Concord, Massachusetts, that the British were set to move, and this message prompted the people of Concord to move their military weapons and ammunition to a different area. On April 18, word came that the British were setting sail on small boats from Boston to Cambridge before embarking on the road to Lexington and Concord. The time was around 10 p.m. when Revere set out on his horse to warn of the British attack. Riding through places such as Somerville, Medford, and Arlington, Revere let everyone know of the impending attack. This bold and brave move set off a chain of riders heading in different directions to get the word out. It is said that up to forty riders in total were advising of the British attack by the night's end. Revere is one of our Founding Fathers. And largely due to Revere's diligence in being informed, engaged, and committed to self-governance at any price, we stand as a free nation today.

ELIZABETH CADY STANTON[20]

"Nothing strengthens the judgment and quickens the conscience like individual responsibility."
—*Elizabeth Cady Stanton*

Fast-forward seventy-three years after the colonists started and won the American Revolution. Women still had few rights (in a nation that was founded upon principles of equality and justice for all) and they still could not vote. Founding Mothers like Abigail Adams had long since attempted to get their powerful husbands to "remember the women too," as Adams remarked to her husband, John, as he headed to the Constitutional Convention. But her pleas, and those of many other Founding Mothers, like Martha Washington, Dolley Madison, Betsy Ross, Laura Wolcott, Mercy Warren, and Phillis Wheatley, fell mostly on deaf ears. By the time the nation was well into the 1800s, women were starting to get educated outside the home and were raising their voices about equal treatment and having a voice in politics and public affairs. Women began to write poems, books, and pamphlets about American ideals and the promise of her founding, not just for white men, but for women and slaves, too.

Enter Elizabeth Cady Stanton, the daughter of a prominent attorney and judge (Daniel Cady). Young Elizabeth studied at home and at the Johnstown Academy, Johnstown, New York, and was among the first generation of women to gain a higher education. In 1839, she met Henry Brewster Stanton, an abolitionist speaker. Her father opposed their marriage because Stanton supported himself completely through the uncertain income of a traveling orator, working without pay for the American Anti-Slavery Society. Even with her father's opposition, Elizabeth married Stanton in 1840. By that time, she'd already observed enough about the legal relationships between men and women to insist that the word *obey* be dropped from the ceremony.

Stanton would become one of the nation's leading suffragists, along with her peers Lucretia Mott and Susan B. Anthony. Stanton continually educated herself on how to gain freedoms not just for women, but for slaves. After her wedding in 1840,

Stanton and her new husband departed for a transatlantic voyage to England, to attend an abolitionist convention, the World Anti-Slavery Convention, in London. Both had been appointed as delegates of the American Anti-Slavery Society. The convention, however, denied official standing to women delegates, including Stanton and Mott. Not to be denied their right to participate in self-governance, Stanton and Mott met again in 1848 and began planning for a women's rights convention to be held in Seneca Falls, New York.

The convention met at the Wesleyan Chapel in July 1848 in Seneca Falls—the first ever of its kind held in the United States—and began with almost two hundred women in attendance. The famous "Declaration of Sentiments,"[21] written by Mott, was approved there. Stanton is credited with initiating the long struggle for women's rights and women's suffrage. She began writing frequently for women's rights, including advocating for women's property rights after marriage. After 1851, Stanton worked in close partnership with Susan B. Anthony; Stanton often served as the writer, and Anthony as the strategist and public speaker in this effective working relationship.[22]

Like Paul Revere before her, Stanton created an information network and platform for American women and freed slaves, like Harriet Tubman and Sojourner Truth, through which they could raise their voices for equality. Because of Stanton's engagement in writing, protesting, learning, and convening women's conferences, politicians began to pay court to her and her cohorts. Results began to show after 1851, with Stanton working in close partnership with Susan B. Anthony. They won major reforms in 1860, including the right after divorce for a woman to have custody of her children, and economic rights for married women and widows.

During the Civil War, women's rights activity largely stopped, while the women who had been active in the movement worked in various ways, first to support the war and then to work for antislavery legislation after the war. Elizabeth Cady Stanton ran for Congress in 1866, from the 8th Congressional District in New York. Women, including Stanton, were still not eligible to vote. Stanton received 24 votes out of about 22,000 cast.[23]

In 1866, at the Anti-Slavery Society annual meeting, Stanton formed the American Equal Rights Association, which would eventually become the National Woman Suffrage Association, of which Stanton served as president. The rival American Woman Suffrage Association was founded by others, dividing the women's suffrage movement and its strategic vision for decades. Paul Revere and Elizabeth Cady Stanton, separated by more than seven decades, both held fast to and modeled for us the great American Code of the power and effectiveness of a citizen who is informed, engaged, and devoted to the right of self-governance. By educating themselves with information, they were both effective advocates for the cause of liberty. They engaged their fellow citizens of the time, and, in so doing, rallied them to fight for freedom not just for all men, but for all women, too.

★ ★ ★ ★ ★ ★ ★ ★ ★ ★ ★ ★ ★ ★ ★

Reclaiming Our Founders' Vision

Here are ten Action Items that we as citizens of our time can take to heart and practice today. We the people must first commit to being: Informed. Engaged. And Self-Governing. There is no longer an excuse for not being informed—we are surrounded by twenty-four-hour news, media, social media, television, and radio, not to mention the Internet.

1. **Read the Constitution.** Carry a copy of it in your pocket or purse. On your iPad or iPhone. It is our founding document. Hold it close and know it well.

2. **Learn about government:** its functions, its limitations, its responsibilities. Understand the coequal branches of our system—how they work and how they affect our day-to-day lives.

3. **Get active in your local government.** Work at a polling place. Register people to vote. Visit your state capitol. And the nation's capital.

4. **Be connected with your local or regional library.** Read, share books, and encourage your children to do the same. Reading is knowledge. And knowledge is power.

5. **Know who your elected officials are.** Visit their offices. Send emails about important issues you want them to

address. Elected officials have staffs that tally citizens' voices on important policies and issues before voting.

6. **Get involved in causes that interest you.** Support candidates for office. Run for office yourself.

7. **Write. Blog. Post.** Share information about politics and government on your social media platforms. Create a network of information for you, your community, and your friends.

8. **Engage our free press.** Local. Regional. National. Watch the news. Follow both conservative and liberal news outlets on social media. Make yourself aware of all points of view, and absorb the news daily.

9. **Govern yourself** according to the laws and freedoms you have been granted as an American.

10. **Raise your voice.** Exercise your right to protest and to have redress under the law.

★ ★ ★ ★ ★ ★ ★ ★ ★ ★ ★ ★ ★ ★ ★

"Only a virtuous people are

capable of freedom."

—Benjamin Franklin

CODE
2

BE VIRTUOUS AND MORAL

Make no mistake about it: Right and wrong do exist. There are moral absolutes.

There are things that we as human beings should do. And there are things that, deep down at our core, we know we should *not* do. If and when we cease to be good as people, any greatness that is possible within us likewise ceases to exist.

As citizens in a free nation, moral imperatives matter because those very mores and ideals that we subscribe to keep us a great nation. Let us be clear: The success of any great country depends upon the character of its citizenry. There is a reason that America is the envy of the world. We are different. We live different. We worship different. We exercise freedom different. We govern different. And that is because our "different" is predicated upon the belief that America is a virtuous and moral nation. We care about others. We defend others when they are trampled upon. Although we are not perfect—far from it—we actually believe that all men are created equal before almighty God, and that, when our unalienable rights are restrained by other men, such injustice, such immorality must be righted.

Our Founders understood this imperative.

Our Founders understood that to be engaged, informed, and self-governing was more than just a set of rote actions. It is a way of life, a "civic virtue" that requires one to exercise good judgment, compassion, and good morals. To understand and reevaluate our present-day understanding of virtue, however, we must be willing to admire our past heroes and what they laid as the foundation of our greatness as a nation. If we do not honor how we began, and we slowly yet deliberately change the formula of success that has been ours for more than 240 years, we will change what it means to be America the Great.

My challenge to myself and to all of us is that we must be willing to take a stand. We the people must be willing to accept that there are, in fact, some moral absolutes. There are nonnegotiables in public life that stem from our private conduct. Unfortunately, in our modern-day body politic we shy away from such moral imperatives due to "political correctness" or a desire not to appear judgmental. We seem unwilling to "call a thing a thing" because we do not want to be seen as religious zealots, nonconformists, or as intolerant. We laugh at things that should shock us and we are unfazed by conduct in our leaders that should alarm, if not enrage us.

One example of such conduct, which took place during the 2016 presidential primary campaign, was with one of the leading candidates on the Republican side. This candidate actually stood on a nationally (and globally) televised debate stage and in a not-so-veiled way talked about his private parts, defying a remark made by another candidate about his "small hands" indicating "small parts" otherwise. Not only did the accused candidate hold up his hands to show their large size, but indicated that the size of his hands matched other of his body parts.

It was simply jaw-dropping. Families were watching. Children were watching. And all I could think to myself was: *Is this the best we have to offer to America? Is this where we have sunk? Is this the reality TV, voyeuristic America that we have become?* But what struck me as most disturbing about this display of vulgarity was that it became a cocktail-party joke. A news headline. And it had no impact whatsoever on the candidate who uttered the words. He increased his standing in the polls. He became his party's nominee.

Even more disturbing than that exchange was the entire 2016 campaign and the use of name-calling, personal attacks, demeaning rhetoric, scurrilous attacks on spouses, and regular citizens like you and me literally fistfighting, assaulting, and cursing one another at political rallies. Somewhere along the way we the people lost our moral compass and it's time for us to get back on course.

I think it's important for us as Americans living in the twenty-first century to understand how our Founders in the eighteenth century and those Americans living in the nineteenth century understood "virtue" and "morals" and how they applied them when it came to the duties of being a citizen. I have no desire in this work to take us backward. I do desire, however, to challenge us to take a long, hard look at our current state of morals and virtues. Because the most objective observer would have to agree that, when our kids watch another kid being beaten to death in a high school bathroom and videotape the murder in action, we have lost all semblance of morality.

It is likewise very important that we understand that America is an "ideal." We are unique. The "ideal" of our founding is vested in we the people being the fuel that keeps the fires of virtue, goodness, order, and decency glowing. And that ideal must always be in check and balance. By that I mean we have to balance two ideas: On the one hand, because we are a free people vested in liberty, we never want to impose our individual religious morals and personal values on others or look down on others and how they live simply because we disagree with them. On the other hand, we do want to stay true to our founding principles and ideals by keeping them intact. For example, we never want to get rid of religious liberty or of the right to keep and bear arms. Those two founding principles make America unique around the world. Yet what we must do is condemn any conduct and morals that run contrary to our precious freedom. As is oft said, "The only thing necessary for the triumph of evil is for good men to do nothing."[24]

In this Code, then, we will look at two of our founding Codes:

1. virtue
2. morals

as they apply to we the people. And we will look at the lives of two great citizens who exemplified these codes and who helped to set the course of our great nation by living up to the tenets of such virtues and morals. We will see brave expressions of humility, compassion, honesty, loyalty, and responsibility all directed toward the preservation of liberty. I also hope we can come to see that virtues and morals are not a set of rules and regulations, but ideals we should strive for.

Morals and Virtue and Why They Matter

Morals and virtue mean basically the same thing. A moral man or woman may have virtue. And a person of virtue (for example, good character, manners, compassion, work ethic, etc.) is said to be a person with morals.

Now, being virtuous does not necessarily require belief in a supreme being. Although our Founders believed that it certainly helped, they never intended to impose one set of religious beliefs on citizens. So, we do not need to be afraid of the term *virtue*. Despite the occasional misunderstanding that it sometimes conjures up, virtue is really a course of conduct that reflects universal principles of moral and ethical excellence essential to leading a worthwhile life and to effective self-government. For many leading Founders, attributes of character such as justice, responsibility, and perseverance, among others, were thought to flow from an understanding of the rights and obligations of men to one another. Virtue is certainly compatible with, but does not require, religious belief.

America's Founders knew that it would take more than a perfect plan of government to preserve liberty. Something else would be needed to sustain us: It would require the moral principles of the people to unite and strengthen the urge to peaceful observance of law. Our Founders recognized that the basis of a free government are the people who can act morally without compulsion, who do not willfully violate the rights of others, and who love liberty enough to demand that government act the same. The Founders used the word *virtuous* to describe such people. Defined by Webster's, "virtue" is "a conformity to a standard of right." Such a moral standard is the necessary fountainhead of a free society.

It all harks back to the Declaration of Independence, which referred to "Nature's God," the "Creator," the "Supreme judge of the World," and "Divine Providence." Our nation's Founders came together, voluntarily, to create a limited government to secure for themselves and posterity their God-given rights to life, liberty, and property. Such liberty, they believed, rested on three great supports:

1. Natural law and unalienable natural rights granted by the Creator,
2. A written Constitution to assure a government of laws, not of rulers, and
3. VIRTUE among the people—the best defense against tyranny.

Virtue as the Wellspring of Self-Governance

The United States Founders believed that certain civic virtues were required of citizens in order for the Constitution to work. Numerous primary sources—notably *The Federalist Papers* and *The Autobiography of Benjamin Franklin*—point us to the "Founders' Virtues." Some of those virtues that they believed were essential to keep us a free and functioning republic were as follows:

- Justice
- Self-Governance/Moderation
- Humility
- Responsibility/Prudence
- Perseverance
- Courage
- Respect
- Contribution
- Integrity.[25]

Aristotle understood virtue as a "mean" (or middle) between two extremes. The same character trait, when expressed to the extreme, ceases to be a virtue and instead becomes a vice. For example, too little courage is cowardice, while too much makes one foolhardy. A healthy respect for authority becomes blind obedience to power when unquestioned, but descends into unprincipled recalcitrance when completely lacking. That is the beauty of our founding, that we understood that, in order for self-governance to work and to then elect those who would govern us, we must be in balance. Wary of extreme power. Extreme religion. Extreme vice. Extreme control. Virtue, then, is that part in all of us, when taught early in our homes and institutions, that has nothing to do with our religion per se; it has to do with our souls. There are three things I want to say about *how* virtue must play out in our body politic:

- **Virtue is action.** One's thoughts and words alone don't make a person virtuous—one must act on them.
- **Virtue is a habit.** Aristotle also believed that virtue is a habit. Virtuous behavior is not the result of numerous, individual calculations about which course of action would be most advantageous. It becomes a reflex of sorts. Virtue is how we treat ourselves, and each other. While all virtues must be habits, not all habits are virtuous.
- **Virtue requires a just end.** Our Founders believed that virtue is most exemplified in the pursuit of justice. That virtue is more than keeping a set of rules or religious tenets. Virtue requires of us to act in good conscience and in good faith. To come to the rescue of others when needed. To stand up for right versus wrong. To raise our voice in the defense of others.

Two Americans Who Helped Chart the Course for a Moral and Virtuous Citizenry

BENJAMIN FRANKLIN[26]

> *"They who can give up essential liberty to obtain a little*
> *temporary safety deserve neither liberty nor safety."*
> —*Benjamin Franklin*

Benjamin Franklin was a walking contradiction in so many ways. Particularly when it came to his morals and virtues. On the one hand, this Founding Father was the paragon of American idealism, compassion, revolution, social justice, and faith. Dr. Franklin, along with his countryman John Adams, was one of the key voices to speak up against slavery at the nation's birth in 1775–76, but their protests to emancipate the slaves was shot down by the southern delegates. It was Franklin, in 1726 at age twenty, who came up with a structure to develop his "character," which he called the thirteen virtues:

1. **Temperance**. Eat not to dullness; drink not to elevation.
2. **Silence**. Speak not but what may benefit others or yourself; avoid trifling conversation.
3. **Order**. Let all your things have their places; let each part of your business have its time.
4. **Resolution**. Resolve to perform what you ought; perform without fail what you resolve.
5. **Frugality**. Make no expense but to do good to others or yourself; that is, waste nothing.
6. **Industry**. Lose no time; be always employed in something useful; cut off all unnecessary actions.
7. **Sincerity**. Use no hurtful deceit; think innocently and justly, and, if you speak, speak accordingly.
8. **Justice**. Wrong none by doing injuries, or omitting the benefits that are your duty.
9. **Moderation**. Avoid extremes; forbear resenting injuries so much as you think they deserve.
10. **Cleanliness**. Tolerate no uncleanliness in body, clothes, or habitation.
11. **Tranquility**. Be not disturbed at trifles, or at accidents common or unavoidable.
12. **Chastity**. Rarely use venery but for health or offspring,

never to dullness, weakness, or the injury of your own or
another's peace or reputation.

13. **Humility.** Imitate Jesus and Socrates.[27]

I chose Ben Franklin for the virtuous and moral Code
because it was his ideas and principles more than others that
helped shape this once-fledgling nation, and his diplomatic
skills assured that the newly born United States of America
received the respect of the great European countries. Franklin
is often referred to by historians as "the First American." Franklin earned that title for his early and indefatigable campaigning
for colonial unity, initially as an author and spokesman in London for several colonies. As the first United States ambassador
to France, he exemplified the emerging heart and values of the
emerging American nation.

More than that, Franklin was foundational in defining the
American ethos as a marriage of the practical values of thrift, hard
work, education, community spirit, self-governing institutions,
and opposition to authoritarianism both political and religious,
with the scientific and tolerant values of the Enlightenment. In
the words of historian Henry Steele Commager, "In a Franklin
could be merged the virtues of Puritanism without its defects,
the illumination of the Enlightenment without its heat." To
American journalist Walter Isaacson, this makes Franklin "the
most accomplished American of his age and the most influential
in inventing the type of society America would become."[28]

However, like us, Franklin was a flawed man. He was
the model of an American: Founding Father, delegate to the

Constitutional Convention for Pennsylvania, inventor, printer, statesman, diplomat, Freemason, father, husband, patriot. Yet, in his private life, Franklin was known as quite the ladies' man, before he married his wife, Deborah Read, to whom he stayed married for thirty-eight years. Franklin is known to have sired at least one illegitimate son, "William," from his dalliances, but he is believed to have been faithful to his wife during the course of their marriage.

What Benjamin Franklin's life teaches us is that a truly moral and virtuous life is a process of growth, humility, compassion, and care of others. It is not about perfecting a public mask or image that is false in reality. It is about the perfection of the union of our individual states through her people.

How many of our modern-day politicians have deceived us about marriages of convenience, only for us to find out they had children and loves elsewhere? How many of our modern-day politicians—and even clergy—have spoken to us of family values, only to live out very few of them? We have seen some of our finest American presidents get caught up in adulterous liaisons and affairs that rocked the nation. Yet they served the people's interests well. The thing I think we all need to understand is that we are an imperfect people. Our nation started out quite imperfectly, as half-slave and half-free. Yet we righted ourselves, because somewhere in our moral conscience we knew how immoral and evil slavery was. Somehow we knew deep in our American soul that enslaving one man to make profit for another was unjust. Somehow we evolved to understand that Thomas Jefferson's words "All Men Are

Created Equal" meant just that. "All men" and "All women," not just some.

HARRIET BEECHER STOWE[29]

"Perhaps it is impossible for a person who does no good to do no harm." —Harriet Beecher Stowe

Enter Harriet Beecher Stowe. She believed her great purpose in life was to write. And write she did. Her most famous work, *Uncle Tom's Cabin*, is credited as the book that put a vivid face to American slavery. The book that started a "civil war," some would later say.

Stowe was the daughter of a prominent Connecticut family. Her father was a reverend and her mother a homemaker, who passed away when Harriet was just five years old. Her father not only encouraged his sons, but also his two daughters, to make persuasive arguments at the family table. The Beechers took in boarders from Tapping Reeve's law school in Litchfield, Connecticut. Lyman Beecher, Harriet's father, taught religion at Sarah Pierce's Litchfield Female Academy and honed the debating talents of both his students and his children.

Stowe began her formal education at Sarah Pierce's Academy, one of the earliest to encourage girls to study academic subjects and not simply ornamental arts. In 1824, Stowe became first a student and then a teacher at Hartford Female Seminary, founded by her sister, Catharine. There, Stowe furthered her writing talents, spending many hours composing essays.[30]

Stowe would author more than thirty books in her lifetime,

but her most famous work was published when she was in her forties, well into midlife. That book, *Uncle Tom's Cabin,* exposed the truth about the greatest social injustice of her day—slavery. Her passion for writing afforded her a great purpose in helping to perfect the "Union" by exposing the hypocrisy, degradation, immorality, and lack of any virtue in American slavery. Her book depicted the harsh life for African Americans under slavery, and it reached millions as a novel and a play, becoming influential both in the United States and Great Britain. It energized antislavery forces in the American North, while provoking widespread anger in the South.

In 1850, Congress passed the Fugitive Slave Law, prohibiting assistance to fugitives and strengthening sanctions even in free states. At the time, Stowe had moved with her family to Brunswick, Maine, where her husband was teaching at Bowdoin College. Stowe claimed to have had a vision of a dying slave during a communion service at the college chapel, which inspired her to write his story. Historians, however, believe that what allowed her to empathize with slaves was the loss of her eighteen-month-old son, Samuel Charles Stowe, to cholera. She was overheard to have stated the following: "Having experienced losing someone so close to me, I can sympathize with all the poor, powerless slaves at the unjust auctions. You will always be in my heart, Samuel Charles Stowe."[31]

On March 9, 1850, Stowe wrote to Dr. Gamaliel Bailey, Jr., the editor of *National Era,* an abolitionist newspaper in Washington, D.C., that she planned to write a story about the problem of slavery: "I feel now that the time is come when even a woman or a child who can speak a word for freedom and humanity is bound to speak. . . . I hope every woman who can write will not be silent." Bailey contracted with Stowe for a story that would "paint a word picture of slavery" that would run in installments. Stowe expected *Life Among the Lowly* (as it was then called) to be three or four installments. She wrote more than thirty. Eventually those articles would become *Uncle Tom's Cabin*.

Uncle Tom's Cabin not only brought financial security to Stowe, but also enabled her to write full-time. She began publishing multiple works per year, including *The Key to Uncle Tom's Cabin*, which documented the case histories on which she had based her novel, and *Dred: A Tale from the Swamp*, another and more forceful antislavery novel. Stowe's passion for writing allowed her to do something that few women of her time, the 1850s, could do: use her moral (and, yes, religious) upbringing to publicly express her thoughts and beliefs at a time when a woman could not speak publicly, much less vote or hold office. And she was contributing financially to the Stowe family household income.[32]

According to Daniel R. Lincoln, the goal of *Uncle Tom's Cabin* was to educate northerners on the realistic horrors of the things that were happening in the South. The other purpose was to try to make people in the South feel more empathetic toward the people they were forcing into slavery.[33] The book's emotional portrayal of the effects of slavery on individuals captured the nation's attention.

Stowe's portrayal of slavery sparked a national outcry and emboldened the abolitionist movement to grow in strength and power. By standing firm in her morals and virtues she showed the nation that slavery touched all of society, beyond the people directly involved as masters, traders, and slaves. She connected us as Americans. She used her voice through her words, and she called us to rise up to the great call of our founding: *All men are created equal. And endowed by their Creator with certain unalienable rights.*

★ ★ ★ ★ ★ ★ ★ ★ ★ ★ ★ ★ ★ ★ ★ ★

Reclaiming Our Founders' Vision

Morals and virtues do not seem high on our national radar anymore. The 2016 presidential campaign taught us all a lot about the flaws in our leaders, and by default ourselves. Perhaps we need to see morality and virtue much as Franklin and Stowe did, not as absolutes, but as ideals that we as Americans must strive for. Given the past few years of our national and political landscape, here are five critical morals and virtues that we as citizens of our time should strive to model and seek in our leaders to help preserve our great republic:

1. **Justice:** The best way we the people can engage justice is in the electing and appointing of judges. Be informed (Code #1) and engage your elected officials to appoint judges who uphold the fundamental principles of our Constitution, as well as judges who understand that the Constitution is a living, breathing document whose principles must be adapted to our time. Also important is that we get engaged in the causes of our time for racial, economic, and social justice. March. Write. Protest. Speak up. Make a change.

2. **Charity:** The oldest of virtues—it's in the Bible—charity really does begin in our homes. What we teach our kids about giving, love, and helping others lays the foundation for the kind of society we have as Americans.

3. **Respect:** Bullying among our kids and our adults is at an all-time high. Social media posts, texting, and workplace violence are common now. Again, we have to do better at laying the foundations of respect by what we model to our kids, to our colleagues, and in our communities.

4. **Kindness:** We are all dealing with difficulties in life. One of our most basic needs is to have people be kind to us.

5. **Diligence:** Hard work is our foundation. The story of Americans is a story of people who never quit. Who forged ahead. Who dug deep. Blood. Sweat. Tears. Toil. That is how we built our great nation. We need to instill this virtue in our children and in ourselves. America isn't free. You have to want it. And be willing to work for it.

★ ★ ★ ★ ★ ★ ★ ★ ★ ★ ★ ★ ★ ★ ★

"A little rebellion now and

then is a good thing."

—Thomas Jefferson

CODE 3

BE AN INDIVIDUAL—NONCONFORMITY

Our most cherished value as Americans is our desire for individualism and freedom. Of all we value, of all we hold dear, and of all we treasure most, being individuals is at the very core of our founding. We crave nothing more than our ability to be unique. To be different. To not conform to what the rest of the world does and how it does so. Our Founding Fathers and Mothers understood this well because they literally put their lives, their families, and their fortunes on the line to secure the rights of the individual.

One of the great paradoxes of our founding is that from our diversity and our differences have come some of the most amazing individuals in the history of our nation. In the history of the world. Men and women who blazed trails. Who staked out new territory. Who braved the frontier, learned how to fly, and who even walked on the moon. We Americans are trained from a very early age to have a strong individualistic character in order to shape our own destinies. We teach our children about brave heroes and heroines who forged new paths and opened closed doors. People who stood above the mundane. We take pride in the genius of one man or one woman to change the course of human history. We Americans value the freedom and liberty to make our own decisions, to be independent, and to live free.

The Founding Fathers, as we know, were all great thinkers. They studied history, philosophy, economics, political science, and law, among other disciplines, and used what they learned as the basis of the American founding. They were more than just thinkers, however; they were men of action. In their own ways, they discovered the elements of two literally revolutionary ideas that they put into practice for the first time on earth in 1776: the principles of individual rights combined with a republican government. With those two overarching principles in mind, they intended to change history in a phenomenal way that has never been matched since.

The rights of the individual are what make America different from any other nation on the face of the earth. We are avid nonconformists. We are rebels even. And what I see happening today is a soft and slow movement toward conformity. Toward "political correctness." Toward taking away the rights of the individual and moving more toward the rights of the majority. Or the perceived majority. This is not who we are as Americans. It is great individuals who have made America great. It is the power of man's free will to think. To dream. To dare. To challenge. To push. To create. To battle. To undo. To mend. That has made America a nation of inventors, builders, businessmen, scientists, creators, statesmen, aviators, explorers, and educators.

What's important to note is that the Founders believed that men needed rights precisely to exercise their free will, yet act in accordance with natural laws, and with God. How ironic, yet how true. America works precisely because we value the individual but we do so in accordance with moral and virtuous standards. We do so by keeping God at the center, by allowing for and encouraging the exercise of free religion. We do so by being informed, engaged, and self-governing. America works and thrives as a great nation because we don't oppress our people's ideals, rights, thoughts, faith, or enterprise.

In this Code we are going to look at what it means to be an individual and a nonconformist. We are going to look at two great Americans from the twentieth century who model for us the power of the individual. And the power of not conforming to social norms, limitations, or even unjust laws. By not conforming, these individuals changed those social norms. They broke down barriers, and strengthened America by their example.

As with the previous Codes, my goal is to help us to reclaim the greatness of not just America, but of individual Americans. It is, after all, people who built our great nation. Men and women from all walks of life. Immigrants. Former slaves and slave owners. Merchants and laborers. Inventors and writers. People who had vision and who dared to go against the grain and make their dreams come true. And who had the courage to believe, by staking out their place in the world, no matter how daunting or difficult, that they could in fact make the world a better place.

What Are Individual Rights?

In 1787, Thomas Jefferson, the chief architect of the Declaration of Independence, urged the drafters of the Constitution to clearly identify the rights of the people. The rights of the "individual." Jefferson believed, like John Stuart Mill, that the individual was sovereign. Sacrosanct. And critical to the proper functioning of government. Jefferson also believed strongly that historically governments and nations had harshly restricted the rights of people's lives, and that such governments had interfered in questionable areas with no just power to act or with no jurisdictional authority, resulting in a reduction or loss of individual rights. This was the basis upon which the colonies ultimately broke ties with Great Britain.

Like Jefferson, many of the Founding Fathers' generation feared the encompassing and absolute power of a federal government, and they demanded a Bill of Rights to protect the people and limit the powers of a federal government.

The Bill of Rights contains the first ten amendments to the United States Constitution and includes the basic privileges of all United States citizens. Many of the rights written in the amendments resulted from the shared experience of both the British and the American colonists under British rule. All the amendments reflect the close ties between personal freedom and democracy as envisioned by the Founding Fathers' generation. Over the years, the definitions of some rights have changed, and new concepts, such as privacy interests, were added to the Constitution. But the rights of the people are the core of American democracy. In this way, the United States is unique in the world; its tradition of individual rights strongly reflects the American experience.

Written by James Madison, in response to calls from several states for greater constitutional protection for individual liberties, the Bill of Rights lists specific prohibitions on governmental power. The Virginia Declaration of Rights, written by George Mason, strongly influenced Madison. We would do well in this generation to remember that we still have a Bill of Rights as citizens and as individuals.

Lest we forget their value and power in our day-to-day lives, they are as follows:

1. **Amendment I:** Congress shall make no law respecting an establishment of religion, or prohibiting the free exercise thereof; or abridging the freedom of speech, or of the press; or the right of the people peaceably to assemble, and to petition the government for a redress of grievances.
2. **Amendment II:** A well-regulated militia, being necessary to the security of a free state, the right of the people to keep and bear arms, shall not be infringed.
3. **Amendment III:** No soldier shall, in time of peace be quartered in any house, without the consent of the owner, nor in time of war, but in a manner to be prescribed by law.
4. **Amendment IV:** The right of the people to be secure in their persons, houses, papers, and effects, against

unreasonable searches and seizures, shall not be violated, and no warrants shall issue, but upon probable cause, supported by oath or affirmation, and particularly describing the place to be searched, and the persons or things to be seized.

5. **Amendment V:** No person shall be held to answer for a capital, or otherwise infamous crime, unless on a presentment or indictment of a grand jury, except in cases arising in the land or naval forces, or in the militia, when in actual service in time of war or public danger; nor shall any person be subject for the same offense to be twice put in jeopardy of life or limb; nor shall be compelled in any criminal case to be a witness against himself, nor be deprived of life, liberty, or property, without due process of law; nor shall private property be taken for public use, without just compensation.

6. **Amendment VI:** In all criminal prosecutions, the accused shall enjoy the right to a speedy and public trial, by an impartial jury of the state and district wherein the crime shall have been committed, which district shall have been previously ascertained by law, and to be informed of the nature and cause of the accusation; to be confronted with the witnesses against him; to have compulsory process for obtaining witnesses in his favor, and to have the assistance of counsel for his defense.

7. **Amendment VII:** In suits at common law, where the value in controversy shall exceed twenty dollars, the right of trial

by jury shall be preserved, and no fact tried by a jury, shall be otherwise reexamined in any court of the United States, then according to the rules of the common law.

8. **Amendment VIII:** Excessive bail shall not be required, nor excessive fines imposed, nor cruel and unusual punishments inflicted.

9. **Amendment IX:** The enumeration in the Constitution, of certain rights, shall not be construed to deny or disparage others retained by the people.

10. **Amendment X:** The powers not delegated to the United States by the Constitution, nor prohibited by it to the states, are reserved to the states respectively, or to the people.[34]

This Bill of Rights is the foundation of what American liberty and individual rights are all about. Fast-forward to the twenty-first century: We have a large and powerful federal government with more than ninety thousand employees. We have a backlogged federal and state court system, with limited jurists available to serve, and a U.S. Senate that is slow to confirm new judges. We have people marching in the streets against a growing armed police presence that seemingly violates the rights of some citizens at will. The right to keep and bear arms is a hotly debated topic in our current political discourse. How much regulation is enough, and what doesn't go far enough? The issues that we are wrestling with now were settled long ago by our Founders. Yet, two centuries after our birth as a nation, we seem to have veered off course and allowed the precious rights of the individual to be overwhelmed by the power of the mechanisms of government.

The Power of Nonconformity

One of the best ways to learn, and to teach our children how to learn, is by example. We have already established that this nation values freedom and individual liberty above all. And when that freedom or liberty has been oppressed in our past, whether at Lexington and Concord in the 1770s, during the Civil War of the 1860s, the suffragist movement of the early 1900s, or during the Civil Rights Movement of the 1960s, good men and women have answered the call to fight for their rights, believing that, by securing their own individual liberty, they would secure liberty for all other men and women. Our nation started as a nation of rebel rule breakers. They refused to have their rights trampled upon by one of the greatest empires on earth. They refused to conform to what felt unnatural and unholy to their very nature. We of this generation are their heirs. We are their legacy. And we seem to be moving away from the individual and closer to the notion of "group rights."

"Conformity is obligatory," Emerson once wrote, meaning that society expects individuals to conform to its conventions. A man of his time in the 1840s, Ralph Waldo Emerson was known as one of the American transcendentalists, a very formal word that describes a very simple idea: People, men and women equally, have knowledge about themselves and the world around them that transcends, or goes beyond, what they can see, hear, taste, touch, or feel. This knowledge comes through intuition and imagination, not through logic or the senses. People can trust themselves to be their own authority on what is right, and not have to be spoon-fed by others or institutions.

A transcendentalist is a person who accepts these ideas not as religious beliefs but as a way of understanding life relationships. In his famous essay "Self-Reliance," Emerson talks about his belief in the individual being "true to thy self" by giving Americans of his time a way of thinking about the power of individual ideas, beliefs, thoughts, and actions. If I could accurately summarize what Emerson challenged us to become, I would do it with these thirteen nuggets of his pure brilliance on the rights of man that flow from our deepest and innermost sanctuary: *our free will.*

- Trust thyself: every heart vibrates to that iron string.
- Society everywhere is in conspiracy against the manhood of every one of its members.
- Whoso would be a man must be a nonconformist.
- What I must do is all that concerns me, not what the people think.
- A foolish consistency is the hobgoblin of little minds, adored by little statesmen and philosophers and divines. With consistency a great soul has simply nothing to do.
- It is easy to see that a greater self-reliance must work a revolution in all the offices and relations of men; in their

religion; in their education; in their pursuits; their modes of living; their associations; in their property; in their speculative views.

- Insist on yourself; never imitate.
- Society never advances. It recedes as fast on one side as it gains on the other.
- The civilized man has built a coach, but has lost the use of his feet.
- Society is a wave. The wave moves onward, but the water of which it is composed does not.
- And so the reliance on Property, including the reliance on governments which protect it, is the want of self-reliance.
- Nothing can bring you peace but yourself. Nothing can bring you peace but the triumph of principles.[35]

Two Americans Who Broke the Rules to Stand on Their Individual Rights

JACKIE ROBINSON[36]

"A life is not important except in the impact it has on other lives. I'm not concerned with your liking or disliking me. All I ask is that you respect me as a human being." —Jackie Robinson

There is nothing more American than baseball. It is one of our favorite pastimes and allows us to come together across race, religion, region, age, and gender; root for our favorite team;

have a beer; eat a hot dog; and enjoy the game with family and friends.

But there was a time in America, not too long ago, that certain individuals (namely African Americans) could only watch the game in the "Colored" section. And they could not *play* the game regardless of their talent or their ability. Jackie Roosevelt Robinson is best known for being the first African American to ever play major-league professional baseball. In 1947, the second baseman Robinson broke the color barrier by signing with the Brooklyn Dodgers. The Dodgers, by hiring Robinson, heralded the end of racial segregation that had relegated black players to the Negro Leagues since the 1880s.

Robinson would go on to have an exceptional ten-year baseball career: He was the recipient of the inaugural MLB Rookie of the Year Award in 1947; an All-Star for six consecutive seasons from 1949 through 1954; and won the National League's Most Valuable Player Award in 1949, the first black player so honored. But Robinson's becoming a professional baseball player is not what made him great, or what made him a great American. What makes Jackie Robinson the stuff that legends are made of is his refusal to conform to a system of a segregated America, and a segregated sport that he loved and in which he excelled.

Jackie Robinson was not a Founding Father. He was not a statesman or diplomat. He did not hail from wealth or privilege. But he understood that, by standing up for his individual rights, first by serving his country in the military during World War II, as a commissioned officer (he and boxing great Joe Louis had to protest to get their commissions), and then rising up out of the segregated Negro Leagues to play professional baseball, he would be opening the door for others like him to use their individual gifts and talents on the baseball field, and, frankly, anywhere else.

What makes Robinson such a poster child for American individualism is that, through his public character (Code #2), his use of nonviolence, and his unquestionable talent, he effectively challenged the traditional basis of segregation, which then marked many other aspects of American life. By showing up as one man on the *all-American* baseball field, he forced those in the majority—who, at that time, were still blocking African Americans (some eighty years after the Civil War)—to acknowledge that African Americans could succeed on the baseball field, and by extension could succeed in other walks of life.

By accepting Dodger manager Branch Rickey's challenge to join the Dodgers, Robinson created a national pride that had an impact on the culture of, and contributed significantly to, the Civil Rights Movement, which would follow almost a decade later. A lesser-known fact is that Robinson was the first black television analyst in Major League Baseball, and the first black vice president of a major American corporation (*Chock full o'Nuts*, a coffee company). In the 1960s, he helped establish the Freedom National Bank, an African-American-owned financial institution based in Harlem, New York. In recognition of his achievements on and off the field, Robinson was posthumously awarded the Congressional and Presidential Medals of Freedom.[37]

AMELIA EARHART[38]

"The most effective way to do it, is to do it."
—Amelia Earhart

Amelia Earhart was a woman ahead of her time. Yet because her early life convictions were strong, and she believed in being her own person above societal expectations, she was able to do what few women of her time in the 1920s and 1930s could do: prevail against challenging prejudicial and financial obstacles, which awaited her in her quest to become a great American aviator. Raised in an upper-middle-class family, Earhart was something of a tomboy (a real no-no in her day). Defying conventional female behavior, Earhart shunned beautiful dresses, hair ribbons, and social graces, preferring instead to climb trees, run, jump, and hunt with a .22-caliber rifle. She also kept a scrapbook of newspaper clippings about the lives of successful women making strides in predominantly male-oriented fields, including film direction and production, law, advertising, management, and mechanical engineering.

After graduating from Hyde Park High School, in Illinois, in 1915, Earhart attended Ogontz, a girl's finishing school in the suburbs of Philadelphia. She left in the middle of her second year to work as a nurse's aide in a military hospital in

Canada during World War I, attended college, and later became a social worker at Denison House, a settlement house in Boston. Earhart took her first flying lesson on January 3, 1921, and, in six months, managed to save enough money to buy her first plane. The secondhand Kinner Airster was a two-seater biplane painted bright yellow. Earhart named her newest obsession *The Canary* and used it to set her first women's record by rising to an altitude of 14,000 feet. On May 15, 1923, Amelia Earhart became the sixteenth woman to be issued a pilot's license by the world governing body for aeronautics, the Fédération Aéronautique Internationale. She was the first woman to fly across the Atlantic Ocean, in 1928, as well as the first person to fly over both the Atlantic and Pacific Oceans.

What made Earhart such a good model of American individualism was her belief in herself, and her talents, despite convention. As a woman of her time, she was expected to marry (she did marry publisher George Putnam), have a family, and tend to her societal duties as a woman of a prominent husband. (Conformity was indeed obligatory.) However, what Earhart did was model for a generation of American women the power of their dreams. The power of being an individual over being a woman. The power of the possible.

Through her celebrity endorsements, she gained notoriety and acceptance in the public eye. She accepted a position as associate editor at *Cosmopolitan* magazine, using the media outlet to campaign for commercial air travel. From this forum, she became a promoter for Transcontinental Air Transport, later known as Trans World Airlines (TWA), and was a vice president of National Airways, which flew routes in the Northeast. She truly paved the way for women in nontraditional fields such as aeronautics, engineering, mathematics, and aviation, proving once again the power of the individual when left to pursue life, liberty, and happiness as he or she sees fit.[39]

★　★　★　★　★　★　★　★　★　★　★　★　★　★　★

Reclaiming Our Founders' Vision

The concept of a **right** relates to the freedom from interference by other individuals or the government. **Individual rights** refer to the liberties of each individual to pursue life and goals without interference from other individuals or the government. Examples of individual rights include the right to life, liberty, and the pursuit of happiness, as stated in the United States Declaration of Independence. Here is a summary of our rights as individuals in our time that we seem to be wresting with as a nation when it comes to our politics, the Supreme Court, and our public discourse and debate:

1. **The right to privacy.** This one is huge. And the one most in danger of being eradicated by a global super information highway. Computer hacking. Identity theft. And a government that seeks more and more rights to intrude on our privacy to "protect" the republic.

2. **The right to free speech.** This one is central to our founding as a nation. The right to raise your voice, assemble peaceably, and not fear arrest or retribution—or worse, as we see happening now, if you disagree with another's opinion, you're a hater, squashing dissent in our public discourse and privately held beliefs. As was once famously said, "I disapprove of what you say, but I will defend to the death your right to say it."[40]

3. **The right to free religion.** This fundamental American right—unlike any other country in the world—is to me our most sacred. The right to worship God as you see Him. The right to live out that faith freely at your place of employment, in the public sphere, and in your house of worship is what makes America special. The right of the individual to be unafraid to read his Bible, his Koran, or any other sacred text in a public place, to wear a cross or symbol of faith on his garments, to be able to speak about his faith and share it with others is what makes America different. We must guard against the notion that for one Christian man to speak of his faith and by so doing offend a Muslim man and his faith, that means one of the faiths must bow to the other. That is wrong. That is not who we are. We honor all men's faiths. We honor all men's religions. One is not superior to the other, and not one has the right to limit the other.

★ ★ ★ ★ ★ ★ ★ ★ ★ ★ ★ ★ ★ ★ ★

"Government is not reason; it is not eloquence. It is force. And force, like fire, is a dangerous servant and a fearful master."

—George Washington

CODE

4

BE VIGILANT: KEEP WATCH ON THE GOVERNMENT, ESTABLISH A FREE PRESS, AND OPEN COURTS OF REDRESS

One of the things I am most passionate about, as you can probably tell by now, is history, and specifically, American history. The early history of America is legion with revolutionary men and women, some wealthy, some humble and poor, but all thinkers. They founded this country on the powerful principle of self-governance, small government, the fundamental "unalienable rights" that we all naturally possess, and the "duty" we the people have to knock our government down a peg or two when it begins to restrain us or to restrict our rights.

Think about it for a moment. Our Founders put the duty on us. Not the government. Not those who would govern or preside over the affairs of state. What a radical idea. What a radical notion that men and women from whatever station in life are equipped by their Creator to govern themselves. To keep watch.

To be vigilant and, if necessary, "refresh the tree of liberty" by whatever means necessary to keep the people free, and to keep the government of the people, by the people, and for the people.

Our most sacred duty as Americans, then, is to stay free and to preserve our liberty. To preserve the republic for which it stands. Our most obvious foe in this effort, whether intended or not, always has been and will always be government. The government, as envisioned by our Founders in 1776, is nothing like what we have today in 2016. We have more than ninety thousand federal employees, in more than thirty agencies that we know of. We have an $18 trillion national debt (and climbing) and we the people are more and more burdened with excessive taxes at all levels of government.

The Founders were clear that the government's role was essential, but that it must also be diligently controlled by the people lest the government become too big for the people. In short, and with good reason, as we saw in the first few Codes in this book, the Founders distrusted strong government. Period. Their own experience with a tyrannical monarch in King George, and a study of history, taught them that overly powerful governments turn oppressive. That overly powerful men placed into power would try to exercise absolute power. That people could never be safe or free if turned over to the care of a powerful government.

In fact, two of our nation's Founders were very clear on this. One, the governor of New Jersey (also a signer of the Declaration of Independence), William Livingston, shared firsthand family accounts of fleeing oppression in Europe in his journal during the 1750s. His writings were key in turning the colonists' minds toward revolution. In one such entry, Livingston reminded his readers how "the countless Sufferings of your pious Predecessors for Liberty of Conscience, and the Right of private Judgment," drove them "to this country, then a dreary Waste and barren Desert."[41] Livingston's own Presbyterian grandfather was among those pious predecessors who fled to America seeking a better life, free of the oppression so flagrant in European governments of the time.

Similarly, John Jay, our first chief justice of the U.S. Supreme Court, once wrote a gripping account of how his paternal grandfather, a French Protestant, returned home to La Rochelle, France, from a trading voyage abroad to find his parents, siblings, and neighbors gone. Their houses were occupied by soldiers, their church destroyed, their savings confiscated. While he had been away, he learned, France had revoked its toleration of the Huguenots. He was lucky to be able to sneak aboard a ship and sail away to freedom in the New World. Similarly, Jay's maternal grandparents had to flee anti-Protestant persecution, one of them from Paris and one of them from Bohemia. Justice Jay's son and biographer shared the story proudly, as it was a living family legend.[42]

The point is this: Our Founders understood the gravity of a nation being governed first by the people, and yet they also knew a government was necessary. In fact, they ended up by opting for a stronger government than that which had been adopted by the Congress in November 1777. By the time the Constitutional Convention convened in May 1787, a consensus had developed that the Articles of Confederation were severely flawed, but there was uncertainty about what kind of government could sustain a republic through the ages. They knew it couldn't be too weak, but it also couldn't be too strong. The Articles of Confederation (formally the Articles of Confederation and Perpetual Union) was an agreement among all thirteen original states that served as America's first Constitution. Its drafting by a committee, appointed by the Second Continental Congress, began on July 12, 1776, and an approved version was sent to the states for ratification in late 1777. The formal ratification by all thirteen states was completed in early 1781. Government under the Articles was superseded by a new constitution and a federal form of government in 1789.[43]

Even unratified, the Articles provided a system for the Continental Congress to direct the American Revolutionary War, conduct diplomacy with Europe, and deal with territorial issues and Native American relations. Nevertheless, the weakness of the government created by the Articles became a matter of concern for key nationalists. On March 4, 1789, the general government under the Articles was replaced with the federal government under the United States Constitution. The new Constitution provided for a much stronger federal government, with a chief executive (a president), courts, and taxing powers.

This is a key point because it explains the foundation for the huge federal bureaucracy that we now see in 2016. In order to protect the principle of self-governance, the Founders designed an elaborate set of *checks and balances* so that they could give the government enough power to govern, while harnessing it with multiple layers of accountability that would hold it in place so it didn't trample upon the rights of the people. From our high school civics class, we all learned about the checks and balances among the three branches. But teachers seldom mention the intended check of the national government by the states. Nor, were we taught that the Founders wanted our national leaders selected and elected by different means as yet another check on a runaway government. Lastly, the Constitution ratified by the people was supposed to be the premier check to prevent our government from becoming oppressive.

I think that we can all agree, regardless of political party affiliation, that our federal government has become overly large, burdensome, and in many ways oppressive. Consider President Bill Clinton in the 1990s declaring "the era of big government is over." Whether you like Bill Clinton or not, ironically he was a conservative Democrat who tried to downsize government. He also had a Republican congress to check him and hold him accountable. Sometimes, then, divided government is the best government. Our leaders seem to thrive best when they are checked and balanced by leaders with opposite points of views and perspectives on how best to move America forward.[44]

In this Code we are going to look at two of our most important founding principles explaining how we the people are to keep watch on the federal, state, and local governments, as well as the people we elect and give power to in Washington, D.C.:

1. Freedom of the press
2. Power of the courts to fight unjust laws.

In this Code, unlike the previous ones, although we will highlight famous Americans who helped to shape our nation's history and move us toward a more perfect union, we will do so in the context of two of the most fundamental principles in the amendments to the U.S. Constitution.

Freedom of the Press

The First Amendment to the U.S. Constitution reads as follows:

> *Congress shall make no law* respecting an establishment of religion, or prohibiting the free exercise thereof; or *abridging the freedom* of speech, or *of the press*; or the right of the people peaceably to assemble, and to petition the government for a redress of grievances. [Emphasis mine.]

I think it wise and brave of our Founders to have placed up front in our Constitution the importance of a free press, and a citizen-based media (in addition to the traditional news outlets, we now have bloggers and social-media exchanges) that would be a watchdog of sorts on the federal government. Be clear that this is exactly what the Founders intended. Supreme Court

Justices Hugo Black and William O. Douglas explained in their concurring opinion in *New York Times Co. v. United States* (1971):

> In the First Amendment, the Founding Fathers gave the free press the protection it must have to fulfill its essential role in our democracy. *The press was to serve the governed, not the governors. The Government's power to censor the press was abolished so that the press would remain forever free to censure the Government.* The press was protected so that it could bare the secrets of government and inform the people. [Emphasis mine.]

In layman's terms what that means is this: The purpose of the free press clause of the First Amendment was *to keep an eye on people in power and maintain a check on corruption.* Period. Our Founders understood power because they had been oppressed by the great power of their time. And they took great pains to ensure in our founding documents and Codes that we the people would forever be free if we followed their wisdom and instruction. There is no better example of the power and importance of a free press preserving democracy in the history of our nation than in the 1972 Watergate scandal.

BOB WOODWARD and CARL BERNSTEIN[45]

"A reporter's ability to keep the bond of confidentiality often enables him to learn the hidden or secret aspects of government." —Bob Woodward

"You can't serve the public good without the truth as a
bottom line." —Carl Bernstein

B ob Woodward and Carl Bernstein were two young reporters in their twenties when they were assigned a story about a
burglary that took place at the Democratic National Committee
headquarters in Washington, D.C., at the Watergate Hotel and
office complex in June 1972.

"Five Held in Plot to Bug Democrats' Offices Here," said
the *Washington Post* headline at the bottom of page one on Sun-
day, June 18, 1972. The story by *Post* staff writer Alfred E.
Lewis reported that a team of burglars had been arrested inside
the Watergate offices of the DNC. This story would, in fact, be
the first in a serious and stunning chain of events that would
rock Washington and the nation to its core. For the two years
that followed, Woodward and Bernstein would make journal-
istic history by unmasking a cover-up that led all the way up to
the president of the United States of America. The initial story
intrigued the two young reporters Woodward and Bernstein,
who were called in to work on it.

The rest, as we know, is, of course, history. Literally. The
two enterprising and unyielding journalists risked life, limb, and
career as they worked for more than a year to piece together
information, sources, reports—anything that could lead to
the true source of the break-ins. After being able to trace the
break-in to Nixon campaign aides, and selling it to their legendary tough editor at the *Washington Post,* Ben Bradlee, the reporters realized that what had first appeared as a low-level break-in

by political hacks could quite possibly lead to the highest officials in the land. In fact, to the highest official in the land: President Richard M. Nixon.

Their famous, or rather infamous, source, was "Deep
Throat," who we would learn much later, in 2005, was a
high-ranking FBI official, Mark Felt. Felt helped the two young
reporters create timelines, find witnesses, and gather the critical information needed to expose the wrongdoers within the
government—and ultimately the thirty-seventh president of
the United States. Felt held several posts in the FBI, ultimately
becoming Associate Director, the number one job in the bureau
during the administration of President Richard M. Nixon. He
had the means and the motive to help uncover the web of internal spies, secret surveillance, dirty tricks, and cover-ups that led
to Nixon's unprecedented resignation on August 9, 1974, and to
prison sentences for some of Nixon's highest-ranking aides.

The importance of what Woodward and Bernstein did as
members of a free press cannot be overstated. They did exactly
what the Founding Fathers envisioned might someday be
necessary to protect the people from a corrupt president and
high-ranking government officials. Two young, unassuming
reporters with everything to lose challenged the most powerful man in the world. They also started a national firestorm
that tested the checks and balances of our great democratic
republic. During the Watergate scandal every branch of government was involved: the judicial, the executive, and the legislative. Each branch worked in concert, yet each carefully

checked the others so as not to overstep their constitutional authority. Ultimately the free press prevailed by shining the light of day on government abuse of power for all Americans to see. Rather than being impeached, President Nixon resigned, the only American president ever to do so. The free press today seems to be much more concerned with punditry, opining, and celebrity rather than bringing government abuse to light. For example, take someone like Edward Snowden. Whether or not you agree with what he did, from the Founding Fathers' point of view he would be a patriot because he exposed that the government was infringing upon Americans' fundamental liberty: our right to privacy.

The key takeaway from these two citizen journalists is that our Founders got it right. The First Amendment to the Constitution is the foundation of all we Americans hold dear. The free press is the investigative and accountability arm of we the people to hold the government honest and within the limits of its constitutional power.

Due Process of the Judicial System against Unjust Laws

The free press is just one important aspect of our Bill of Rights. The judicial branch was set up expressly for the citizens to have the right to *due process* (or their day in court, their right to be heard). Again, our Founders understood what it was like, as I shared earlier in this Code, to have their families, property, wealth, and rights taken away at the whim of a king or rogue governments.

The Fifth and Fourteenth Amendments to the United States Constitution each contain a due process clause. Due process deals with the administration of justice, and the due process clause acts as a safeguard from arbitrary denial of life, liberty, or property by the government outside the sanction of law. The Supreme Court of the United States tends to interpret due process clauses more broadly in its case history because these clauses provide four protections:

1. procedural due process (in civil and criminal proceedings),
2. substantive due process (the protection of rights, a speedy trial, etc.)
3. a prohibition against vague laws, and as the vehicle for the incorporation of the Bill of Rights, and
4. ensuring the rights and equality of all citizens.

One of America's greatest defects at the time of our founding was slavery. Once slavery ended in 1863, by presidential proclamation, and once the Civil War was fought and won by the Union in 1865, the nation adopted a code of "separate but equal" segregation, also known as "Jim Crow." It plagued African Americans in this nation for almost one hundred years. That is, until a young attorney named Thurgood Marshall and his cohorts at the National Association for the Advancement of Colored People (NAACP) decided that they had had enough of segregation and the effects it was having on black children and their right to an "equal" education.

THURGOOD MARSHALL[46]

"Our whole constitutional heritage rebels at the thought of giving government the power to control men's minds." —*Thurgood Marshall*

Young Thurgood Marshall grew up in a segregated America. Everything in his world was black and white. Literally. He grew up in an America that lived under *Plessy v. Ferguson*, a landmark Supreme Court case decided in 1896, post-Reconstruction, that established the law of "separate but equal" in the United States. The basic tenet of this law was that black people (then called "colored") would have separate transportation, bathrooms, food counters, hotels, and, most egregiously, schools, separated from whites as long as they were equal. This doctrine was most rampantly enforced in the South, leaving millions of black men and women, who had served their country in two world wars, paid their taxes, and obeyed the laws, left out of a good and equal education.[47]

Born on July 2, 1908, in Baltimore, Maryland, Marshall attended the city's Colored High and Training School (later renamed Frederick Douglass High School), where he was an above-average student, and where he put his finely honed skills of argument to use as a star member of the debate team. The teenaged Marshall was also something of a mischievous trouble-maker. His greatest high school accomplishment, memorizing the entire United States Constitution, was actually a teacher's punishment for misbehaving in class. After graduating in 1926,

Marshall attended Lincoln University, an historically black college in Pennsylvania. There he joined a remarkably distinguished student body that included Kwame Nkrumah, the future president of Ghana; Langston Hughes, the great poet; and Cab Calloway, the famous jazz singer and bandleader. After graduating from Lincoln with honors in 1930, Marshall applied to the University of Maryland Law School. Despite being overqualified academically, Marshall was rejected because of his race.[48]

This firsthand experience with discrimination in education made a lasting impression on Marshall and helped determine the future course of his career. Instead of Maryland, Marshall attended law school in Washington, D.C., at Howard University, another historically black school. The dean of Howard Law School at the time was the pioneering civil rights lawyer Charles Houston. Marshall quickly fell under the tutelage of Houston, a notorious disciplinarian and extraordinarily demanding professor. Marshall recalled of Houston, "He would not be satisfied until he went to a dance on the campus and found all of his students sitting around the wall reading law books instead of partying." Marshall graduated magna cum laude from Howard in 1933.

As counsel to the NAACP, he utilized the judiciary to champion equality for African Americans. Starting with a series of cases that led all the way up to the United States Supreme Court, Marshall is most famous for his role as lead counsel in the historic and landmark Supreme Court case *Brown v. Board of Education* (1954), in which the Supreme Court ended racial segregation in public schools. Marshall and his associates used the courts as their platform and battlefield over a series of decades to ultimately end racial segregation in America. And not just in education—but in all forms of transportation, and the right of African Americans to shop, eat, and sleep wherever they wanted as free citizens of the United States.

Marshall and his cadre of attorneys at the NAACP started a movement in America. A movement to push back against the powerful and mighty federal government that had written and codified unjust and unconstitutional laws against its own black citizens. They masterfully used the courts. Case by case. Jurisdiction by jurisdiction. And they won, challenging and chipping away at government-sanctioned racial segregation in America through the guarantee of "due process" of law. Ultimately their efforts launched a civil rights movement that birthed Rosa Parks, Martin Luther King, Jr., and Medgar Evers, and lasted from the 1950s to 1970s, resulting in civil rights and voting rights legislation in 1964 and 1965.

In an historic move, President Lyndon B. Johnson appointed Thurgood Marshall in 1967 to the Supreme Court, where he served for twenty-four years. He died in Maryland on January 24, 1993.

Both Woodward and Bernstein, as citizen journalists, and Justice Marshall, as a citizen lawyer, tested and trusted the guarantees of the Constitution that all men are entitled to a free press and information about their government, as well as due process in the courts. And, by doing so, by standing for truth, justice, and integrity, they advanced our great republic higher, moving us ever closer to a more perfect union.

I chose these three American men because they inspired me to become first an attorney and ultimately a journalist. They inspired me by their courage to challenge the status quo and to put themselves on the line in order to see the Constitution fulfilled. Candidly, I am not sure that among my peers of journalists that there is another Bob Woodward or Carl Bernstein. We all seem so focused now on celebrity and popularity. We all so want to be on TV, have a show, have our columns featured, that we have forgotten about what the Constitution charges us to do: keep the government and our leaders honest and accountable. I am also not convinced that there is another Thurgood Marshall among us. A man who literally put his life on the line every time he dared to fight a court case against segregation and unjust laws in America. My hope, however, in sharing their stories is that a new generation of Americans will get to know them and by doing so, aspire to be like them.

★ ★ ★ ★ ★ ★ ★ ★ ★ ★ ★ ★ ★ ★ ★ ★

Reclaiming Our Founders' Vision

The questions many pundits and analysts have been asking since the 2016 presidential campaign are: What role did the media play in electing the new president? What role do journalists play in the kind of information we get as the public, and is that information fair and unbiased? The reality is that, in the information age, we have access to news 24/7. There are liberal channels and conservative channels. Liberal pundits and conservative ones. We can follow the nominations of our Supreme Court justices and watch, in real time, arguments before the Court. We can see everything now, thanks to the first Amendment, and if we don't like what we see, or how we are treated, we can seek redress of the courts.

Yet, something seems amiss. We the people seem powerless. Can one man or one woman still make a difference? Do journalists like Woodward and Bernstein still exist? Do lawyers like Thurgood Marshall still take on the impossible cases that change the law? I still believe that they do. Here are three things we as citizens can do to engage our First and Fourth Amendment rights:

1. Going back to Code #1, we the people must be engaged in keeping vigilant watch on our government. We do it by reading, and by listening to and watching the reporting

of journalists through a myriad of sources now available to us. And we ourselves can blog, write, periscope, chat—whatever it takes to be informed and engaged.

2. The courts are our most precious source of justice on many levels. We need to hold our elected officials to account to make sure more judges get confirmed and placed in areas where we have shortages of them.

3. We must educate our children and their children about the Constitution so that they know their rights as they grow into adulthood. Arm the next generations with information so that, like Justice Marshall and those two young reporters, they can change the world for the good of us all.

★ ★ ★ ★ ★ ★ ★ ★ ★ ★ ★ ★ ★ ★ ★ ★

"A people . . . who are possessed of the spirit of commerce, who see and who will pursue their advantages may achieve almost anything."

—George Washington

CODE 5

BE FREE IN ENTERPRISE AND COMMERCE

I believe that what makes America truly great—beyond our ability to self-govern, to be freethinking, to worship God as we choose, to keep and to bear arms, and to pursue our own individual happiness—is our free market, free enterprise, capitalistic, "can do" entrepreneurial spirit.

The American spirit of invention, ingenuity, opportunity, and capitalism is the envy of the world. It is this ideal—that anyone, from anywhere, can come to America and become the richest man or the wealthiest woman—that sets this nation apart. It is this ideal that any boy or girl can grow up in the poorest of neighborhoods and become the owner of a small business. Or a great Fortune 500 company. Or secretary of the Treasury. Or the owner of a professional sports team, or a great manufacturing plant. Or anything else the human mind can conceive!

Our American history is filled with amazing men and women who hail from humble roots, who were "possessed" (in George Washington's words) with the spirit of commerce. The spirit of creativity, discovery, and invention. The spirit of manufacturing goods, buying goods, selling goods, and providing jobs and products for their fellow citizens. That is what makes us great. We are a free people who thrive not on what the government gives us, or takes from us, not on what we are told to do, or told we cannot do. We are free because we can see and pursue our dreams. We can pursue and create our own businesses. Our own technologies. Our own laboratories. We can be Steve Jobs or Bill Gates, Henry Ford or Thomas Edison. We can come up with an idea in our college dormitory, as Mark Zuckerberg did when he created Facebook, which has revolutionized the way people "connect and make friends" around the world.

Our Founders understood this principle well. They understood that our "liberty" was about much more than just securing our political and personal freedoms. True liberty requires economic and entrepreneurial freedom—the ability to profit from our own ideas and labor, to work, produce, consume, own, trade, and invest according to our own gifts. Thomas Jefferson underscored that point when he observed that "a wise and frugal Government, which shall restrain men from injuring one another, shall leave them otherwise free to regulate their own pursuits of industry and improvement."[49]

Many of those who founded this nation bled and died so that we could experience "life, liberty and the pursuit of happiness." Our Founders knew well the economic tyranny of big government (the monarchy) and the tyranny of the big banks and feudal lords of their day, and they wanted something very different for America. True, capitalism and corporations of today, and the impact they have on our day-to-day lives, are vastly different from anything our Founders could have imagined. Yet presidents from George Washington to Theodore Roosevelt worried about the delicate balance between free commerce, trade, economic freedom, and big corporate governance, on the one hand, and protecting the rights of we the people on the other against economic oppression and classism. In short, they wanted the little guy to have as great a chance as the big guy to be successful financially in the marketplace of ideas and industry.

Before the Civil War, corporations had been limited in their charters (twenty to thirty years was the maximum corporate charter granted). From the 1500s until the 1880s, corporations were considered the artificial creations of their owners and the state legislatures that authorized them. In American republican democracy, government's role is to serve the people and protect them from threats—both domestic and foreign—to their life, liberty, and pursuit of happiness. This has historically included control of corporate behavior.

After the Civil War, with America's expansion westward and industry booming, corporations grew in their power and influence, particularly political influence, which was feared by the Founding Fathers. Corporations had free rein and total power over their workforce and could sell virtually anything they wanted, even if the product was unsafe. Corporations treated workers like slaves, only they were paid extremely low wages. Workers received no benefits, no vacation days, no health insurance, and no worker's compensation.[50] To put it bluntly, corporations didn't care about their workers or the people who bought their products. The only rule of the game was to make as much profit as possible, no matter what.

As the nineteenth century ended and the twentieth century began, corporations were getting bigger and bigger. Many began buying up smaller companies, becoming monopolies that controlled whole industries. This practice eliminated competition and, as a result, prices skyrocketed and no one could challenge them. The greatest example of this event in our history centers on the lives of four American men who became known as "the men who built America":[51] Cornelius Vanderbilt, John D. Rockefeller, Andrew Carnegie, and J. P. Morgan. And beyond them, the men they invested in. Men like Thomas Edison and Henry Ford. These men paved the way for free enterprise and American domination in commerce and industry for generations to come. They were a new breed of leaders. A new kind of businessman. They set the standard for the American Dream. Men of insight, of innovation, they ushered in an age of advancement. This new breed, with the ingenuity the likes of which the world had never seen, propelled the United States of America to greatness. Men of vision, they not only built America but helped to connect and build the world.

Cornelius Vanderbilt was first a shipping magnate, then he built the American railroad system. He was referred to as "the Commodore." He contracted with a young struggling oil refinery businessman named John D. Rockefeller, in Ohio (then considered the Middle East oil of its day). Vanderbilt and Rockefeller had an exclusive deal to fill the trains supplying oil throughout the nation. Rockefeller went into business with Tom Scott (Andrew Carnegie's mentor) and when Scott and Rockefeller parted ways, Carnegie was the beneficiary. Rockefeller became known as the richest man the world had ever seen. And Carnegie became the great steel baron of his time, building bridges, railroads, and anything else you can imagine. He also became one of the richest men on earth at the time.

Enter J. P. Morgan, also known as "America's Banker." The heir to the famed "The House of Morgan" (which endures to this day) he bailed out the U.S. government with a $100 million loan in the early 1900s. He financed Thomas Edison and the lightbulb, which led to electricity in every home in the United States. He was the man who helped Henry Ford put an affordable car in everyone's garage. These four men produced many of the products and industries that we enjoy to this day. Yet these titans of industry fast became a symbol of all that was wrong with America, destroying competition and crushing American workers with grueling hours and unfair wages.[52]

That is, until Theodore Roosevelt became president in 1901. Roosevelt believed in honest competition and fair prices, but he also believed in just treatment of workers. Informally known as a trustbuster, Roosevelt frequently went against popular political opinion to protect the American people. As noted by writer Laurel King, when Roosevelt took office in 1901, the Sherman Antitrust Act had been in place for more than a decade. However, despite its goal of encouraging fair competition in the marketplace, the act had so far been an ineffective weapon.[53] Established to prevent monopolies—or dismantle those already in existence—and encourage fair competition and prices for average citizens, the statute was far-reaching and would have been very effective. Unfortunately, most politicians ignored the law and refused to enforce it. Then Roosevelt took office and immediately set to work putting the act to good use. He went after none other than John D. Rockefeller himself.[54] Roosevelt believed that government had not only a duty but indeed a right to regulate corporations, just as the founding generation had done:

> Our aim is not to do away with corporations; on the contrary, these big aggregations are an inevitable development of modern industrialism, and the effort to destroy them would be futile unless accomplished in ways that would work the utmost mischief to the entire body politic. We can do nothing of good in the way of regulating and supervising these corporations until we fix clearly in our minds that we are not attacking the corporations, but endeavoring to do away with any evil in them. We are not hostile to them; we are merely determined that they shall be so handled as to serve the public good. We draw the line against misconduct, not against wealth.[55]

Whatever your political leanings, I think we can all agree that what our Founders envisioned was a country where individual talent could be developed, creative commerce could flourish, and hard work could be rewarded. They wanted a country where the individual was empowered, and where everyone could own land and start businesses. Property rights were the true economic equalizer in the early days of America, but eventually that shifted toward commerce and trade, the marketplace, and corporate wealth. While no system is ever perfect, the experiment that our Founders originally set up has worked beyond their wildest dreams. And in many ways it still thrives today.

In this Code, we will look at the principles of economic freedom and capitalism in America, and why they matter so much to who we are and what we symbolize around the world. We will also look at how two Americans, one man and one woman, who hailed from humble beginnings armed only with the power of their dreams, hard work, and ingenuity, created two major enterprises (industries) that still endure to this day.

Free Enterprise and Commerce

America's free enterprise system is, and has always been, unique. That is because we do not have an economy run by the state or the central government, as in most of the other nations in the world. Ours is run by the ingenuity and toil of the people. In the most basic of terms, a free enterprise economic system is one in which the government places very few restrictions on the types of business activities in which citizens participate. In a free enterprise system, we the people are allowed to spend our money in the way we want. We believe in the competition of the marketplace: Walmart versus Target. Exxon versus Shell. We love to have different companies competing for our business, which often leads to lower prices and better-quality products. We also have a free public education system that educates our citizens and allows us to be free to pursue any type of career or work we desire. Here are a few characteristics of our free enterprise system that made America both great and rich:

- Businesses and the marketplace respond to consumer preferences and spending, and it is the consumer—not the government—that drives what types of products and services companies offer.
- The market allows you to buy land, buildings, and property with very few restrictions.
- As a business owner, you have the right to set your own prices and determine your own profit levels.
- As a business owner, you have the ability to choose suppliers and other people you do business with.
- As a nonprofit organization, you are tax exempt and can serve your community or nation with services and goods, while still retaining enough funds to continue to grow.

Think of it like this: Our Founders so valued commerce and the free exercise of it that James Madison ensured it was placed in Article I, Section 8 of the Constitution. This one simple clause gives the Congress the power to regulate "interstate commerce" when it is clear (or maybe not so clear) that the states or some policy of a state is negatively impacting and affecting the commerce.

The commerce clause authorizes Congress to regulate commerce so that the flow of interstate commerce is free from local restraints imposed by the states. When Jim Crow laws did not allow black citizens to use public restrooms, restaurants, or stay in certain hotels, this had a huge interstate commerce impact. A large group of the citizens were being denied the right to shop, travel, eat, and lodge. This one clause in the Constitution has changed the course of American history many times. Our Founders, in their wisdom, understood that, in order for Americans to truly be free to pursue life, liberty, and happiness, we would need to be equally free in our commerce.

Although the Constitution places some limits on states' powers, the Tenth Amendment guarantees certain rights to the states. Although a state has the right to regulate its domestic commerce, that right must be exercised in a manner consistent with the vision of the Founders, that is, it may not interfere with, or place a burden on, interstate commerce. If it does, Congress may act to regulate that commerce.

The commerce clause has been the basis of some of the most historic and sweeping Supreme Court decisions in the history of America, from civil rights cases to, most recently, "Obamacare." Some say that the commerce clause is being used to justify federal actions that the Founders never envisioned. That may or may not be true. But, for our purposes here, we want to celebrate the notion of free enterprise and American capitalism, both of which have been the light and envy of the rest of the civilized world since we became a nation.

Many politicians and economists have tried to persuade Americans that there is a better way—socialism, communism, and every other kind of "ism" has been thrown our way for centuries. Capitalism is derided as an evil. Corporations are viewed as greedy oligarchs. Free enterprise and free markets are seen as instruments of the wealthy and privileged to oppress the poor. Yet, we know from history that those other isms, that is, socialism and communism, ultimately become burdensome to their citizens, expensive to manage, and lead to the erosion of freedom and the basic human rights given us by our Creator. As the Supreme Court rightly noted in *U.S. vs. Lopez* (1995), federal authority to regulate interstate commerce cannot be extended to the point that it creates centralized government rule over commerce. That is my point: America is different. We are unique. By setting in motion a free system, just as we the people are free, America has the world's most successful economy. We are the world's richest nation. We are the light that draws ordinary men and women from around the world to our shores in the hopes that they too can share in the "American Dream" of free enterprise, free markets, and the ability to make one's dreams come true.[56]

Two Regular Americans Who Made Good: Richard W. Sears and Madam C. J. Walker

RICHARD W. SEARS[57]

> *"The surest way to gain the unswerving loyalty of employees is to show them from the start that they will*

be allowed to make the most of themselves. A man
wants to stay with the firm with which he can reach
his greatest efficiency."—Richard W. Sears

If you are an American over the age of forty, you are old
enough to remember the Sears, Roebuck catalog. I remember as a child when my parents would order products and we
would wait eagerly for them to come in the mail. At one point
in our nation's history, this catalog was a unifying instrument of
American commerce. Americans from all walks of life used it.
It became a way of life from the late 1800s through the 1970s.

But it is the story of how the Sears catalog (and ultimately
the Sears retail company, which stands to this day) was born
that intrigues and excites me as an American. Richard Sears was
born in Stewartville, Minnesota. His father was James Warren
Sears, born circa 1828 in New York, a blacksmith and wagon
maker; his mother was Eliza Burton Sears, born in Ohio circa
1843. Young Sears entered the railroad service, which was at
the time the hottest new mode for the transportation of goods
and products outside of shipping. Sears moved up in the railroad service, and in 1886, at age twenty-three, his career path
and his life changed forever: A shipment of gold watches from
a Chicago manufacturer was refused by a retailer, Edward Stegerson.[58]

A common scam existing at the time involved wholesalers
who would ship their products to retailers who had not ordered
them. Upon refusal, the wholesaler would offer the already
price-hiked items to the retailer at a lower consignment cost

in the guise of alleviating the cost to ship the items back. The unsuspecting retailer would then agree to take this newfound bargain off the wholesaler's hands, mark up the items, and sell them to the public, making a small profit in the transaction. But Stegerson, a retailer savvy to the scam, flatly refused the watches. Young Sears, however, jumped at the opportunity and made an agreement with the wholesaler to keep any profit he reaped above $12. Then he set about offering his wares to other station agents along the railroad line for $14. The watches were considered an item of urban sophistication, and, because of the growth of railways, and the recent application of time zones, farmers needed to keep time accurately, unnecessary until then. For those two reasons, the station agents had no trouble selling the watches. Within six months, Sears had netted $5,000 and felt so confident in this venture that he founded the R. W. Sears Watch Company. Placing advertisements in farm publications and making fliers for potential clients, he spoke directly to rural and small-town communities, persuading them to purchase by mail order.[59]

In 1887, Sears moved his company to Chicago, an important transportation center for the Midwest. And he hired watch repairman Alvah Curtis Roebuck to repair any watches being returned. Roebuck was Sears's first employee, and he later became cofounder of Sears, Roebuck & Company, which was formed in 1893, when Sears was thirty years old. The company was incorporated in Illinois as Sears, Roebuck & Company of Illinois on September 7, 1895. The first Sears catalog was published in 1893 and offered only watches. By 1897, items such as men's and ladies' clothing, plows, silverware, bicycles, and athletic equipment were added to the offering. The five-hundred-page catalog was sent to some 300,000 homes. Sears catered to the rural customer because he had been raised on a farm and he knew what the rural customer needed. Because of his experience with the railroad, he knew how to ship merchandise to remote areas. In 1908, Sears made another move forward: He began selling mail order homes through the catalog, making Sears— at the time and for many generations to come—the largest and most successful company of its kind. All born from one man's ingenuity and vision, Sears continues to be one of the largest Fortune 500 companies in America, and one of the largest domestic employers across the continental United States.[60]

A Black Woman Ahead of Her Time

MADAM C. J. WALKER[61]

"Don't sit and wait for the opportunities to come. Get up and make them." —Madam C. J. Walker

In the post–Civil War South, opportunity was slim, and commerce was shifting from slave labor to industry. Most blacks, post-Reconstruction, took to sharecropping and domestic services that they had learned in slavery. Times were hard for all Americans, but particularly hard for black Americans. Many, if not all, freed slaves could not read or write. The South was ravaged by the war, and had to be rebuilt. Shortly after Reconstruction, the United States sanctioned Jim Crow segregation via the landmark *Plessy vs. Ferguson* case in 1896, which ultimately would be struck down in *Brown v. Board of Education* in 1954, in part by the commerce clause. Until that time, however, segregation ruled the South and black men and women had to live "separate but equal" lives.

Sarah Breedlove was born on December 23, 1867, on a Louisiana plantation. The daughter of former slaves, Breedlove would transform herself from an uneducated farm laborer and laundress into one of the twentieth century's most successful, self-made women entrepreneurs and the first self-made female millionaire. Breedlove would later be known as "Madam C. J. Walker," and leave a legacy for the black community of invention, entrepreneurship, manufacturing, job creation, free enterprise, political activism, and giving back to the community that is in many ways unparalleled since.

Orphaned at age seven, she often said of herself, "I got my start by giving myself a start." She and her older sister, Louvenia, survived by working in the cotton fields of the Delta and nearby Vicksburg, Mississippi. Her only daughter, Lelia (later known as "A'Lelia" Walker) was born on June 6, 1885. When Sarah's husband died two years later, she moved to St. Louis to join her four brothers, who had established themselves as barbers. Working for as little as $1.50 a day, Sarah managed to save enough money to educate her daughter in the city's public schools.

Friendships with other black women who were members of St. Paul AME Church and the National Association of Colored Women exposed Breedlove to a new way of viewing the world. Realizing that the marketplace did not cater to the specific needs of black people, she began to develop products to deal with her own hair loss (something that was common to black women of her day). To promote her products, the new "Madam C. J. Walker" traveled for a year and a half on a dizzying crusade throughout the heavily black South and Southeast, selling her products door-to-door, demonstrating her scalp treatments in churches and lodges, and devising sales and marketing strategies. In 1908, she temporarily moved her base to Pittsburgh, where she opened Lelia College to train Walker "hair culturists." By early 1910, she had settled in Indianapolis, then the nation's largest inland manufacturing center, where she built a factory, a hair and manicure salon, and another training school. Less than a year later, Walker grabbed national headlines in the black press when she contributed one thousand dollars to the building fund of the "colored" YMCA in Indianapolis.

In 1913, while Walker traveled to Central America and the Caribbean to expand her business, A'Lelia moved to Harlem, New York. Walker herself moved to New York in 1916, leaving the day-to-day operations of the Madam C. J. Walker Manufacturing Company in Indianapolis to Freeman B. Ransom, her attorney, and Alice Kelly, her factory forelady. She continued to oversee the business and to work in the New York office. Once in Harlem, she quickly became involved in Harlem's social and political life, taking special interest in the NAACP's anti-lynching movement, to which she contributed five thousand dollars.

As her business continued to grow, Walker organized her agents into local and state clubs. Her Madam C. J. Walker Hair

Culturists Union of America convention in Philadelphia in 1917 was most likely one of the first national meetings of business-women in the country. Walker used the gathering not only to reward her agents for their business success, but to encourage their political activism as well. "This is the greatest country under the sun," she told them. "But we must not let our love of country, our patriotic loyalty cause us to abate our protest against wrong and injustice. We should protest until the American sense of justice is so aroused that such affairs as the East St. Louis riot be forever impossible."[62]

By the time she died at her estate, Villa Lewaro, in Irvington-on-Hudson, New York, Walker had helped create the role of the twentieth-century, self-made American businesswoman. She established herself as a pioneer of the modern black hair-care and cosmetics industry, and set standards in the African-American community for corporate and community giving. Tenacity and perseverance, faith in herself and in God, quality products, and "honest business dealings" were the elements and strategies she prescribed for aspiring entrepreneurs who requested the secret to her rags-to-riches ascent. "There is no royal flower-strewn path to success," she once commented. "And if there is, I have not found it for if I have accomplished anything in life it is because I have been willing to work hard."[63]

Like the four great men briefly profiled in this Code who birthed industry in America, both Richard Sears and Madam C. J. Walker embody the spirit of what is possible in a freethinking, free-enterprise system. Two people, from humble roots, became icons of their time and left a legacy that is still with us in the twenty-first century. Their vision and their willingness to take risks to create successful businesses prove that the power of a free and open marketplace can work for anyone. Sears the retail giant endures, and Madam C. J. Walker's beauty and hair-care products are available online and in retail stores throughout the United States.

*   *   *   *   *   *   *   *   *   *   *   *   *   *   *

Reclaiming Our Founders' Vision

One of the greatest attributes of freedom is the ability to be free not just in our person, or on our property, but in our ability to create, build, invent, buy, and sell goods and services. America is a capitalist country. We are not socialists. We are not communists. We are Americans. For much of the nineteenth and twentieth centuries, America was the place everyone on earth wanted to go to, seeking their own "American Dream." The election of 2016 showcased not just the difference between two big political personalities, but an American electorate fed up with America being seen as a second-rate power, including a second-rate economic power. America has become a place riddled with a huge national debt, too much regulation, excessive taxes, with small businesses unable to procure capital and create good-paying jobs.

This Code teaches us about our Founding Fathers' implicit and express understanding that we also be free in our finances, commerce, and markets. Key takeaways for us as citizens:

1. Engage your respective state legislators and members of Congress to support legislation that helps grow, support, and fund small businesses.

2. Support STEM (Science, Technology, Engineering, and Math) education in your children's elementary and high schools, so that they will be equipped to work in a twenty-first-century, high-tech/global workforce.

3. Educate yourself and your workforce about the free market system, in particular the Commerce Clause, because it is being applied much more broadly as of late by the U.S. Supreme Court, the most notable case, of course, being Obamacare.

4. Support free and fair competition of businesses in your community, your state, and your country.

★ ★ ★ ★ ★ ★ ★ ★ ★ ★ ★ ★ ★ ★ ★ ★

"We hold these truths to be self-evident,

that all men are created equal, that they

are endowed by their Creator with certain

unalienable Rights, that among these are

Life, Liberty and the pursuit of Happiness."

—Thomas Jefferson,
Declaration of Independence

CODE

6

BE COURAGEOUS AND WILLING TO FIGHT
FOR ESTABLISHED RIGHTS

O f all the rights that human beings have ever desired to possess, none were ever so divinely inspired and then eloquently stated as these penned by Thomas Jefferson at the very outset of our fledgling nation: ". . . that all men are created equal, that they are endowed by their Creator with certain unalienable Rights, that among these are Life, Liberty and the pursuit of Happiness."

These words, written well over 235 years ago, have given hope and inspiration to men and women, not just here at home, but to nations and people all around the world. But how do we see them today, and how do they apply in our everyday lives? Many would argue that we no longer have to fight for our liberty. We are Americans, after all, and our liberty is guaranteed by the blood and sweat of our forefathers and embedded in the Constitution. Many might argue that we are secure in our persons (or lives) as the world's greatest super power, and as the nation with the world's highest standard of living.

Of course none of us can guarantee another person's "happiness," a deeply personal endeavor meaning something different to everyone. But certainly happiness is not even possible unless we daily guard and honor the virtues of life, liberty, and the pursuit of happiness (it's interesting to note that the phrase "the pursuit of Happiness" came about when Thomas Jefferson took British philosopher John Locke's notion that governments are responsible for "life, liberty, and property" and replaced "property" with "the pursuit of Happiness").[64]

We need to respect the fact that we are indeed human. That we all need to do what humans do: Laugh. Sing. Play. Love. Succeed. Serve. Interact. Accomplish. Explore. Find. Seek. Desire. Our Founders understood that our rights could never come from kings, legislatures, deliberative bodies, statesmen, corporate giants, rich men, wise men, religious men, military men, or any kind of men. They understood that we the people were born out of a conviction that our rights were natural, that they came from a Creator wiser, smarter, and more just than any man could ever be. James Madison said it best:

> What is government itself but the greatest of all reflections on human nature? If men were angels, no government would be necessary. If angels were to govern men, neither external nor internal controls on government would be necessary. In framing a government which is to be administered by men over men, the great diffi-

culty lies in this: you must first enable the government to control the governed; and in the next place oblige it to control itself.[65]

In this Code we will look at essential principles of our founding and the men and women who modeled them when it mattered the most:

1. Life
2. Liberty
3. Happiness

and what they mean in the context of our founding. The Declaration specifically mentions these three rights as that which we possess by virtue of our birth. These are rights that no man can deny us, and, as such, since they are "unalienable" (or not able to be denied), we cannot surrender them. What a powerful concept and ideal Thomas Jefferson expressed when he wrote these transformative words. But it's more than that, my fellow Americans. These unalienable rights, I must note, are not granted by the Declaration of Independence. Let me be clear, as our Founders were clear: Our rights do not depend upon government for their existence. They are not owing to the largesse of the state or the beneficence of any institution. The rights of man are the gifts of God. The Creator endows; the state exists to protect what He has given. These unalienable rights can be suppressed or denied, as they have been many times in our history, but they can never be annulled. We possess them no matter what kings or parliaments say, or presidents and congress decree, because they are given us by our Creator.

What Is Life? What Is Liberty? And How Does One Pursue Happiness?

LIFE

What is the right to life? What is it that Thomas Jefferson meant when he opened with the right to life? In its most basic form, our life is our physical existence. It is our heartbeat, our breath. And if that breath is taken or infringed upon by another, it is the responsibility of the government (in its various forms) to protect our physical life and impose punishment on those who have taken or infringed upon it.

The right to life is most directly linked to the final prong of the three: the pursuit of happiness. I will address that later in this section, but it is important that we first understand what a life is before we can pursue happiness with that life. And the great genius of what Jefferson wrote is that it says our liberty comes from being both alive, and being able to live that life as we so please, as long as we do not harm or infringe upon another's right to his life.

LIBERTY

The great beacon of light that makes us Americans different from all the rest of the world is that we value our liberty most, above all our other virtues. Liberty is more than just a theory, or a constitution, or a set of laws. Liberty is that precious gift that allows you to be free to move about as you will, free to speak your mind as you will. Free to express and write your opinions. It is the freedom to own property, to educate yourself and your children, to work, to earn income, and to create wealth. Liberty is being secure in our homes, in our communities, in our nation. Liberty is the freedom to fall in love, get married, and create a family of your own. Liberty is the ability to assemble with others and form associations, share information, create organizations, and feel secure that you will not be blackballed, blacklisted, or tracked down by the government for doing so.

Our liberty as Americans is the envy of the world. Never let anyone tell you different. We are not a perfect nation, but we are one nation. We don't imprison women or throw acid on them when they reject a marriage proposal, as some nations still do. One young woman was murdered in this way in May 2016 in Pakistan for rejecting a man's marriage proposal.[66] We do not build walls in America, as the Germans once did between East and West Berlin. We do not roll tanks over our people in the streets as the Chinese did in Tiananmen Square because people dared raise their voices in protest against their government. We encourage dissent. We encourage peaceful protest. We encourage the writing of provocative books and journals that keep watch on the government. We can do all of this only because we are free. We are liberated. We are a nation of more than 300 million individuals who stand under one flag, and who believe that because we are free, nothing that we dare imagine is impossible for us to achieve.

THE PURSUIT OF HAPPINESS

To pursue happiness! Wow! What a finish. What a charge. What a challenge.

Not only did Jefferson proclaim that we have a right to "life," but he followed it with the most perfect turn of phrase ever written: *the pursuit of happiness*. Let's define quickly the words *happiness* and *pursuit*. The word *happiness* comes from the Old Norse word *happ*, meaning "luck" or "chance." It's also related to the Old English word *hæpic*, meaning "equal." While early senses of "happiness," dating from the 1500s, are still very much in use—such as "good luck," "success," and "contentment"—Francis Hutcheson, an Irish reverend, brought a new, more political interpretation of *happiness* to English speakers with his 1725 treatise *An Inquiry into the Origin of Our Ideas of Beauty and Virtue*.[67] His political philosophy: "that Action is *best* which accomplishes the *greatest Happiness* for the *greatest Numbers*; and that worst, which in like manner occasions Misery."[68] [Emphasis mine.]

The popularity of Hutcheson's philosophies helped tie the concepts of civic responsibility and happiness to one another in the minds of the great political thinkers of the eighteenth century, including the main writer of the Declaration of Independence, Thomas Jefferson.

U.S. Supreme Court justice Anthony Kennedy once explained this often forgotten sense of happiness in his 2005 lecture at the National Conference on Citizenship. Kennedy noted that while in modern times there is a "hedonistic component" to the definition of happiness, for the framers of the Declaration of Independence "happiness meant that feeling of self-worth and dignity you acquire by contributing to your community and to its civic life." In the context of the Declaration of Independence, "happiness" was about an individual's contribution to society rather than the pursuit of self-gratification. While this sense has largely fallen out of use today, it's important to keep these connotations of happiness in mind when studying political documents from the eighteenth century.[69]

As to the meaning of the word *pursuit,* it indicates that we desire something. We want something. We are intentional about something, and we run after it. We Americans love our freedom. We love our happiness. But in our pursuit of freedom and happiness we neglect other things. The current generation, unlike many others in our nation's past, does not seem to grasp the notion of civic responsibility, civic provocation, and civic sacrifice. Liberty and freedom are never free. Our pursuit of life, liberty, and happiness is a right we must always be willing to defend and to expand when it is called into question or comes under attack.

The men and women we will meet in this Code are familiar names to many Americans, although perhaps not to the current generation of Americans. I feel strongly that these individuals embody the best as "citizens" who fought to keep these three God-given and well-established rights honored and enduring at different times in our nation's conscience.

Four Americans Who Modeled Our Values

TECUMSEH[70]

> *"Show respect to all people, but grovel to none."*
> —*Chief Tecumseh*

Tecumseh was a Native American leader of the Shawnee and a large tribal confederacy (known as "Tecumseh's Confederacy") that opposed the United States during Tecumseh's War and became an ally of Britain in the War of 1812. He was a brave leader in the resistance to American colonization. Now, you may ask yourself why would I include someone like this in a book about America, and why would I highlight him as a patriot who was dedicated to defending life, liberty, and the pursuit of happiness. Because he was here first. His people were here first. Native Americans are the rightful first people and inhabitants of America.

Chief Tecumseh was one of his people's greatest advocates because he too understood the notions of life, liberty, and happiness. His people enjoyed those rights for centuries before America became an established colony in Jamestown, Virginia, in 1619. Tecumseh grew up in the Ohio Country during the American Revolutionary War and the Northwest Indian War, during which he was constantly exposed to warfare. With Americans continuing to move west after the British ceded the Ohio Valley to the new United States in 1783, the Shawnee moved farther northwest. In 1808, they settled Prophetstown, in present-day

Indiana. With a vision of establishing an independent Native American nation east of the Mississippi under British protection, Tecumseh worked to recruit additional support.

But what he is most famously remembered for is a speech he gave during the War of 1812. Chief Tecumseh delivered a powerful speech that to this day is still preserved upon a rock at Fort Malden, Ontario. His words about the preservation of Indian lands, their way of life, their belief in God, and their liberty made him a legendary folk hero in American history. To put it more bluntly, Tecumseh's words spoken to General Proctor at Fort Malden echo our own credo as American colonists—life, liberty, and the freedom to pursue our own happiness. Here is an excerpt of his words:

> Father, listen. . . . You always told us to remain here and take care of our lands. It made our hearts glad to hear that was your wish; our great father the king is the head, you represent him. You always told us you would never draw your foot off the British ground; but now, father, we see you drawing back, and we are sorry to see our father doing so without seeing the enemy. We must compare our father's conduct to a fat animal, that carries its tail upon its back; but when affrighted, it drops it between its legs and runs off. Father. You have got the arms and ammunition which our great father sent for his red children. If you have any idea of going away, give them to us and you may go and welcome. For us, our

lives are in the hands of the Great Spirit; we are determined to defend our lands; and if it is his will we wish
to leave our bones upon them.[71]

ALICE PAUL[72]

"There will never be a new world order until women
are a part of it." —Alice Paul

Alice Paul was very likely the most transformative woman of
her time. She is credited with helping to secure the Nineteenth Amendment (the right to vote) for women in this country, and in seeking the Equal Rights Amendment for women.
Few individuals, much less women, have had a bigger impact on
history than Paul. Her life symbolized a passionate dedication
to a simple notion: that women and men could and should be
equals. Although a conservative in her lifestyle and beliefs, Paul
once quipped: "I think if we get freedom for women, then they
are probably going to do a lot of things that I wish they wouldn't
do. But it seems to me that isn't our business to say what they
should do with it. It is our business to see that they get it."

Harking back to the call of our founding, Paul believed that
women, like men, had the right of life, liberty, and the pursuit of
happiness. In her words: *freedom*. For almost 150 years after the
nation had been formed, women were still disenfranchised and
unable to vote. It brings to mind Abigail Adams's admonition to
her husband, John Adams, as he prepared to head off to Philadelphia to help form a new nation: "remember the ladies, and be

more generous and favorable to them than your ancestors. Do not put such unlimited power into the hands of the Husbands. Remember all Men would be tyrants if they could. If particular care and attention is not paid to the Ladies we are determined to foment a Rebellion, and will not hold ourselves bound by any Laws in which we have no voice, or Representation."

That all changed in 1919: Both the House and Senate passed the Nineteenth Amendment and the battle for state ratification commenced. Three-fourths of the states were needed to ratify the amendment, and the battle came down to Tennessee in the summer of 1920. If a majority of the state legislature voted for the amendment, it would become law. The deciding vote was cast by twenty-four-year-old Harry Burn, the youngest member of the Tennessee assembly. Originally intending to vote no, Burn changed his vote after receiving a telegram from his mother asking him to support women's suffrage. On August 18, 1920, Tennessee ratified the Nineteenth Amendment. Six days later, Secretary of State Bainbridge Colby certified the ratification and, with the stroke of his pen, American women gained the right to vote after a seventy-two-year battle. August 26 is now celebrated as Women's Equality Day in the United States.

ROSA PARKS[73]

"I have learned over the years that when one's mind is made up this diminishes fear, knowing what must be done does away with fear." —Rosa Parks

"The only tired I was, was tired of giving in."

—*Rosa Parks (on her decision to stay seated on the bus*
that day in Montgomery, Alabama)

I had the chance to meet Rosa Parks, a personal hero of mine, in 1993 in Washington, D.C., on the thirtieth anniversary of the March on Washington at the Lincoln Memorial. I was a young law student and I snuck off from class that day to head to the Capitol and watch some of the speeches. As fate would have it, I saw Congressman John Lewis (D-GA), who asked me if I wanted to meet Rosa Parks, and he took me over to her. She was in a wheelchair. But still beautiful. Still humble. Still a quiet fighter for freedom.

As was the case for many black people of her time who lived in the South, Rosa's childhood brought her early experiences with racial discrimination and a quiet yet steadily growing activism for racial equality. After her parents separated, Rosa's mother moved the family to Pine Level, Alabama, to live with her parents, Rose and Sylvester Edwards—both former slaves and strong advocates for racial equality. The family lived on the Edwardses' farm, where Rosa would spend her youth. In one experience, her grandfather stood in front of their house with a shotgun while Ku Klux Klan members marched down the street.

Segregated schools, stores, transportation, and lodging were the norm in young Rosa's life. In 1932, at age nineteen, she met and married Raymond Parks, a barber and an active member of the National Association for the Advancement of Colored People. With Raymond's support, Rosa earned her high school degree in 1933. She soon became actively involved in civil rights issues by joining the Montgomery chapter of the NAACP in 1943, serving as the chapter's youth leader as well as secretary to chapter president E. D. Nixon, a post she held until 1957.

Beginning on December 1, 1955, the world of the segregated South would forever change. After a long day at a Montgomery department store, where she worked as a seamstress, Rosa Parks boarded the Cleveland Avenue bus for home. She took a seat in the first of several rows designated for "colored" passengers. Though the city's bus ordinance did give drivers the authority to assign seats, it didn't specifically give them the authority to demand a passenger to give up a seat to anyone (regardless of color). However, Montgomery bus drivers had adopted the custom of requiring black passengers to give up their seats to white passengers when no other seats were available. As the bus continued on its route, it began to fill with white passengers. Eventually, the bus was full and the driver noticed that several white passengers were standing in the aisle. He stopped the bus and moved the sign separating the two sections back one row and asked four black passengers to give up their seats. Three complied, but Rosa refused and remained seated. The driver demanded, "Why don't you stand up?" to which Rosa replied, "I don't think I should have to stand up." The driver called the police and had her arrested. The police arrested her at the scene and charged her with violation of Chapter 6, Section 11 of the Montgomery City Code. She was taken to police headquarters, where, later that night, she was released on bail by the NAACP.[74]

This one act of defiance by a quiet seamstress on her way home from work launched the Civil Rights Movement. And it gave rise to a young preacher from Atlanta, Georgia, who would lead that movement. Rosa's refusal to give up her seat (her liberty) sparked a fire that could no longer be contained in the black community. Or in America. The Montgomery Bus Boycott lasted for thirteen months, and ultimately segregation in transportation was struck down by the U.S. Supreme Court, proving that one woman (or man) can make a difference by simply refusing to relinquish their God-given rights to life and liberty.

MARTIN LUTHER KING, JR. [75]

> *"Darkness cannot drive out darkness; only light can do that. Hate cannot drive out hate; only love can do that." —Martin Luther King, Jr.*

Where does one start with Martin Luther King? His impact on American civil rights, religion, and American society are so profound that no author of any book could do him justice. Yet I wanted to include Dr. King in this section of this book because he, more than any other American who has ever lived (except for maybe Abraham Lincoln), believed in the "oneness" of our great American union. He believed deeply in the promise of "life, liberty, and the pursuit of happiness." And he became a mirror to our nation. A mirror to our collective national soul. He made us hold that mirror up to take a long, hard look at ourselves. He showed us that the reflection was not a good one. He showed us that this nation, despite ending slavery a century earlier, had still not lived up to the great call of our founding: "All men are created equal," and we are "all" endowed with certain rights of life, liberty, and the pursuit of happiness.

Dr. King believed so greatly in Thomas Jefferson's words that he paid for them, quite literally, with his life. The young preacher from Georgia had a gift. A gift of the heart. A gift of speech. A gift of civil disobedience in the spirit of Gandhi. A son of the segregated South, his father also a preacher, Martin Luther King, Jr., was born on January 15, 1929. He had settled on a career in ministry, with his lovely wife, Coretta, at his side, when history beckoned and changed his course.

It was the refusal of Rosa Parks to give up her seat on the bus in Montgomery on December 1, 1955, that changed everything for King. In 1954, while still working on his dissertation, King had become pastor of the Dexter Avenue Baptist Church of Montgomery. He completed his PhD and was awarded his degree in 1955. King was only twenty-five years old. On the night that Rosa Parks was arrested, E. D. Nixon, head of the local NAACP chapter, met with King and other local civil rights leaders to plan a city-wide bus boycott. King was elected to lead the boycott because he was young, well trained, had solid family connections, and had professional standing. But he was also new to the community and had few enemies, so it was felt he would have strong credibility with the black community.

In his first speech as the group's president, King declared, "We have no alternative but to protest. For many years we have shown an amazing patience. We have sometimes given our white brothers the feeling that we liked the way we were being treated. But we come here tonight to be saved from that patience that makes us patient with anything less than freedom and justice."[76] King's fresh and skillful rhetoric put a new energy into the civil rights struggle in Alabama. The bus boycott would be 382 days of walking to work, harassment, violence, and intimidation for the Montgomery's African-American community. Both King's and E. D. Nixon's homes were attacked. But the African-American community also took legal action against the city ordinance, arguing that it was unconstitutional based on the Supreme Court's "separate is never equal" decision in *Brown v. Board of Education*. After being defeated in several lower-court rulings and suffering large financial losses, the city of Montgomery lifted the law mandating segregated public transportation.

Among King's many contributions to our nation, the most enduring is the pivotal role he played in ending the legal segregation of African-American citizens in the South and other areas of the nation. His love of liberty and every citizen's right to the pursuit of happiness led to the hard-fought victories of the Civil Rights Act of 1964 and the Voting Rights Act of 1965. King received the Nobel Peace Prize in 1964, among several other honors. King was assassinated in April 1968, and continues to be remembered as one of the most lauded American citizen leaders in history, often referenced by his famous 1963 speech, "I Have a Dream."[77] This section of King's speech resonates most with the founding principles of our great nation:

In a sense we've come to our nation's capital to cash a check. When the architects of our republic wrote the magnificent words of the Constitution and the Declaration of Independence, they were signing a promissory note to which every American was to fall heir. This note was a promise that all men, yes, black men as well as white men, would be guaranteed the "unalienable Rights" of "Life, Liberty and the pursuit of Happiness." It is obvious today that America has defaulted on this promissory note, insofar as her citizens of color are concerned. Instead of honoring this sacred obligation, America has given the Negro people a bad check, a check which has come back marked "insufficient funds." But we refuse to believe that the bank of justice is bankrupt. We refuse to believe that there are insufficient funds in the great vaults of opportunity of this nation. And so, we've come to cash this check, a check that will give us upon demand the riches of freedom and the security of justice.[78]

★ ★ ★ ★ ★ ★ ★ ★ ★ ★ ★ ★ ★ ★ ★ ★

Reclaiming Our Founders' Vision

We hold these "truths" to be self-evident. What are truths? A truth is something undeniable. It is fact. It is firm. It is resolved. Truths are absolute. So when Thomas Jefferson wrote the Preamble to the Declaration of Independence, he was standing on firm, resolved, absolute truths. Our union, now almost 240 years old, has become more perfect because of those who pushed back and fought for their rights, like Tecumseh. For those, like Alice Paul, who forged a path to voting rights for women. And for citizens like Rosa Parks and Dr. King, who, through nonviolent protests, claimed what was rightfully theirs. And in doing so they gave us a road map for how to protect our life, liberty, and happiness.

Here are some things we as citizens can learn from these four great individuals:

1. Our liberty is a gift not from men, or wars, or documents. Our liberty comes from our Creator. And our liberty can only be preserved and expanded when we dare to have the courage to fight for it.

2. Life is the right to exist. To breathe. To be. All human beings have that right.

3. Happiness is more than being able to own a home. Go
   to a job. Educate your children. Take a vacation. Travel.
   Happiness is about ensuring that we all have a sense of
   dignity. Worth. Value. And most important, that we are all
   contributing members of society.

★ ★ ★ ★ ★ ★ ★ ★ ★ ★ ★ ★ ★ ★ ★ ★

"Children should be educated and instructed

in the principles of freedom."

—JOHN ADAMS

CODE
7

KEEP THE FAMILY UNIT AND AMERICAN CULTURE STRONG

Our politicians have argued for centuries about the notion of "family" and more recently about "family values." During the 1980s and 1990s, "family values" reigned supreme in our political rhetoric and in our political campaigns. But all of that has changed. The definition of "family" has changed dramatically over the past twenty years or more. "Family" no longer means what it once did in America: one man, one woman, and some children. Single moms now number 10 million or more in this country. Families cohabitating outside of wedlock number in the millions. "Family" now includes same-sex couples, who have children of their own. The old nuclear family concept has all but disappeared, but whatever family looks like for you, the family is the nucleus of our lives.

Few changes in America's political culture in the past hundred years have been as profound as the changes in how Americans experience family life. Fewer marriages occur, and, when they do, they occur later in life. Marriages are much more likely to end in divorce. Childlessness is much more common, as is living alone. The total fertility rate has dipped below replacement rates. Living together outside of wedlock has gone from forbidden, to rare, to almost expected, sometimes as a prelude to marriage, sometimes not. Surveys show that family no longer has the hold on the human heart it once did. Scarcely any area of public policy is unaffected by the decline in marriage and family life. The attainment of education for children raised outside of marriage suffers; the job teachers face is more complicated; and crime is connected with fatherlessness. There is state aid in various forms for children because many think it necessary for the state to step in where families fail. Americans expect the state to provide for old age instead of expecting grown children to provide aid to their parents directly. As the family declines, many, like me, believe that the government has, perhaps, unwittingly taken its place; hence, ironically, as the government rises to take its place, the family declines further.

Marriage and family make an *institution,* connecting such important human aspects as affection, sex, procreation, and parenthood. Marriage is an exercise of freedom, not only an end in itself, but also a necessary means toward securing a self-governing people. Marriage and family life are ends in and of themselves because government is designed to protect the natural rights of the individual, and one of the most important and noble exercises of those rights is consensual marriage and the formation of a family. Marriage and family life are important means as well because they provide invaluable education in, and preparation for, the responsibilities of a self-governing citizenship. Without this moral education, people are poorer, more dependent, and less equipped to become citizens.[79] The Founders' statements and their actions generally show that they held marriage and family life to be, in Founder and signer of the Declaration of Independence, James Wilson's words, "the true origin of society," or the first and most vital foundation on which civil society rests. Many states undertook modest reforms in family law during the revolutionary period and the early republic. These reforms reveal how, for the Founders, the principles of natural rights affected marriage and family life, and how marriage and family life support a republic based on the idea of natural rights.[80]

The Founders believed strongly that children must be educated early about the power of freedom. The price of liberty. I couldn't agree with them more. It is the young who always spark the greatest social movements and reforms, not just here at home but around the world. It was young men and women who launched and fought the American Revolution. It was young men who fought and died in the Civil War. It was young women, and men like John Lewis and Martin Luther King, who led the civil rights struggle in this nation.

The All-American Family

One of the things that makes America so different from the rest of the world is that, in times of crisis, want, war, or other challenge, we come together as one big American family. We are known for our generosity of spirit when our neighbors get hit with hurricanes, earthquakes, floods, or famine.

All one has to do is read ancient texts, the Bible, or the writings of our Founders to understand that great value has always been placed on the strength and sanctity of the family and on the culture in which that family must exist. In the beginning of this book, I shared with you fifteen founding principles (of the twenty-eight founding principles gleaned from our founding documents and our Founding Fathers). Our Founders believed deeply in "natural law," or God-given, divine law. I will discuss that more in Code #8, when we talk about the importance of free exercise of religion. But there is a great intersection between Code #6, "Life, Liberty, and Pursuit of Happiness," and this Code dealing with the strength of the family unit and American culture. You cannot have one without the other, and Code #8, which follows, is actually the footstool upon which our liberties rest.

In the twenty-eight founding principles of America, one of the core Codes of our founding was that the family is the strength of any society. Yet our Founders took it a step further in that they made it the business and duty of government to help "foster and protect" the integrity of the family: "The core unit which determines the strength of any society is the family; therefore, the government should foster and protect its integrity."[81]

There are many think tanks and organizations in Washington, D.C., and around the nation dedicated to "preserving" the

American family and our "values" or "American culture." However, I think we need to be clear about what the Founders were and were not saying here. It should be clear by now to everyone reading this book that our Founders believed in a small federal government. Period. They believed in the individual. In local and self-governance. They believed in the power of individual liberty and freedom. They gave the government to the people to choose their leaders from among their ranks. So, when they suggested that the government should "foster and protect" the integrity of the family, what they never meant to suggest was the government would take the place of parents. Or that the government would step in for parents. Or that the government could raise families. That is not what the Founders meant. What they meant was that the family must stay together. It must be the center of American life and culture.

Beyond making clear that the family was essential to the success of the republic, our Founders set out to establish a uniquely American culture. That culture is one that affords us, as Americans, rights and privileges that most people around the world can only dream of. As I discussed in Code #6, Thomas Jefferson set this nation on a powerful course like none other with this turn of phrase: "We hold these truths to be self-evident, that all men are created equal, that they are endowed by their Creator with certain unalienable Rights, that among these are Life, Liberty and the pursuit of Happiness."

While America's Founding Fathers had their differences, they agreed that there were certain principles essential to sustaining a free society. These principles can be grouped into three categories—**limited constitutional government, free enterprise,** and **traditional values (the core of this Code)**—but, in the end, they are all tied together. Take away one and a free society collapses. It is because of these values—which I like to call "Founding Father Values"—that the United States has flourished, and will continue to prosper only, I believe, as long as we hold fast to our founding principles.

American Culture

American culture is not easy to define, for one very important reason: our diversity. Unlike China, the Middle East, and even parts of Europe, whose cultures are mostly monolithic, the United States is a great melting pot. We are not one kind of people united by language, custom, religion, family, and region. We are a vastly diverse people, and out of that diversity flows our great uniqueness and, of course, our great strength.

The United States is the third-largest country in the world, with a population of more than 320 million, according to the U.S. Census Bureau.[82] And the United States is one of the most culturally diverse countries in the world because nearly every region of the world has influenced American culture. This is a country of immigrants who colonized the country beginning in the early 1600s. U.S. culture has also been shaped by the cultures of Native Americans, Latin Americans, Africans, Asians, and Europeans. The United States is a place to which different cultures have contributed their own distinct "flavors." Just as cultures from around the world have influenced American culture, today American culture influences the world. The term "Western culture" often refers broadly to the cultures of the United States and Europe.

Culture is what people do. How they think. How they engage one another in public and private discourse, courtship, and commerce. Culture is how we see things. What we value. What we create. And what we practice as ritual. American culture is unique because it is always evolving and shifting. There was a time in America when women could not vote. Ninety-six years later, the Democratic Party nominated a woman for president of the United States during the 2016 presidential campaign. There was a time in America where African Americans could not eat in certain restaurants or ride in the front of a train or bus. Now we have an African-American president. That is what makes us so special as a culture. We constantly evolve to perfect our union through the great diversity of our people.

In the context of what our Founders believed about culture, it all goes back to liberty. To freedom. To having in our possession something, about which Thomas Jefferson once quipped: "My God! How little do my countrymen know what precious blessing they are in possession of, and which no other people on the earth enjoy."[83]

In the final analysis, the point of this Code is to remind us that our family unit and our culture keep us Americans grounded, more unified, and free. The Founders knew that a free society could only remain stable—and free—if its people could govern themselves (Code #1). To govern themselves, people need religion (Code #8), morality (Code #2), and family (Code #7).

Three Americans Who Fought to Preserve the American Family and Culture

RICHARD and MILDRED LOVING[84]

> *"Almighty God created the races white, black, yellow, Malay and red, and he placed them on separate continents. And but for the interference with his arrangement there would be no cause for such marriages. The fact that he separated the races shows that he did not intend for the races to mix."*
> —*Virginia trial judge Leon M. Bazile*

> *"Marriage is one of the 'basic civil rights of man', fundamental to our very existence and survival. . . . Under our Constitution, the freedom to marry, or not marry, a person of another race resides with the individual and cannot be infringed by the State. These convictions must be reversed."*
> —*United States Supreme Court,* Loving v. Virginia, *1967*

Two thousand seventeen marks the fiftieth anniversary of the landmark Supreme Court case *Loving v. Virginia*. On June 12, 1967, the U.S. Supreme Court unanimously struck down Virginia's law prohibiting interracial marriages, as a violation of the Fourteenth Amendment, also known as the "equal protection clause." The two American citizens who brought this historic case were Richard P. Loving, a white man, and Mildred Jeter Loving, an African-American woman, both natives of Virginia, who grew up in Caroline County under segregation. They married in Washington, D.C., in June 1958 and were arrested shortly thereafter, in July, when they returned to their home state of Virginia. They were sentenced to twenty-five years in jail after being charged with violating the state's antiquated miscegenation laws and the Virginia laws prohibiting interracial marriage.

Anti-miscegenation laws in the United States had been in place in certain states since colonial days. Marriage to a slave was never legal. In the Reconstruction era in 1865, the "Black Codes" across the seven states of the lower South made interracial marriage illegal. The new Republican legislatures in six states repealed the restrictive laws. After the Democrats returned to power, the restriction was re-imposed. A major concern was how to draw the line between black and white in a society in which white men had many children with black slave women. On the one hand, a person's reputation as black or white was usually decisive in practical matters. On the other hand, most laws used a "one drop of blood" rule, which meant that one black ancestor made a person black in the view of the law. In 1967, sixteen states, all southern, still had anti-miscegenation laws.

In the case of the Lovings, the trial judge, Leone Bazile, sentenced them to twenty-five years in jail but agreed to suspend their sentence if they would leave Virginia. So they left and moved to Washington, D.C. In 1964, frustrated by their inability to travel together to visit their families in Virginia, and their social isolation and financial difficulties in Washington, Mildred Loving wrote in protest to Attorney General Robert F. Kennedy. Kennedy referred her to the American Civil Liberties Union

(ACLU). The ACLU filed a motion on behalf of the Lovings in the Virginia trial court to vacate the judgment and set aside the sentence on the grounds that the violated statutes ran counter to the Fourteenth Amendment.

On October 28, 1964, while waiting for a response from the court to their motion, they brought a class-action suit in U.S. District Court for the Eastern District of Virginia. On January 22, 1965, a three-judge district court panel decided to allow the Lovings to present their constitutional claims to the Virginia Supreme Court of Appeals. Virginia Supreme Court justice Harry L. Carrico (later chief justice of the court) wrote an opinion for the court upholding the constitutionality of the anti-miscegenation statutes and, after modifying the Lovings' sentence, affirmed their criminal convictions. The Lovings, supported by the ACLU, appealed the decision to the United States Supreme Court. They did not attend the oral arguments in Washington, but their lawyer, Bernard S. Cohen, conveyed the message he had been given by Richard Loving to the Court: "Mr. Cohen, tell the Court I love my wife, and it is just unfair that I can't live with her in Virginia."

Richard and Mildred Loving are both gone now. But the impact and the legacy of their bold assertion to define marriage in America as between two people who love each other regardless of race changed the way we looked at "family" and ultimately served as legal precedent to the controversial 2015 Supreme Court ruling *Obergefell v. Hodges*, legalizing same-sex couples' right to marry. Whether you agree with the latter definition of marriage or not, the point is that the Lovings understood a principle near and dear to our Founders' hearts: that each of us has the God-given right to have life, liberty (considered a right as defined by the Supreme Court), and the pursuit of happiness as we deem appropriate and fitting. For the Lovings, they fell in love. They were childhood friends, and they wanted to be married just like any other couple. Their case opened the door for mixed-race couples and families to live out their liberty and their love, and by doing so redefined the American culture not just for their time, but for all times to come.

CESAR CHAVEZ[85]

> *"Preservation of one's own culture does not require contempt or disrespect for other cultures."*
> —*Cesar Chavez*

Those words, spoken by the late Cesar Chavez, are powerful. And they sum up in a sentence the heart of our motto: *Out of many we are one.* Born near Yuma, Arizona, to immigrant parents, Chavez moved to California with his family in 1939. For the next ten years they moved up and down the state, working in the fields. During this period, Chavez encountered the conditions that he would dedicate his life to changing: wretched migrant camps, corrupt labor contractors, meager wages for backbreaking work, and bitter racism.

A major turning point came in September 1965, when the fledgling Farm Workers Association voted to join a strike that had been initiated by Filipino farmworkers in Delano, California's grape fields. Within months Chavez and his union became nationally known. Drawing on the imagery of the Civil Rights Movement, Chavez's insistence on nonviolence, his reliance on volunteers from urban universities and religious organizations, his alliance with organized labor, and his use of mass mobilizing techniques—such as a famous march on Sacramento in 1966— brought the grape strike and consumer boycott into the national consciousness. The boycott in particular was responsible for pressuring the growers to recognize the United Farm Workers (the UFW, renamed after the union joined the AFL-CIO). The first contracts were signed in 1966 but were followed by more years of strife. In 1968, Chavez went on a fast for twenty-five days to protest the increasing advocacy of violence within the union. Victory finally came on July 29, 1970, when twenty-six Delano growers formally signed contracts recognizing the UFW and bringing peace to the vineyards.

In short, Chavez's bravery in standing up for the treatment of the people in his community was transformational to American culture, bringing to light how our nation treated migrant workers (mostly Hispanic) and the conditions in which they and their families were forced to live and work. But more than that important achievement, Chavez made the nation take a look in the mirror and hold true to the motto of our founding when he reminded us that pride in, and preservation of, one's own culture must never mean disrespect or contempt for another's.

ALEX HALEY [86]

"In every conceivable manner, the family is the link to our past, the bridge to our future." —Alex Haley

I am old enough to remember the original *Roots* miniseries on television in 1977. I was just nine years old when it aired. Like everyone in my generation, I sat with my family for five nights, spellbound by the epic adaptation of Alex Haley's bestselling book, *Roots: The Saga of an American Family*. *Roots* was transformational to the American culture. More than 130 million people watched the series over the course of a week. Americans of every race and background watched in awe, and at times in horror, at the graphic depictions of the slave trade and the transatlantic crossing. Black and white Americans learned about our ancestry, our complicated history and lineages as a result of American slavery. The History Channel aired a new "reimagined" version of *Roots* as a Memorial Day weekend special in May 2016, and it was watched by as many as 10 million people over the four nights that it aired, proving the impact and power that the original had on our culture over 40 years ago.

In 1976, Haley had published *Roots: The Saga of an American Family*, a novel based on his family's history, going back to slavery days. It started with the story of Kunta Kinte, who was kidnapped in the Gambia in 1767 and transported to the province of Maryland to be sold as a slave. Haley claimed to be a seventh-generation descendant of Kunta Kinte, and his work on the novel involved twelve years of research, intercontinental travel, and writing. He went to the village of Juffure, where Kunta Kinte grew up, and listened to a tribal historian (griot) tell the story of Kinte's capture. Haley also traced the records of the ship, *The Lord Ligonier*, which he said carried his ancestor to the Americas. Haley has stated that the most emotional moment of his life occurred on September 29, 1967, when he stood at the site in Annapolis, Maryland, where his ancestor had arrived from Africa in chains exactly two hundred years before. A memorial depicting Haley reading a story to young children gathered at his feet has since been erected in the center of Annapolis. *Roots* was eventually published in thirty-seven languages. Haley won a special Pulitzer Prize for the work in 1977.

The great contribution of Haley through *Roots* is twofold: First, it emphasized that African Americans have a long history, and that not all that history starts in slavery in America, as many believed. It starts in Africa, where Africans were free to marry, have families, have property, and worship with a deep, abiding faith in their Creator (sound familiar?). Second, *Roots*'s popularity also sparked a greatly increased public interest in genealogy, giving rise to websites such as ancestry.com, and TV series like *Who Do You Think You Are*, created by Henry Louis Gates, Jr. Alex Haley redefined American culture by sharing his American story, once again proving that we are more alike than different in that many of us share bloodlines and ancestry across the races, and the many cultures that immigrated to this nation.

* * * * * * * * * * * * * * * * * *

Reclaiming Our Founders' Vision

Who are we and what do we value as Americans? That is the question. By reflecting on what our Founders envisioned America to be, we rediscover who we were meant to be as a great nation unlike any other before. There can be no doubt that we have a distinctly "American culture," and a big part of that culture is the evolving virtue of family. Here are some key takeaways and traits that we Americans value in our culture, traits that have endured since our founding:

1. Family

2. Individuality

3. Liberty

4. Equality

5. Privacy

6. Time

7. Informality

8. Laughter

9. Directness/Candor

10. Success

* * * * * * * * * * * * * * * * * *

"Religion is the basis and

foundation of Government."

—James Madison, 1775

CODE 8

BE ENGAGED IN THE FREE EXERCISE OF RELIGION

Freedom of religion is the cornerstone of our nation's founding. Yes, we celebrate liberty and freedom, as we should. Yes, we celebrate that *all of us are created equal.* And, yes, we celebrate the right to keep and bear arms. But what our Founding Fathers did in 1776 was radical. It was, in fact, unthinkable in an age of monarchs. The fifty-five men who signed the Declaration of Independence declared that God was supreme, not kings. And that God, not man, endowed His creation with certain unalienable rights. Rights that could not be dissolved. Rights that could not be given away. Rights that came through Him, and Him alone.

Our Founders believed strongly in "natural law." That's evident in all our founding documents, and the debates during the Continental Congress about what we wanted in our Constitution. It is evident in the writings of Jefferson, Washington, Madison, Adams, and Franklin. Their belief that our rights are given to us at birth by an omnipotent God was something the earth had never seen in an established government. While slavery may have been this nation's great birth defect, faith, belief, and religious doctrine was this nation's saving grace.

The right to freedom of religion was so central to our American democracy that it was enshrined in the First Amendment to the U.S. Constitution. We would do well as a nation founded on a unique set of faith and freedom principles not to shy away from, or, worse, try to run away from our Founders' belief that religious freedom is in fact what keeps men free.

The Founders framed the First Amendment in response to almost two centuries of religious conflict and oppression in America by the British Crown. And, beyond that, they had a keen understanding of the religious persecution of the citizenry in Europe dating back to the sixth century and earlier, as many of their family had descended from there. The result of religious persecution, of course, was disastrous: religious wars, burnings, property seizures, kingdoms toppled, and worse. With this backdrop, and understanding the unique and intimate nature of religion, the Founding Fathers wisely put religion on a different footing from other forms of speech and observance, mandating strict separation of religion and government to ensure religious freedom for all individuals and faiths. In other words, our Founders had a vision that the best way to keep America and Americans united was not to force them to worship by fiat. Largely because of the First Amendment's prohibition against government regulation or endorsement of religion, diverse faiths have flourished and thrived in America since the founding of the republic. James Madison, our nation's fourth president and "Father of the Constitution," concisely summed up the reasons for, and benefits of, the First Amendment's unique treatment of religion:

> Because we hold it for a fundamental and undeniable truth, that Religion or the duty which we owe to our Creator and the manner of discharging it, can be directed only by reason and conviction, not by force or violence. The Religion then of every man must be left to the conviction and conscience of every man: and it is the right of every man to exercise it as these may dictate.[87]

Madison was the great champion of religious freedom and small government at the founding of our great nation. Madison did not speak of religious liberty in clichés, although he did speak emphatically from principle. Religious freedom was central to him personally and to his understanding of the United States. He agreed with Jefferson that a republic without religious freedom was impossible. Religious freedom was essential for political freedom and academic freedom.

Madison understood well that 1639 represented a defining moment in Americans' religious heritage, when a group of New England Puritans drafted a constitution affirming their faith in God and their intention to organize a Christian nation. Delegates from the towns of Windsor, Hartford, and Wethersfield drew up the "Fundamental Orders of Connecticut," which made clear that their government rested on divine authority and pursued godly purposes.[88] But Madison also knew that 1787 was another defining moment. In that year, our Founders drafted a new constitution that, unlike that of their Puritan forebears of New England, made no reference at all to God or divine providence, citing as its sole authority "the people of the United States." Further, its stated purposes were secular and political: "to form a more perfect Union, establish Justice, insure domestic Tranquility, provide for the common defense, promote the general Welfare, and secure the Blessings of Liberty."

So, our Founders again did something radical: Instead of building a "Christian Commonwealth," the supreme law of the land established a secular state. The opening clause of the First Amendment introduced the radical notion that the government had no voice concerning matters of conscience: "Congress shall make no law respecting an establishment of religion or prohibiting the free exercise thereof." Two years later, in April 1789, George Washington took another oath, swearing to "faithfully execute the office of the President of the United States" and pledging to the best of his ability to "preserve, protect and defend the Constitution of the United States." Although the Presidential Oath ends "So help me God," our Founders took great pains to ensure that there was no requirement of the government to force religion upon its officeholders or citizenry.

Hence, while the Puritan fathers gave us the symbols of America as a haven of religious freedom, the Founding Fathers provided us with something more enduring: the idea that all men were allowed to worship freely (whether Muslim, Jewish, Christian, or atheist) and decide their own fate. Their ideas of separation of church and state and the free exercise of religion extended to people of all faiths or no faith. These men were framers of a religious revolution, rejecting the idea of an established or official religion, which was the organizing principle informing church-state relations in the vast majority of countries, as indeed it had been in most of the American colonies. Never before had there been such a total separation of religious and political institutions. But the ban on an established or official church was not the Founders' only legacy in church-state matters. Regarding religion as a natural right that the governed need never surrender to government, they prohibited any interference in citizens' rights to the free exercise of religion.

To Madison, "the separation between Religion and Government in the Constitution of the United States" was the surest guarantee of "the sacred principle of religious liberty." History was filled with examples of unholy alliances between church and state as religious and political leaders sought to curry each other's favor for their own selfish ends. Indeed, the Puritan fathers themselves had fled England when King Charles I's strict enforcement of religious conformity violated the Puritans' liberty of conscience. While delegates like William Williams of Connecticut were primarily worried about America as a "Christian Nation," Madison was more concerned about America as a haven of religious liberty.[89]

In this Code we will look at two key principles concerning the freedom of religion in America. And we will look at the lives of two well-known Americans who used their religious freedoms as a means to free others and preserve the right of religious conscience and the right to object to those things that may offend any religion in American culture. The two key principles we will review are the First Amendment and the Establishment Clause.

The First Amendment

In the spring of 1778, the Constitutional Convention was held in Philadelphia. This convention resolved three main religious controversies:

- There would be no religious test or oath or confirmation required to hold any federal office.
- Quakers and others could affirm, not "swear," their religious beliefs.
- Christianity, or one of its denominations, would not be recognized as an established state church.

Although these core tenets were agreed upon, there was no specific guarantee of religious freedom. Thomas Jefferson was pleased with the Constitution but felt it was incomplete. He pushed for legislation that would guarantee individual rights, including what he felt was the prime guarantee: freedom of and from religion. Madison promised to promote such a bill in order to gain support for the ratification of the Constitution by the state of Virginia. In 1789, the first of ten amendments were written to the Constitution; they have since been known as the Bill of Rights. Here is a timeline of the early draft language showing how our Founders arrived at the religious liberties clause of the Constitution[90]:

- **James Madison, June 7, 1789:** "The Civil Rights of none shall be abridged on account of religious belief or worship, nor shall any national religion be established, nor shall the full and equal rights of conscience be in any manner, nor on any pretext infringed. No state shall violate the equal rights of conscience or the freedom of the press, or the trial by jury in criminal cases."

- **House Select Committee, July 28, 1789:** "No religion shall be established by law, nor shall the equal rights of conscience be infringed."

- **Samuel Livermore, August 15, 1789:** "Congress shall make no laws touching religion, or infringing the rights of conscience."

- **House version, August 20, 1789:** "Congress shall make no law establishing religion, or to prevent the free exercise thereof, or to infringe the rights of conscience." (moved by Fisher Ames)

- **Initial Senate version, September 3, 1789:** "Congress shall make no law establishing religion, or prohibiting the free exercise thereof."

- **Final Senate version, September 9, 1789:** "Congress shall make no law establishing articles of faith or a mode of worship, or prohibiting the free exercise of religion."
- **Conference Committee, September 24, 1789:** "Congress shall make no law respecting an establishment of religion, or prohibiting the free exercise thereof."

The final wording that we now have in our Constitution was accepted by the House of Representatives at the Conference Committee on September 24, 1789, and by the Senate on September 25, 1789. It was ratified by the states in 1791.

The Establishment Clause

There has been and continues to be great debate in America about the religious "Establishment Clause" of the Constitution. As mentioned earlier in this Code, James Madison proposed three religion clauses in his June 8 speech in the First Congress.[91] He proposed the addition to the Constitution of three clauses, to be inserted in Article I, Section 9: "1) The civil rights of none shall be abridged on account of religious belief or worship," "2) nor shall any national religion be established," and "3) nor shall the full and equal rights of conscience be in any manner, or on any pretext, infringed." What we ended up with was the Establishment Clause: "Congress shall make no law respecting an establishment of religion. . . ."

The Establishment Clause was written by Congressman Fisher Ames in 1789. He derived it from discussions in the First Congress of various drafts that would become the amendments making up the Bill of Rights. The second half of the Establishment Clause includes the "Free Exercise Clause," which guarantees freedom from governmental interference in both private and public religious affairs of all kinds. The Establishment Clause is a limitation placed upon the United States Congress, preventing it from passing legislation respecting an establishment of religion. The second half of the Establishment Clause inherently prohibits the government from preferring any one religion over another. While the Establishment Clause does prohibit Congress from preferring or elevating one religion over another, still it does not prohibit the government's entry into the religious domain to make accommodations for religious observances and practices in order to achieve the purposes of the Free Exercise Clause.

Note that the Establishment Clause is absolute. It allows *no* law to be made that would establish a religion. It is also noteworthy that the clause forbids more than just the establishment of religion by the government. It forbids even laws *respecting* an establishment of religion. The Establishment Clause sets up a line of demarcation between the functions and operations of the institutions of religion and government in our society. It does so because the framers of the First Amendment recognized that when the roles of the government and religion were intertwined, the result too often had been bloodshed or oppression.

Many have come to interpret this controversial clause as limiting the sanctioning of religion in any public way, shape, or form. For example, prayers at high school sports or graduations. The wearing of religious symbols. Christmas or religious displays on public property or in government offices. Many lawsuits have been filed, and the Supreme Court has visited the issue so many times it created what is called the "Lemon test." In *Lemon v. Kurtzman* (1971), the Court provided a three-part test for Establishment Clause analysis, which is used to assess whether a law violates the Establishment Clause. The three-part test asks:

1. Does the law have a secular purpose? If not, it violates the Establishment Clause.
2. Is the primary effect either to advance religion or to inhibit religion? If so, it violates the Establishment Clause.
3. Does the law foster an excessive governmental entanglement with religion? If so, it violates the Establishment Clause.

The bottom line with respect to freedom of religion in this nation is that our Founders believed it was the cornerstone of how America would keep a free and strong republican form of government. They understood that the government should never be able to mandate a man's religious beliefs or practices. We may argue in our present day about whether America is a Judeo-Christian nation or not, but one thing we can and should all agree on is the vision of our Founders, particularly James Madison, that has set the course for America for the past 240 years. We are the great city on a hill. We are the light. We are the salt. And it is so because we are free, all of us, to worship our Creator, or not, in the way that we believe is best for us.

Two Americans Who Put it on the Line for Their Faith

MUHAMMAD ALI[92]

"He who is not courageous enough to take risks will accomplish nothing in life." —Muhammad Ali

Born Cassius Marcellus Clay, Jr., Muhammad Ali (January 17, 1942–June 3, 2016) became a true American hero after winning a gold medal in Boxing in the 1960 Olympics in Rome. Cassius Clay the man became even more famous for taking a stance for his right to religious freedom, when he objected to being drafted to serve in the Vietnam War in 1966.

Ali was born and raised in Louisville, Kentucky, and began training as a boxer when he was just twelve years old. At eighteen, he won the light heavyweight gold medal in the 1960 Summer Olympics in Rome, and converted to Islam shortly afterward. At twenty-two, in 1964, he won the WBC and WBA heavyweight championships from Sonny Liston in an upset. After joining the Nation of Islam, Clay changed his legal name from Cassius Clay—which he called his "slave name"—to "Muhammad Ali." Under the tutelage of Malcolm X, Ali became an unabashed voice of racial pride and resistance to "white domination" for African Americans during the 1960s Civil Rights Movement.

In 1966, two years after winning the heavyweight title, Ali further antagonized the establishment by refusing to be drafted into the U.S. military, citing his religious beliefs and opposition to American involvement in the Vietnam War. He was eventually arrested, found guilty on draft-evasion charges, and stripped of his boxing titles. It is here that we should pause and reflect on what our Founders fought for with respect to religious freedom. Here was the heavyweight champion of the world, and he was a practicing Muslim. The federal government prosecuted him because his religious beliefs forbade him to go into military service, and, in this case, the Vietnam War. Ali successfully appealed his case to the U.S. Supreme Court, which overturned his conviction in 1971. By that time, he had not fought for nearly four years—losing a period of peak performance as an athlete. Ali's actions as a conscientious objector to the war made him an icon for the large counterculture generation of the time.

Ali attended his first Nation of Islam meeting in 1961. He continued to attend meetings, although keeping his involvement hidden from the public. In fact, Clay was initially refused entry to the Nation of Islam (often called the "Black Muslims" at the time) due to his boxing career. However, after he won the championship from Liston in 1964, the Nation of Islam was more receptive. Shortly afterward, Nation of Islam leader Elijah Muhammad released a statement that Clay would be renamed "Muhammad" ("one who is worthy of praise") "Ali" (the most important figure after the Prophet Muhammad in the Shia view, and the fourth "rightly guided caliph" in the Sunni view). Around that time Ali moved to the south side of Chicago and lived in a series of houses, always near the Nation of Islam's Mosque Maryam or Elijah Muhammad's residence. He stayed in Chicago for about twelve years. Not afraid to antagonize the white establishment, Ali stated, "I am America. I am the part you won't recognize. But get used to me. Black, confident, cocky; my name, not yours; my religion, not yours; my goals, my own; get used to me."

Ali passed away in June 2016, to great respect from around the world. His memorial service exemplified the heart of our great motto: *E Pluribus Unum*. Eulogized by former president Bill Clinton and an array of great citizens of the Mormon, Christian, Jewish, and Muslim faiths, he was most remembered for his great stance on his faith. Ali is regarded as one of the greatest boxers of all time, and he remains the only three-time "lineal world heavyweight champion" (meaning the undisputed champion), winning a title in 1964, 1974, and 1978. Nicknamed "The Greatest," he was involved in several historic boxing matches. After retiring from boxing in 1981, Ali devoted his life to religious and charitable work. In 1984, Ali was diagnosed with Parkinson's disease, which he attributed to boxing-related brain injuries.

SOJOURNER TRUTH[93]

"Ain't I a woman too?" —*Sojourner Truth*

Sojourner Truth is most notably remembered for being a former slave who became a great abolitionist. But what many do not know about her is that it was her religious faith that propelled her to greatness in the annals of American history. Born into slavery about 1797, in Ulster County, New York, she was named Isabella. Her parents were James and Betsey, the property of Colonel Johannes Hardenbergh. As a child she spoke only Low Dutch and, like most slaves, never learned to read or write. About 1815 Isabella married Thomas, a fellow slave, and bore five children: Diana (b. 1815), Peter (b. 1821), Elizabeth (b. 1825), Sophia (b. 1826), and a fifth child who may have died in infancy.

Over the course of her life, Isabella was sold to four more owners, until she finally walked to freedom in 1826, carrying her infant daughter, Sophia. She settled in New York City until 1843, when she changed her name to Sojourner Truth, announcing she would travel the land as an itinerant preacher, telling the truth and working against injustice. It is here that her true story as an American hero begins.

During the next several years, Truth traveled throughout the East and the Midwest, preaching for human rights. As an illiterate ex-slave, Truth became a powerful figure in several national social movements, speaking forcefully for the abolition of slavery, women's rights and suffrage, the rights of freedmen, temperance, prison reform, and the termination of capital punishment.

Almost six feet tall, Truth was a striking woman with a charismatic presence. When she addressed an audience, legend has it that her low, resonant voice, especially when raised in song, could still the most hostile of crowds. Sojourner Truth often testified to the demeaning nature of slavery and the redeeming power of faith. She declared that her soul was "beclouded and crushed" while in slavery, but "how good and wise is God, for if slaves knowed what their true condition was, it would be more than the mind could bear. While the race is sold of all their rights—what is there on God's footstool to bring them up?" "But I believe," she said, "in the next world. When we get up yonder, we shall have all them rights 'stored to us again."[94]

What makes Truth a hero, and earned her a marble bust in the rotunda of the U.S. Capitol, is that she held a mirror up to America's soul at a time when it seemed soulless. Truth was unwilling to wait to get to heaven to have her rights—or those of any persecuted person—restored. Preaching for racial equality, she asked, "Does not God love colored children as well as white children? And did not the same Savior die to save the one as well as the other?"[95] Truth was not intimidated by convention or authority. She learned to manipulate establishment institutions to effect reforms.

Probably her most famous address, known as "Ain't I a Woman," was made at a Women's Rights Convention in Akron, Ohio, on May 28, 1851. Truth asserted that women deserved equal rights with men because they were equal in capability to men. "I have plowed and reaped and husked and chopped and mowed, and can any man do more than that?" She concluded her argument, saying, "And how came Jesus into the world? Through God who created him and the woman who bore him. Man, where was your part?"[96] Truth used her faith and her belief in God to hold America's feet to the fire on the promise of her birth. She was a preacher without a color, a powerful priest with the American conscience as her pulpit.

★ ★ ★ ★ ★ ★ ★ ★ ★ ★ ★ ★ ★ ★ ★ ★

Reclaiming Our Founders' Vision

The religion clauses of the First Amendment guarantee religious liberty, or freedom of conscience, for all Americans: people of all faiths and those who have no professed faith. Our nation was indeed founded upon religious freedom. Our Founders fled religious persecution by the British Crown and many of the monarchs of Europe. The notion that a government should not only respect a man's faith, but also protect it, was indeed radical.

Here are some key takeaways that we as Americans must honor and protect as citizens when it comes to our religious liberties:

1. Practice and defend the right of free religious expression in America for all citizens; not just Christians, but all Americans of faith.

2. Or those who have no beliefs.

3. Be vigilant against government intrusion of any kind into the rights of freedom of religious expression guaranteed in the Constitution.

4. Monitor closely your children's school dress codes, codes of conduct, and make sure that they do not infringe on your child's religious liberties.

5. Form employee resource groups (ERGs) for people of faith as they have with other groups of Americans (women, blacks, Latinos, LGBT, etc.).

6. Run for political office. Get engaged in your local and state organizations that work to protect religious liberties.

★　★　★　★　★　★　★　★　★　★ · ★　★　★　★　★　★

"*The right of the people to keep and bear arms shall not be infringed. A well-regulated militia, composed of the body of the people, trained to arms, is the best and most natural defense of a free country.*"

—JAMES MADISON, I *ANNALS OF CONGRESS 434*, JUNE 8, 1789

CODE
9

THE RIGHT TO KEEP AND BEAR ARMS: REFLECTIONS ON THE SECOND AMENDMENT

The Second Amendment: Where Do We Go from Here?

How could I possibly write a book about America and the freedom that makes us so great, and the most admired nation on earth, without talking about one of our most central freedoms: the right to be licensed for, carry, purchase, and keep arms in our homes or on our person?

This is the one place in the book where I will use my voice to discuss one of our founding principles differently than I have the others. The reason is that this founding principle is a hotbed of opinions and controversy in our modern-day country. Truth be told, I had originally decided to leave this Code out. I didn't want to deal with it. I didn't want my book to be considered as partisan or controversial. And yet, how does one talk about the greatness of America without addressing one of the three most fundamental principles of our founding:

1. freedom of speech,
2. freedom of religion, and
3. freedom to own fire arms.

The truth is, I was afraid to say out loud that I am a proud gun owner. That I go to the shooting range, and that my father kept guns in our home (as did my grandfather, and my uncles, all of whom, by the way, served honorably in the United States Army from World War II to the Persian Gulf War). I was afraid that my book would not be well received by some of my friends in the media, and some of my favorite politicians on the left, and that mattered to me because this book is an attempt to unify us, to bring us together. I did not want those reviewing this book to focus on the Code about the Second Amendment and miss every other important virtue about our founding. I want to be a uniter, not a divider. My country is in pain. It has hit a midlife crisis of the soul, and we need to be able to dialogue openly and honestly about some deeply difficult issues such as race relations, gender equality, policing, and, yes, guns.

It is time we addressed the elephant in the room, and discussed this important issue respectfully for those of us who own guns, and with a keen ear of empathy for the other side that seeks to restrict gun ownership for those who would commit heinous crimes, including acts of murder or terrorism.

I am a member of the National Rifle Association (NRA), dating back on and off to the 1990s (the NRA is headquartered down the street from my home in the great commonwealth of Virginia). I believe deeply in the Second Amendment, as I do all the other Amendments contained in the Bill of Rights. I am a sworn officer of the court. I took an oath to the Constitution when I became an attorney and a member of the United States Supreme Court Bar. I have read with awe the lessons of history and how the colonists defeated the greatest empire on earth at the time, because they had guns. They could form militias and they could defend their freedom. They could never have secured the liberties you and I enjoy today without the rights they enjoyed because of English common law—the right to bear arms in the colonies.[97]

It is important for us in our time to understand that guns were integral to the American experience. Every able-bodied white male between the ages of eighteen and forty-five *was required to own a gun* and serve in the militia. Black men were enslaved and could not own arms legally, and women certainly could not own them, but they were often taught to use them by their militiamen husbands. Guns could be, and were, regulated in the colonies. But the fact remains that the people had guns.

It is difficult to know how the Founding Fathers would react today to matters relative to our military might and our free access to weapons. Or how they would react to the fact that we have an incredibly powerful standing army (which they did not want), and that we are now rife with handguns, machine guns, and weapons that have no relationship to militias. It is worth noting that the Constitution allowed for a permanent navy, but not a standing army. Note also that the Constitution explicitly states what militias do: *They make sure the laws are followed, suppress insurrections, and repel invasions.*[98]

The role of the militia was made explicit because our Founders had learned painful lessons after Shays' Rebellion of 1786–87 and the Whiskey Rebellion of 1791–94. The Militia Act of 1792[99] also explicitly directed the president's use of militias or force. The Constitution made sure that there was nothing to fear from the federal government, because there was no standing army at the time. The Founders rightly feared insurrection and invasions of all sorts. The militias were empowered by the Constitution to protect against these in the absence of an army. Every single speaker in the U.S. House of Representatives who commented on the Second Amendment before its ratification spoke only about militias. This is critical, because it gives us a context for our Second Amendment rights from the very men who granted them to us more than 240 years ago.[100]

After the Boston Tea Party in 1773, the Crown became concerned about the colonists and their acts of rebellion. The king and his soldiers desperately wanted to strip the colonists of their arms when they realized that the citizens of Boston were starting to assemble and protest. The British realized that they could not control the people with only two thousand troops in Boston. So what did they do? They sought to eliminate the people's ability to acquire firearms and gunpowder. Remember, at one time it was law in the colonies for militiamen to own their own firearms and have a minimum quantity of gunpowder on hand, though not all could afford it.[101]

In Massachusetts, the royal governor, General Thomas Gage, forbade town meetings from taking place more than once a year. So when an "illegal meeting" was taking place in Salem, he sent in the British Redcoats to break it up. They were met with three thousand armed Americans and they retreated. Interestingly enough, Gage's aide, John Andrews, said that everyone in the area who was age sixteen or older owned a firearm and had gunpowder. The militia at the time produced twenty thousand men who mobilized and began marching toward Boston. American colonists believed that if the British were going to use force or violence to seize arms or powder, it would be an act of war and they would respond in kind.[102] As a result of this protest, Parliament, with the direct encouragement of King George III, passed the Coercive Acts, or, as they were properly known, the Restraining Acts (aka "the Intolerable Acts"), in 1774. The purposes of the Intolerable Acts:

- The purpose of the Boston Port Act of the Intolerable Acts was to close the port of Boston until the tea that had been destroyed at the Boston Tea Party had been paid for. Only food and firewood were permitted into the port of Boston.
- The purpose of the Massachusetts Government Act was to effectively suspend the right of self-government in the Massachusetts colony and revoke the colony's 1691 charter.
- The purpose of the Administration of Justice Act of the Intolerable Acts allowed the Governor to send rebellious colonists for trial in other colonies or in Great Britain.
- The purpose of the Quartering Act of 1774 of the Intolerable Acts was to extend the provisions of the previous 1765

Quartering Act, giving the governor, rather than the
assembly, the authority to enforce arrangements to ensure
that the colonists supplied billeting for the troops.
- The purpose of the 1765 Quartering Act was to require
colonial governments to absorb the costs associated with
quartering British troops, which included food, shelter,
bedding, cooking utensils, firewood, salt, vinegar, beer or
cider, and candles.
- The purpose of the Quartering Act of 1774 was to avoid
a repetition of the defiant actions taken by the New York
Provincial Assembly, who had at one point refused to comply
with the 1765 Quartering Act.[103]

Similarly, once the patriots heard about the acts, they made
it clear that they would fight and die rather than see such laws
enforced upon them by the British Army. The patriots of Lancaster County, Pennsylvania, resolved: "That in the event of
Great Britain attempting to force unjust laws upon us by the
strength of arms, our cause we leave to heaven and our rifles."[104]
So you see, "gun control" is not new. The British Crown
sought to seize weapons from citizens, and the strong arm of the
government attempting to impose its power on the people not to
assemble, is centuries old. That's right, gun control is nothing
new. It was very much alive in the eighteenth century. Nor was
it new even in the twentieth century. But what made the "united
colonies" (ultimately the "United States") different was that the
people did not allow themselves to be bullied or to compromise on what they understood was a fundamental, God-given

right: the right to protect themselves, and defend their liberty. As Continental Congress President Richard Henry Lee wrote:

> A militia when properly formed are in fact the people themselves . . . and include, according to the past and general usage of the states, all men capable of bearing arms. . . . To preserve liberty, it is essential that the whole body of the people always possess arms, and be taught alike, especially when young, how to use them.[105]

Modern scholars Thomas B. McAffee and Michael J. Quinlan agree that James Madison "did not invent the right to keep and bear arms when he drafted the Second Amendment; the right was pre-existing at both Common Law and in the early state constitutions." In contrast, historian Jack Rakove suggests that Madison's intention in framing the Second Amendment was to provide assurances to moderate Anti-Federalists that the militias would not be disarmed.[106]

One aspect of the gun control debate is the conflict between gun control laws and the right to rebel against unjust governments. In his *Commentaries*, Sir William Blackstone, jurist, judge, and Tory politician, alluded to this right to rebel as the natural right of resistance and self-preservation, to be used only as a last resort, exercisable when "the sanctions of society and laws are found insufficient to restrain the violence of oppression."[107]

The Second Amendment, then, was created so that the states could form militias or armies to destroy insurrections or slave rebellions because the federal government had no standing military for a long time. The Founding Fathers were fearful of the notion of a standing army, because they were wary of a military coup. Without a standing army, the only protection the people and the government had were militias. The U. S. Constitution, Article 1, Section 8, states:

> The Congress shall have Power . . . To raise and support Armies, but no Appropriation of Money to that Use shall be for a longer Term than two Years; To provide and maintain a Navy; . . . to make Rules for the Government and Regulation of the land and naval Forces; To provide for calling forth the Militia to execute the Laws of the Union, suppress Insurrections and repel Invasions;

The Second Amendment, then, protects the right of the people to keep and bear arms. It was adopted on December 15, 1791, as part of the first ten amendments, the Bill of Rights. The Supreme Court of the United States has ruled in several cases over the years that the "right belongs to individuals," while also ruling that the "right is not unlimited and does not prohibit all regulation of either firearms or similar devices." State and local governments are limited to the same extent as the federal government from infringing this right, per the incorporation of the Bill of Rights.[108] The Second Amendment was based partially on the right to keep and bear arms in English common law and was influenced by the English Bill of Rights of

1689, as we will see below. Sir William Blackstone described this right as an auxiliary right, supporting the natural rights of self-defense, resistance to oppression (as we saw in the quote above), and the civic duty to act in concert in defense of the state.

Thomas Jefferson wrote:

> The laws that forbid the carrying of arms are laws of such a nature. They disarm only those who are neither inclined nor determined to commit crimes. Such laws make things worse for the assaulted and better for the assailants; they serve rather to encourage than to prevent homicides, for an unarmed man may be attacked with greater confidence than an armed man.[109]

What Jefferson wrote after the American Revolution, however, goes back to English common law, which is where many of the original rights we enjoy today emanate from. Our Bill of Rights was based on an act of the Parliament of England, and it dealt with constitutional matters and set out certain basic civil rights. Passed on December 16, 1689, it is a restatement in statutory form of the "Declaration of Rights" presented by the Convention Parliament to King William and Queen Mary in February 1689, inviting them to become joint sovereigns of England. It laid down limits on the powers of the monarch and set out the rights of Parliament, including the requirement for regular parliaments, free elections, and freedom of speech in Parliament. It also set forth certain rights of individuals, including the prohibition of cruel and unusual punishment, and it reestablished the liberty of Protestants to have arms for their defense within the rule of law.

In the United States, which has an English common law tradition, the concept of a right to keep and bear arms was recognized prior to the creation of a written national constitution. When colonists in the thirteen colonies rebelled against British control during the American Revolution, they cited the 1689 English Bill of Rights as an example. Early English settlers in America viewed the right to arms and/or the right to bear arms and/or state militias as important for one or more of the following purposes:

- to enable the people to organize a militia system;
- for participation in law enforcement;
- to deter tyrannical government;
- to repel invasion;
- to suppress insurrection, including slave revolts;
- to facilitate a natural right of self-defense.

Which of these considerations were thought of as most important and ultimately found expression in the Second Amendment is unclear. Some of these purposes were explicitly mentioned in early state constitutions; for example, the Pennsylvania Constitution of 1776 asserted that "the people have a right to bear arms for the defense of themselves and the state."[110] During the 1760s, in the prerevolutionary period, the established colonial militia was composed of colonists, including many who were loyal to British imperial rule. As defiance and opposition to British rule developed, a distrust of these loyalists in the militia became widespread among the colonists, known as "patriots," who favored independence from British rule. As a result, some patriots created their own militias that excluded the loyalists and then sought to stock independent armories for their militias. In response to this arms buildup, the British Parliament established an embargo on firearms, parts, and ammunition on the American colonies.[111]

It is clear to me, at least, that our Founders believed we the people must always have the right to keep arms, and, if necessary, form lawful citizen groups to protect our rights. Founding Father and cofounder of the Sons of Liberty Samuel Adams said it best in 1778 at the ratifying convention: "The Constitution shall never be construed to prevent the people of the United States who are peaceable citizens from keeping their own arms."[112]

Yet, as I reflect on the horrific shootings that have plagued this nation over the past two decades, beginning with the Columbine High School shooting in Colorado in 1999; to the 2015 shootings at the historic AME Church in Charleston, South Carolina, which claimed the lives of two of my Alpha Kappa Alpha sorority sisters; to the 2016 nightclub shooting in Orlando, Florida, I am also reminded of the horrific shooting deaths of the children at Sandy Hook Elementary School in Connecticut in 2012, and I begin to cry. My heart breaks. I think of my two nieces when they started school, and how much I loved them, as I do now. Then I think about the parents of those children at Sandy Hook, and I cannot imagine their grief. No parent should lose their child in such a way. No child should die in such a way. We can do better. We the people must demand better.

I am of the belief that the guns per se are not the problem. Every act of violence or terrorism that we face in the twenty-first century, as in centuries gone by, is perpetrated by madmen or madwomen filled with hatred, violence, disillusion, and anger toward their fellow man. We all know that something has gone wrong here in America with respect to guns and violence. Policemen have been gunned down in anger over what is perceived as a criminal justice and community policing system that is badly broken. The summer of 2016 saw eight policemen shot to death by former military men in the cities of Dallas and Baton Rouge. Young black men and women have been gunned down by each other in the streets of Chicago and Baltimore, in addition to the hundreds killed at the hands of police caught on tape in scenes that stun and shock us fellow Americans.

America, we indeed have a problem, but it is not one easily solved. Our Founders warned us that to easily give up our arms, or even to limit our access to them, was unwise.

General George Washington, who was the commander of all forces during the Revolutionary War, said in his First Annual Address to both Houses of Congress in 1790: *"A free people ought not only to be armed, but disciplined* [Emphasis mine.]; to which end a uniform and a well-digested plan is requisite; and their safety and interests require that they should promote such manufactories as tend to render them independent of others for essential, particularly military, supplies."

Some believe that the framers of the Bill of Rights sought to balance not just political power, but also military power, between the people, the states, and the nation. As Alexander Hamilton explained in 1788: "[I]f circumstances should at any time oblige the government to form an army of any magnitude, that army can never be formidable to the liberties of the people while there is a large body of citizens, little, if at all, inferior to them in discipline and the use of arms, who stand ready to defend their own rights and those of their fellow-citizens."

This code is the one place in this book that I am going to raise my voice, and attempt to sway you as my fellow Americans to come to some fundamental agreement. The gun debate is a source of great division in America right now. I can see the wisdom of both sides. I get it. We have been beset by violence with guns. What I want us to consider as we move forward into a new presidency, and a new direction for America, is how we come together on this issue, how we can sit down at the table of reason and honor a few core principles essential to the well-being of our republic. Consider these from our Founding Fathers:

- Principle #1: "They that can give up essential liberty to obtain a little temporary safety deserve neither liberty nor safety." —Benjamin Franklin, *Historical Review of Pennsylvania*, 1759

- Principle #2: "The Constitution shall never be construed . . . to prevent the people of the United States who are peaceable citizens from keeping their own arms."

  —Alexander Hamilton

- Principle #3: "The Constitution preserves the advantage of being armed which Americans possess over the people of almost every other nation (where) . . . the governments are afraid to trust the people with arms."   —James Madison

My bottom line is this: The most basic reason our Founders codified the right to keep and bear arms was to protect us from tyrannical governments and madmen who might try to do to us what King George and his armies did to them. And we must never, ever yield our guns, for that very reason. That being said, however, our political leaders, the NRA, and groups that want gun control must come together to find a middle ground that does not in any way compromise the lawful rights of those of us who are law-abiding American citizens to keep weapons in our homes, while still addressing how we keep guns out of the hands of possible terrorists, madmen, the mentally ill, or simply those who are not law-abiding Americans. I would suggest starting here:

1. **Crack down on the illegal transfer of, and access to, guns in the United States.** It is a fact that people who kill other people with guns in America acquire only 3 percent of their guns at gun stores (or legally). The other 97 percent

are obtained through other means. Rarely is a gun used in a homicide in possession of its original owner (who may or may not have purchased it legally). Hold those with legal title accountable for lending or selling guns to people who should not or who cannot purchase them legally. Impose strict laws and fines governing the sale and ownership of guns in all fifty states. With freedom comes responsibility.

2. **Improve the safety of guns.** Most gun-related deaths in the United States involve handguns. Provide free community training for citizens who purchase guns.

3. **Enact state and federal laws that require a background check.** Require that guns be registered and traceable in a database, and if not a federal database, a state database where, for example, officials in West Virginia could trace a gun registered in California. Create terrorist watch lists and criminal watch lists. I would also strongly suggest a mental health database cross-checking system that would alert the appropriate, relevant authorities.

SECTION II

THE LEADERSHIP CODES

★ ★ ★ ★ ★ ★ ★ ★ ★ ★ ★ ★ ★ ★ ★ ★ ★ ★

O ur nation was born from men of valor, courage, and Codes. They created America in the midst of revolution. They led by sacrificing their fortunes, careers, and time with their families, and with the threat of being hanged for treason, should they be captured or defeated by the British Crown. These Codes signify what true profiles in political courage should be about. They are the critical elements we need in the men and women who serve at the highest levels of government, elected office, the military, and corporations.

★ ★ ★ ★ ★ ★ ★ ★ ★ ★ ★ ★ ★ ★ ★ ★ ★ ★

"Our greatest happiness does not depend on the condition of life in which chance has placed us, but is always the result of a good conscience, good health, occupation, and freedom in all just pursuits."

—THOMAS JEFFERSON

CODE

1

PUBLIC SERVICE (NOBLESSE OBLIGE)

With Wealth and Power Come Responsibilities

Our Founders, for the most part, were men of privilege, wealth, and means. Not all, but most. Some were farmers or planters, but they owned slaves, which afforded them free labor and great financial reward. Some, like Paul Revere, were silversmiths, or, like Samuel Adams, tavern owners. But many were attorneys, merchants, bankers, or of "noble" professions, families, and birth. Our nation was formed because our Founding Fathers wanted to escape the clutches of British royalty and nobility, and build a nation that was free to govern itself and thrive on its own, without royal dictatorship.

They felt so strongly about the noble class, aristocrats, and monarchs usurping the power of the people that in the Constitution there is a Title of Nobility Clause, a provision in Article I, Section 9, Clause 8, that forbids our government from granting titles of nobility, and restricts members of the government from receiving gifts from foreign countries without the consent of the Congress. This clause is also sometimes called the "federal" Nobility Clause, because a similar clause in Article I, Section 10, Clause 1, bars the states (rather than the federal government) from granting titles of nobility. The Title of Nobility Clause is also one of the clauses that is sometimes called the "Emoluments Clause": "No Title of Nobility shall be granted by the United States: And no Person holding any Office of Profit or Trust under them, shall, without the Consent of the Congress, accept of any present, Emolument, Office, or Title, of any kind whatever, from any King, Prince, or foreign State."

Very few men of wealth and privilege are willing to set in motion systems of governance that limit their own advancement or power. Yet that is exactly what the Founders did. Much of the progress that America experienced during the Revolutionary War happened as a direct result of the Founding Fathers' counterintuitive actions. Yes, men had formed democracies and republics before. But none ever went as far as our Founders did to enfranchise and empower "the people" as when they created this great nation.

In this way, the Founding Fathers were the progenitors of their own disempowerment, not the victims. As Gordon Wood notes in his book *Revolutionary Characters: What Made the Founders Different*, "they created the changes that led eventually to their own undoing, to the breakup of the kind of political and intellectual coherence they represented." In other words, "they willingly destroyed the sources of their own greatness."[113]

This premise is where I want to open the Leadership Codes that will follow. Because, as with the Citizens' Codes we rediscovered in Section I, our Founders birthed this nation by doing radical, righteous, and revolutionary things. For example, in comparison with the founding of governments around the world, it is difficult to think of a comparable case where men of power opted to create a government *of the people*. Of course, the Founding Fathers did not absolutely eliminate the influence of nobility or aristocracy in America. America has had its share of wealthy and powerful political families, like the Adamses, the Vanderbilts, the Morgans, the Rockefellers, the Roosevelts, the Kennedys, and, more recently, the Bushes. But our Founders made sure there was no king, no omnipotent ruler, no dictator, and no title that could be given to elevate one man or group of men into permanent power.

The foresight of the Founding Fathers is admirable in this way. Few politicians before or since have dedicated their actions toward establishing a more equal, more just system of government that empowered the people at the lowest rungs of society to have a voice, to be able themselves to run for office, and to participate directly in their government. Yet, what we have seen since our founding is that most of our presidents, diplomats, and elected officials come from wealthy or privileged backgrounds.

The 2016 primary and presidential election was no different. We had two candidates for president who were multimillionaires or billionaires, from what we would consider the wealthy class in America. The truth is that, despite our Founders' best efforts to level the playing field, the expense of running for public office makes it improbable (not impossible) for a regular citizen to emerge into high public office. Yet, as history has proven, some of our greatest leaders in America emerged from the so-called "noble class."

The truth is the aristocratic class will always find ways to preserve its power and influence in government. That's why, time and time again, as Wood noted in his book, there have been efforts to control royalty and nobility in America. From Lincoln's land-grant colleges, to Theodore Roosevelt's and Taft's "trust-busting," Franklin Delano Roosevelt's "New Deal," Johnson's "Great Society," the goal of America has always been to ensure that everyone has an equal opportunity (not outcome) at living a happy and comfortable life.

In this Code we are going to explore the principles of duty and responsibility on the part of those who claim the mantle of leadership in our great nation, whether those leaders were born to privilege or whether they earned it through hard work and perseverance. I want to begin by breaking down the French phrase *noblesse oblige*—literally "nobility obliges"—meaning that with wealth and power come responsibilities. Here are two key takeaways that are a must for those who lead and serve in public life:

1. Power demands responsibility.
2. Responsibility demands service. A servant leader is responsible to those they serve.

Power Demands Purpose

What is power anyway?

How is it wielded?

Who has it?

And how should it be used in a democratic republic?

These are the questions our Founders asked when their king kept taxing them, oppressing them, and not allowing them the right to be heard. They were tired of being oppressed. Bullied. And at times literally bludgeoned to death by British soldiers in taverns and gatherings in Boston before and after the Boston Tea Party and leading up to the Revolutionary War.[114] A monarch is the highest of the noble class, and the highest form of absolute power. Our Founders understood absolute power because they were subject to its tyranny. They believed that the soul of government should be to place power in the hands of the people, and let the people elect from among themselves their leaders. Hence, the great news is that we the people, from our inception, understood that power must be limited. Power must be contained. Power must be balanced with checks and balances so that no leader, no executive, no legislature, no court can become so powerful that they could overtake and usurp the people. If, in fact we are looking for solutions that will help our leaders exercise their power more appropriately, then we should consider some successful leadership models used throughout the world, and in some of the world's most successful global corporations. All of the models of power start with the two cornerstones of any successful team, organization, or even any successful country: *responsible leadership* and *responsive leadership*.

If we were, for example, to analyze the United States, we could see this at work very clearly. America has for some time now been one of the most dominant countries in the world, hence being rightfully titled a "world power." I believe that good leadership complements power, and power complements good leadership. When these two qualities are exercised in a responsible manner, success soon follows. Good leadership and a responsible use of power have created some of our greatest presidents: Washington, Jefferson, Lincoln, both Roosevelts, Truman, Eisenhower, Reagan. Good leaders understand implicitly that power must be exercised hand in hand with responsibility.

Our leaders today seem to take power as a means of punishing political enemies and creating personal platforms and further wealth (look at the financial data around former presidents, senators, members of Congress, and see how much money they earn from book deals, speeches, and corporate boards once they leave office). Power has come to be synonymous with personal gain. That is not what the wealthy families of old believed about their duty to serve. They believed that because they were blessed with so much wealth, power, and position, they owed something back to the people. They did not need to gain more wealth or position. They already had both. And they, like our Founders, understood the old biblical axiom, "To whom much is given, much is required."

Responsibility Demands Service

Savvy political leaders know that there is a lot more to leadership than wielding power. Power must be used judiciously and responsibly. *Leadership brings with it both opportunity and responsibility.* No matter what the level of leadership, or the type of organization, the opportunity of leadership is the power to make a difference. Only a leader has license to focus vision, establish goals, and implement actions that determine the future of the group. The power of leadership, however, comes with a price. And that price is the responsibility to provide for the greater good, for those who cannot serve themselves. It requires compassion and care. Foresight and loyalty. Commitment and consistency. Those who lead must be held accountable by the people. They are not in power to fill their own pockets, or to serve their own interests. They are there to serve us, the people. You cannot be a true leader unless you respond to the opportunity and accept the responsibility to provide responsible leadership. Unadulterated power does not make a leader; rather, it spawns an environment ripe for despots and demagogues. Despots offer only the leadership of tyranny; demagogues exercise power by appealing to people's emotions, instincts, and prejudices in a way that is manipulative and dangerous. Simply having the power to make a difference does not qualify one as a leader. It is power used responsibly that defines leadership. True power is the result of responsible leadership.

In the 2016 campaign we witnessed one of the most raucous and nasty campaigns in American history. The Republican nominee, Donald Trump, was viewed by many as ill-tempered, foul-mouthed, and immature when it came to understanding the responsibilities of being president of the United States. Others lauded him for being plainspoken and direct. Leadership is more than what we do. It is also what we speak. It is how we say things.

It is how we engage leaders around the world. Responsible leadership is about vision and purpose. It is about follow-through and execution. It is about role-modeling for young people.

When Power Corrupts

Unfortunately, we have recently been presented with far too many examples of feckless leaders in both the national and local body politic who have embraced the intoxication of power, while shunning the responsibility of leadership. One of the most potent powers of leadership is the ability to create an environment, set a tone, define the discussion, and set the direction of the group. When this power is used responsibly, progress can be achieved; but when it is abused, chaos and conflict follow. This is what the United States is dealing with right now on a social justice front and beyond. For example, you see protests in many of our nation's major cities around policing and the shooting deaths of black men, as well as the vigilante shootings of the police themselves. This is why you see social justice movements like "Black Lives Matter" and movements around illegal immigration in places like Arizona and Texas, demanding that leaders begin to actually lead on these important issues.

These types of protests have become common reactions of certain segments of our citizenry. Americans are tired of those with power wielding that power as a police state. Or with the IRS taking people's businesses, homes, and income, and placing the burden of proof on the citizens. Somehow, somewhere, those in power have become too powerful. They believe that they are more important than the people. Like King George in the 1700s, they believe they can treat the citizens any way they want to, and that the citizenry will just accept the rule of power and submit to it. I think the past two years in America have proven that the people are *not* willing to just take it anymore, and that they are willing to push back against abuses of power.

The key, then, for leaders who wish to serve in high office is to stop looking at the people as plebeians to be discarded by the noble class, and start seeing them as citizens to be served. The great families of America, such as our second president and Founding Father, John Adams, instilled in their children the duty to serve. John Quincy Adams, his son, traveled and studied abroad under his father's guidance and later became our nation's sixth president. Teddy Roosevelt began his service in political office in the New York State legislature, as well as serving as an assistant secretary of the Navy. His cousin Franklin also served in the same role before becoming governor of New York. The Tiffanys (yes, *those* Tiffanys) had a son who served in World War II. And let us not forget America's Camelot family, the Kennedys. Spurred to service by the family patriarch and millionaire, Joseph P. Kennedy, Sr., the Kennedy sons served in the military, and they served their nation in the highest office, the presidency, and as U.S. attorney general, and in the U.S. Senate.

The point is that our Founders and their offspring, as well as future generations of the American wealthy class, served nation nobly and well. They risked life and limb to honor the ideals of America. They helped found charities (President George H. W. Bush's Points of Light Foundation, President Clinton's Clinton Global Initiative, President Kennedy's Peace Corps), and initiated countless other articles of legislation that helped the poor, hurting, unemployed, and disenfranchised. The new generation of corporate leaders, Wall Street power brokers, and the wealthy class need to return to the call of their forebears, men and women blessed beyond measure who understood the duty of service to their country.

President John F. Kennedy and Jacqueline Bouvier Kennedy Onassis

PRESIDENT JOHN F. KENNEDY[115]

> *"Ask not what your country can do for you. Ask what you can do for your country." —President John F. Kennedy*

President Kennedy is best remembered for his great call to Americans in his January 1961 inaugural address: "And so, my fellow Americans, ask not what your country can do for you. Ask what you can do for your country." It was a call that he himself, being a member of the gentry or noble class of Boston, answered.

Born John Fitzgerald Kennedy in Brookline, Massachusetts, in 1917, he was the second son born to Rose Fitzgerald (daughter of the mayor of Boston) and Joseph P. Kennedy (son of an Irish saloon owner). Young JFK attended the best prep schools in the Northeast and eventually landed at Harvard. Graduating from Harvard in 1940, he entered the Navy. In 1943, when his PT boat was rammed and sunk by a Japanese destroyer, Kennedy, despite grave injuries, led the survivors through perilous waters to safety. He became a bona fide war hero, winning the Navy's Distinguished Service Cross. Kennedy's plan was to write books, teach, maybe start a magazine (something his own son and namesake, John F. Kennedy, Jr., would do in the 1990s). But when his older brother, Joseph P. Kennedy, Jr., was killed in action during World War II, the mantle of leadership fell to young John. Once back from the war, he became a Democratic congressman from the Boston area, advancing in 1953 to the U.S. Senate (defeating another wealthy senator, Henry Cabot Lodge). Kennedy married Jacqueline Bouvier on September 12, 1953, in Rhode Island. In 1955, while recuperating from a back operation, he wrote *Profiles in Courage,* which won him the 1957 Pulitzer Prize in History.

Kennedy, under the steady and often stern hand of his father, former U.S. ambassador to the United Kingdom, ran for the presidency in 1960 and was elected. He was the nation's first Irish Catholic president. During his presidency Kennedy established the U.S. Peace Corps (run by his brother-in-law Sargent Shriver, father of Maria Shriver). The Peace Corps stands to this day as a living testament to humanitarian service around the world. President Kennedy's vision was inspired in part by his "noble" birth. As a young man, he and his siblings lived abroad in England when their father was ambassador to the Court of Saint James's and saw the beginnings of World War II firsthand (it was the inspiration for his college senior thesis and first book, *Why England Slept*). Kennedy saw the evils of Hitler and Mussolini and the brilliance of Winston Churchill. He never forgot the lessons of World War II and of history, making him one of America's most beloved presidents.

Kennedy's great hour of testing as president came during

the Cuban Missile Crisis. He used a combination of diplomacy and military power to force the Russians to back down after they violated international treaties and deployed missiles to Cuba. Yet, what Americans of his time remember about him is his youth, vigor, and soaring vision for what he called the "New Frontier" of America, challenging Americans to confront new opportunities to secure peace, to explore space, to address ignorance and poverty. Although Kennedy was never able to finish out his promise, this young president of wealth and station was truly one of our greatest servant leaders. When he was assassinated on November 22, 1963, it was one of the saddest days in modern American history.

FIRST LADY JACQUELINE BOUVIER KENNEDY[116]

"I have been through a lot and have suffered a great deal.
But I have had lots of happy moments, as well. Every
moment one lives is different from the other. The good, the
bad, hardship, the joy, the tragedy, love, and happiness are all
interwoven into one single, indescribable whole that is called
life. You cannot separate the good from the bad. And perhaps
there is no need to do so, either." —Jacqueline Kennedy

No president is complete without his first lady, but Jacqueline Bouvier was much more than that. One of our nation's youngest first ladies (she was only thirty-one years old when her husband was elected president), she changed the culture of the

White House and challenged Americans to reengage with our great legacy of art and literature.

Jacqueline Lee Bouvier was born on July 28, 1929, in Southampton, New York, the daughter of wealthy parents. Her father, John Bouvier (also known as "Black Jack"), was a wealthy stockbroker on Wall Street whose family had come from France in the early 1800s. Her mother, Janet, was from Irish and English ancestry. Jackie was raised with all the wealth and privileges of a rich princess. She was an accomplished equestrian, winning contests as early as eleven years old, and was being written about in the *New York Times*.

She and President Kennedy met when he was a young congressman from Boston and she was a roving reporter and photographer. Educated at the finest schools for girls in the United States and abroad, Jacqueline was a great match for her ambitious husband. They married in 1953, with more than one thousand guests present, the social event of the time. Jackie was beloved on the campaign trail during the 1960 campaign, while she was pregnant with their son, John F. Kennedy, Jr. But it wasn't until the Kennedys moved into the White House that Jackie blossomed into her own woman and became a great asset to our nation by refurbishing the White House and restoring our love of the arts and humanities.

Whether it was abroad in France, bedazzling General Charles de Gaulle, or charming a bully like Nikita Khrushchev, Jackie represented the best of American femininity, charm, and grace. Although she is best known for her efforts to renovate the White House and remake it into a beautiful mansion with fine art, fine furnishings, and history, after her husband's death, she established the John F. Kennedy Library Profiles in Courage Award and the Kennedy Center for the Performing Arts, which is still operating in Washington, D.C. In fact, after the president's death in November 1963 yet another Jackie emerged. She became more of a private person, often hiding her children, Caroline and John, from onlookers. So frustrated with the public stalking and the assassination of her brother-in-law Robert F. Kennedy in 1968, she married Aristotle Onassis and moved to Europe. She eventually divorced Onassis and returned to the United States and became an editor at Viking Press and later at Doubleday in New York City. She championed many causes, often quietly. But she raised both of her children to be "normal" people who loved public service and who honored the legacy of their father. Caroline Kennedy served as U.S. ambassador to Japan under President Obama, and John F. Kennedy Jr., started a magazine, *George*, dedicated to American politics, before his tragic death in 1999.

Throughout her life, Jacqueline Kennedy sought to preserve and protect America's cultural heritage. The results of her work are still visible in Lafayette Square, across from the White House in Washington, D.C. While she was first lady, she helped to stop the destruction of historic buildings along the Square, including the Renwick Building, now part of the Smithsonian Institution. In New York City, she led a campaign to save and renovate Grand Central Terminal. Today, more than half a million people pass through the station each day and enjoy its restored beauty, thanks to her efforts. In short, Jacqueline Kennedy captivated the nation and the rest of the world with her intelligence, beauty, and grace. With a deep sense of devotion to her family and country, she dedicated herself to raising her children and to making the world a better place through art, literature, and a respect for history and public service.

Both President Kennedy and Jackie Kennedy were born of wealth and privilege, yet they served their nation in lasting ways we still honor and remember to this day. Their lives remind us that regardless of our birth or rank, we are all "fellow Americans," and that we all have a duty to public service.

★ ★ ★ ★ ★ ★ ★ ★ ★ ★ ★ ★ ★ ★ ★

Key Leadership Code Points

Noblesse oblige is a French phrase literally meaning "nobility obliges." It is the concept that nobility extends beyond mere entitlements and requires the person who holds such status to fulfill social responsibilities, particularly in leadership roles. The *Dictionnaire de l'Académie Française* defines it thus:

1. Whoever claims to be noble must conduct himself nobly.
2. (Figuratively) One must act in a fashion that conforms to one's position, and with the reputation that one has earned.

As the Founding Fathers well understood, America was never to be a place where monarchs, titled individuals, or those with great wealth could control those who had none. America is great because America is a place where a poor man like Abraham Lincoln can rise to be the president. Or a man from humble beginnings, like Harry Truman, can start as a clothier and become vice president and be elevated to the presidency. Yet America is a place that was formed and forged by men who were the power brokers of their day. They understood that rich men could still be good and virtuous men, and that rank, station, or birth should never be a hindrance to a man's service. There are three core things we must remember about power and those to whom we give it:

• Power can never be absolute.
• Power should be checked. And power cannot rest in one individual. It must be shared and balanced.

★ ★ ★ ★ ★ ★ ★ ★ ★ ★ ★ ★ ★ ★ ★ ★

"The Constitution is not an instrument

for the government to restrain the people,

it is an instrument for the people to

restrain the government."

—PATRICK HENRY

CODE
2

ACCOUNTABILITY: SUBMISSION TO THE WILL OF THE PEOPLE

Our Founding Fathers did not trust government. Period. It doesn't matter if you are liberal or conservative. Black or white. Rich or poor. Democrat or Republican. The Founders did not want the federal or "centralized" government to ever become too large or too powerful. They were men who had just fled the oppression of a greedy, abusive, and tyrannical king. They were overtaxed, overburdened, and overrun by an intrusive police force of British troops who routinely beat, and at times murdered, their fellow colonists. The Founders wanted America to be a republic. It is not a democracy. They chose a republican form of government because they wanted a government that was close to the people, and that gave the people the power to choose their representatives. The Constitution itself makes this desire very clear: Article IV, Section 4 declares: "The United States shall guarantee to every State in this Union a Republican Form of Government."

There is a big distinction, however, between those who, in our current day, despise government and believe it has no role in American life, and those who understand the proper role and function of government. They are very different. Let me be clear: The Founders did not despise government, because they understood that all men, and thus all nations, must be governed by laws. As we saw earlier, James Madison once remarked, "If men were angels, no government would be necessary. If Angels were to govern men, neither external nor internal controls on government would be necessary."[117] The Founders believed in the ideal of we the people controlling our own destiny, and our leaders, men and women like us chosen from among our ranks—whether wealthy and powerful, as we covered in the previous Code, or those with no rank and no wealth—being our advocates, our mouthpieces. Our leaders should answer to us, not us to them. We are their bosses. They are not our bosses.

George Washington, our nation's first president, said it best: "Government is not reason; it is not eloquence. It is force. And force, like fire, is a dangerous servant and a fearful master." Our Founding Fathers didn't like big government for the very reasons Washington stated. They understood, perhaps better than any group of men who had ever lived before, the consequences of their actions as they undertook to create this new nation we call America. They understood that there was a very delicate balancing act between those who would be governed and those who would govern.

Our Founding Fathers wanted to make the citizens of the United States of America their own masters, and government their servants. This is why we are indeed an exceptional nation. No other nation in the world has the freedoms and the Bill of Rights that we inherited and to this day possess. Our Founding Fathers made individual freedom the keystone of our constitutional republic, for they knew that big government cannot be trusted. Like kings and dictators, governments with power can abuse that power, and power can corrupt the rulers. As historian and moralist Lord Acton said in 1887, "Power tends to corrupt, and absolute power corrupts absolutely. Great men are almost always bad men." The Earl of Chatham, British prime minister in 1770, said: "Unlimited power is apt to corrupt the minds of those who possess it."

So our Founders did something extraordinary: They created a government but they limited the power of that government through a system of accountability, a system of checks and balances. They were intentional about the leaders being accountable to the people.

In this Code we will look at two key principles of a republic:

1. Addressing the will of the people (listening and governing)
2. Submitting to the will of the people (accountability).

To secure our freedom, the Founding Fathers gave us the U.S. Constitution as the cornerstone of our rights, liberties, and obligations. They made it the supreme law of the land that limits the power of government and gives its citizens a Bill of Rights. The Preamble to the Constitution reads as follows:

We the People of the United States, in Order to form a
more perfect Union, establish Justice, insure domestic
Tranquility, provide for the common defenses, promote
the general Welfare, and secure the Blessings of Liberty
to ourselves and our Posterity, do ordain and establish
this Constitution for the United States of America.

Addressing the Will of the People

It is very clear in *The Federalist Papers* that the American government was designed *not* to mirror the democracy of the Greeks.
Instead our Founders favored the Roman form of a republic.
They had great concern that a purely democratic government
would be detrimental to America. They feared mob rule, and,
as Ben Franklin once quipped, "Democracy is two wolves and a
lamb voting on what to have for lunch. Liberty is a well-armed
lamb contesting the vote." The Founders wanted a government
that was listening to, and responsive toward, the people, not a
government that would run over them or avoid their express will.

No doubt there were fierce debates at the Constitutional
Convention about the difference between a republic and a
democracy. The fact of the matter is that a republic and a democracy are identical in every aspect except one. In a republic the
sovereignty of the government rests in the rights of the individual. In a democracy, the sovereignty is in the rights of the group.
(Even though our republic was modeled on the ancient Roman
model, still the Founders felt that it didn't completely reflect
their vision for America.)

While the Greeks had a form of democracy and England a form of representative government, neither nation truly modeled a real republic. The Federalists were keenly aware of the turbulence that a democracy would cause if all people in a nation were assembled to decide matters for themselves. Instead, they advocated that we select representatives from among ourselves, people we can trust to be wise, committed, patriotic, and brave. Our Founders were so focused in this regard that they staggered the terms of these representatives to protect us from their gaining too much power; in addition, they allowed us to replace those who failed to adequately perform their duties in the best interests of the people. Madison eloquently showcased the power of the people in the Constitution by thus empowering us to select representatives whose duty it was to represent the people who selected them.

In a republic, the views of the people are expressed through their representatives and given a voice. There is no "mob rule," as there is in a democracy. The rights of the minority matter as much as those of the majority. Despite clear historical evidence showing that the United States was established as a republic and not a democracy, there is still confusion regarding the difference between these two different systems of government. Some confusion stems because the word *democracy* is used to describe both a "type" and a form of government. As a "type" of government, it means that free elections are held periodically, which is what we have in America. But as a "form" of government, it means rule by the majority, which we do not have in America.

Let me say it again: America is a republic. A republic has been defined as:

> A government in which a restricted group of citizens form a political unit, usually under the auspice of a charter, which directs them to elect representatives who will govern the state. Republics, by their very nature, tend to be free polities, not because they are elected by the citizens of the polity, but because they are bound by charters, which limit the responsibilities and powers of the state. The fact that people vote for representatives has nothing to do with making anything free. The logical consistency and rationality of the charter, as well as the willingness of the people to live by it, is what keeps people free.[118]

Whatever your political beliefs or leanings, we would do well as a nation living in this time to remember the vision of our Founders. The Constitution is not outdated. The Founders are not just a group of old, white, privileged dead men. Or merely slave owners, as many have relegated them to being. They were men of intellect, wisdom, and vision. They built our Constitution and our nation to last, and it has for 240 years, specifically because it was designed by them to keep we the people in control of it.

Submitting to the Will of the People

The words "we the people" echo through time, and they remind us of what makes us unique as Americans. Our government is bound to submit to our will. And to be held accountable at the ballot box, or through other carefully crafted checks and balances when it does not.

Our elected officials are duty- and honor-bound to submit to the will of the people. In short, they are accountable to us. Our leaders take an oath of office that swears allegiance to the U.S. Constitution. They swear to "preserve, protect and defend" the Constitution. In case you haven't realized it, our Constitution is one of the greatest documents ever written in the history of man. James Madison said it best:

> In framing a government which is to be administered by men over men, the great difficulty lies in this: you must first enable the government to control the governed; and in the next place, oblige it to control itself.[119]

Madison summed up the great American paradox: a government that is strong and central, but that is totally and completely beholden to the will of the people. As author and historian James Best summarized in his study of the Founders, concentrated political power frightened them. They believed that only by limiting government could liberty survive the natural tendency of man to dictate the habits of other men. They balanced separation of powers with checks designed to prevent tyranny. Each branch was given delineated powers, and then each of these powers was limited and checked by another branch or entity. The system was purposely designed to slow governmental actions enough to allow due deliberation. This frustrates those who want the government to always "do something" about every problem, but it also hampers the government from doing something grievous that affects our life, liberty, and pursuit of happiness.[120]

By putting in place a system of election, and removal from office, as well as the manner in which elected officials in coequal branches would have to interact with and work with each other, the Founders ensured that the government would be accountable. This Code most directly links to Citizens' Code #1, because both the citizenry and its leaders share equal responsibility and accountability to guard their duties as outlined in the Constitution. The republic stands only (notice we recite in our Pledge of Allegiance—"and to the republic for which it stands") when we do our part and keep vigilant by being informed, engaged, and knowledgeable about the business and affairs of our nation.

Our republic still stands after all this time because, for the most part, we have adhered to the framers' intent of how we were to run this great experiment. Our leaders must be reminded by the people often of their duty to be *our* voice, not their own voice. Not for their *own* material gain, but for what is in the best interests of the nation, as desired by the people. The way we hold our leaders to account is best modeled by two Americans born more than two hundred years apart. One of them was a leader in the American Revolution. Indeed, some would say he was the great spark that got the fire started. The other American was a woman born in the midst of the roaring 1920s, and a child of the Great Depression. Both of them were elected leaders of their time, revolutionaries of their day, and both committed to the great vision of our Founders in keeping with their solemn promise to make America special because of our commitment to government by the people, of the people, for the people.

GOVERNOR SAMUEL ADAMS[121]

> *"He who is void of virtuous attachments in private life is, or very soon will be, void of all regard for his country. There is seldom an instance of a man guilty of betraying his country, who had not before lost the feeling of moral obligations in his private connections."*
> —*Samuel Adams*

My favorite Founding Father is American patriot and a signer of the Declaration of Independence, Samuel Adams. Cousin to John Adams, our nation's second president, Samuel Adams was a bit of a rebel. A failed brewer and newspaper publisher before becoming one of the independence movement's most celebrated leaders and statesmen, Adams was an organizer of Boston's The Sons of Liberty[122] movement. Adams conceived the Boston Committee of Correspondence (which, like similar entities in other towns across the colonies, proved a powerful tool for communication and coordination during the Revolutionary War). As if that were not enough, he coordinated Boston's resistance to the Tea Act, which climaxed in the famous Boston Tea Party.

Samuel Adams was born on September 27, 1722, in Boston. A strong opponent of British taxation, Adams played a vital role in organizing the Boston Tea Party. He was a member of the Massachusetts delegation to the Continental Congress, with his cousin John Adams, with whom he urged a final break from Great Britain, and was a signee of the Declaration of Independence. Sam, however, unlike his more reserved and diplomatic cousin, became an ardent and often rabble-rousing advocate for liberty in Boston long before his colleagues would join him. He was truly the proverbial match that lit the revolutionary fire. He became a real thorn in the side of the British hierarchy that occupied Boston. By founding the Sons of Liberty (aka "The Loyal Nine"), Adams and his cohorts began to fight back against British oppression and hold the Crown's proverbial feet to the fire. When their efforts to seek accommodation and representation from the British Crown failed, they decided to follow the brave course of revolt.

Adams understood that those in power were accountable to the people. He understood that the people had to resist in order to gain their liberty. Samuel Adams was a leader in every sense of the word, both as a citizen of the colonies and as a legislator in Massachusetts. Following his run with the state legislature, Adams served as a Massachusetts delegate to the Continental Congress. He represented Massachusetts there from 1774 through 1781 and was elected to the Massachusetts convention on the ratification of the Constitution in 1787. After serving as John Hancock's lieutenant governor from 1789 to 1793, Adams took over as governor, retiring in 1797.

REPRESENTATIVE SHIRLEY CHISHOLM[124]

"I don't measure America by its achievement but by its potential."—Shirley Chisholm

I knew Shirley Chisholm. She was my childhood heroine. It was one of the great privileges of my life to meet her when I was twenty-two years old. I met her in the ladies' lounge at the historic state capitol in Trenton, New Jersey, in the summer of 1991. She was petite and formidable all at once. And she loved America. But, more important, she loved serving Americans.

Known for the famous phrase "unbought and unbossed" (from her autobiography), in 1968 Chisholm was the first African-American woman in history elected to the U.S. House of Representatives. She represented a newly reapportioned U.S. House district centered in Brooklyn, New York. Chisholm was catapulted into the national limelight by virtue of her race, gender, and outspoken personality. In 1972, in a largely symbolic undertaking, she campaigned for the Democratic presidential nomination. But "Fighting Shirley" Chisholm's frontal assault on many congressional traditions, and her reputation as a crusader, limited her influence as a legislator. "I am the people's politician," she once told the *New York Times*. "If the day should ever come when the people can't save me, I'll know I'm finished. That's when I'll go back to being a professional educator."[125]

Shirley Anita St. Hill was born on November 30, 1924, in Brooklyn. She was the oldest of four daughters of Charles St. Hill, a factory laborer from Guyana, and Ruby Seale St. Hill, a seamstress from Barbados. For part of her childhood, Shirley lived in Barbados on her maternal grandparents' farm, receiving a British education while her parents worked during the Great Depression to settle the family in the Bedford-Stuyvesant area of Brooklyn. The most apparent manifestation of her West Indies roots was the slight, clipped British accent she retained throughout her life. She attended public schools in Brooklyn and graduated with high marks. Accepted to Vassar and Oberlin colleges, Shirley St. Hill attended Brooklyn College on a scholarship and graduated cum laude with a BA in sociology in 1946.

Like Sam Adams two hundred years before her, Shirley was a fierce advocate for the people of the United States, particularly the people often left behind. She was a freedom fighter of a different kind, because she was an elected official with the powers granted by the Constitution, and she understood the power entrusted to her on behalf of the people. Chisholm's welcome in the House was not warm, due to her immediate outspokenness. "I have no intention of just sitting quietly and observing," she said. "I intend to focus attention on the nation's problems." She did just that, lashing out against the Vietnam War in her first speech in the House on March 26, 1969. Chisholm vowed to vote against any defense appropriation bill "until the time comes when our values and priorities have been turned right-side up again."

Key Leadership Code Points

The Father of the Constitution, James Madison, and many of our Founders believed strongly in a limited government. A limited government, they reasoned, can only do what the people allow it to do. And they set out to build our nation on the premise of life, liberty, and the pursuit of happiness. The premise of the right to own property. To keep and bear arms. To worship God or not, as we deem right. To be unburdened by excessive taxes and government intrusion. In short, the Founders had a deep distrust of government because they had just fought a Revolutionary War against King George and his tyrannical form of government. Here are some key takeaways from this all-important Code and how the Founders forged a system of governance to keep our leaders accountable to we the people:

1. They balanced power among the three branches.

2. They made sure each branch had robust checks on the other two.

3. They gave the national government only enumerated powers, and retained all other power in the hands of either the people or the states.

4. They used the states to check the national government.

5. The members of each branch were chosen by a different method.

6. The term of office varied by government position.

7. An impeachment process was defined for extreme cases.

"Peace, commerce, and honest friendship

with all nations, entangling

alliances with none . . ."

—THOMAS JEFFERSON

CODE
3

FOREIGN DIPLOMACY AND STATESMANSHIP

It is important to remember that our nation's independence from England was more than just the severing of ties between two countries over political, religious, or moral disagreements. The American Revolution was earth-shattering. It was simply unimaginable not only that a ragtag group of farmers, merchants, and other colonists would, in the first instance, fight back against the British Empire, but that, in the second instance, they would actually beat back Britain and win their independence.

The American Revolution not only birthed a new nation, unlike any the earth had ever seen, but it also established the United States as a unique world power in the community of nations. More than that, our founding as a free nation was the catalyst for the invention of American diplomacy, which for the past two hundred years has made us the light and hope of free nations around the globe. We are America. We stand for hope, opportunity, liberty, and freedom.

Yet many nations around the globe are ruled by some form of socialism, communism, despotism, military regime, radical regime, or tyranny.[125] Just take a look around. Not every nation has free elections. Not every nation allows their people to raise their voices and speak. Not every nation encourages freedom of religion and thought. Very few nations honor their people's right to keep and bear arms. Very few nations provide a free public school system for all their citizens. We are different. I have said it many times throughout this book, and I will continue to say it because we need to remember that truth. America is not like any other place on earth. That truth alone is worth celebrating.

America by birth, then, became a power player in the league of nations. Right from the beginning, America represented peace, commerce, and the extension of friendship with all nations. In fact, one of America's first acts of international partnership, even before we became an "official" nation, was our strategic alliance with France during the Revolutionary War. The United States gained its independence in part because of the support it received from France under the terms of the 1778 Treaty of Alliance. This treaty was negotiated by John Adams and Benjamin Franklin, the nation's first diplomats.

France played a key role in the Revolutionary War. After we captured some British forces and won some victories, France recognized America as a sovereign nation and allied itself with us. In February 1778, France declared war on Britain, provided money and materials to arm the new republic, and sent an army to the United States. French intervention made a decisive contribution to the U.S. victory in the war. Motivated by a longtime rivalry with Britain, and in revenge for its territorial losses during the French and Indian War, France began secretly sending supplies in 1775 to the colonies. Spain and the Netherlands joined France, making it a war in which the British had no major allies.[126]

Benjamin Franklin served as the first American ambassador to France, from 1776 to 1785, meeting with many leading diplomats, aristocrats, intellectuals, scientists, and financiers. Franklin's character and writings caught the French imagination—there were many images of him sold on the market, and he became the cultural icon of the archetypal new American, and even a hero for those who aspired to a new order inside France.

The French supported America for what some might say were unorthodox goals, among them being the desire to weaken Britain and to exact revenge upon them for France's defeat in the French and Indian War. After the American capture of the British invasion army at Saratoga in 1777, and after the French navy had been built up, France was ready. In 1778, France recognized the United States of America as a sovereign nation; signed a military alliance; went to war with Britain; built coalitions with the Netherlands and Spain that kept Britain without a significant ally; provided the Americans with grants, arms, and loans; sent a combat army to serve under George Washington; and sent a navy that prevented the second British army from escaping from Yorktown in 1781.

In this Code we will consider what America's influence abroad meant to our Founders and to us here living today. We will look at two core principles: foreign diplomacy and statesmanship.

But let us be clear that from Yorktown, to Valley Forge, to Charleston Harbor, and Gettysburg; to the European battlefields of World War I, to the Pacific of World War II, to Korea,

Vietnam, and the Persian Gulf, to current military members serving in the Middle East, the goal and function of American diplomacy never changes: It is to secure the perceived national interests of the United States.

Yet, even more fundamental than American interests abroad is that our leaders ensure America remains independent and governed by the American people. And it is precisely because America is a land of liberty founded on universal principles that American diplomats have the responsibility to speak for freedom around the world. American diplomats are, constitutionally and morally, representatives of the American nation and its principles. And our leaders must do a delicate dance between what is in our best security interests and what is in our best interests in terms of liberty.

As John Adams said, "Those who would give up essential Liberty, to purchase a little temporary Safety, deserve neither Liberty nor Safety. The great rule of conduct for us in regard to foreign nations is in extending our commercial relations, to have with them as little political connection as possible. So far as we have already formed engagements, let them be fulfilled with perfect good faith. Here let us stop."

Foreign Diplomacy

Let's start by defining diplomacy and the three-legged stool upon which it must rest. Diplomacy is one of the major tools that a nation uses to promote and effect its position and power in the world. The first leg is direct talks with one's adversaries or allies; the second is indirect talks (through backroom or intermediary diplomatic channels); and the third leg is usually a stick such as sanctions or embargoes. When diplomacy fails, the last resort is usually war.

1. **Domestic tranquility and security.** One of the fundamental guarantees in our Constitution, and entrusted to our leaders, is to provide for the tranquility and security of our nation. That is both a domestic and foreign responsibility. Diplomacy starts at home. And it is protected abroad.

2. **International relations** are just that: the relationships, good, bad, or indifferent, between and among nations.

3. **Foreign policy** is how a country (or group of countries) defines its interests when it comes to other countries or groups of countries.

Foreign diplomacy, then, is an amalgamation of principles that our Founders understood must be addressed and met abroad to keep America safe at home. We live in far different times now, more than two centuries later. We live in a time where technology and connectivity is so great, and so fast, and so accessible, that the world has indeed become smaller. And our foreign "entanglements," to quote Franklin, are far greater. The United States is still considered the world's greatest superpower. Yet protecting the homeland is far more complicated due to terrorism (domestic and international) and the influx of peoples from around the world who come to America but do not necessarily want to be Americans.

The global financial structure of the markets is another "entanglement" that makes it necessary to engage foreign governments like China, who have become economic powerhouses due to the outsourcing of American jobs and merchandise.

Diplomacy is not an end in itself. It is a tool to advance America's interests. It gives the United States some of the instruments it needs to lead like-minded nations, and it provides a means by which our government learns about, speaks to, and negotiates with other powers. As long as American diplomacy is guided by the universal principles on which America was founded, remains dedicated to the best interests of the nation, and receives the consent of the American people and their elected representatives, it will be worthy of the respect the Founders had for it.

Statesmanship

> "A politician and a statesman are not the same."
> —Dr. J. Rufus Fears

I couldn't agree more with that statement made by the late University of Oklahoma classics and history professor J. Rufus Fears. He was right, of course. A politician seeks votes and he seeks to be elected to office. We have a lot of politicians in America. The 2016 presidential primary and election season showed us the raw underside of nasty, mean, divisive politics. Yet we have far fewer statesmen. A statesman seeks neither votes nor high office. A statesman is the natural enemy of a tyrant, because he is a lover of his nation. He is a fierce defender of his nation's principles. He is able. He is wise. And he seeks, most of all, to lead free and empowered people. Fears taught that a true statesman must possess four keen qualities[127]:

1. A bedrock of principles: He or she believes in something greater than self.
2. A moral compass: He or she lives by a set of virtues, absolutes, and leads by them as well.
3. A vision: He or she sees beyond the present and into what is possible through peace.
4. The ability to build a consensus to achieve that vision: He or she listens, counsels, takes counsel, brings people to the table, extends an olive branch, but all while leading from a place of strength.

In modern times, the term *statesman* has come to be synonymous with *conciliation* or *placation*. But that is not what American statesmanship was built on, nor what it should mean today. It was built on the four principles Fears articulates and, even more important, the principles of liberty, justice, and freedom.

GENERAL GEORGE C. MARSHALL[128]

> *"The only way human beings can win a war is to prevent it."* —*General George C. Marshall*

General George Marshall remains, after George Washington, likely the most respected soldier in American history. Not because of his bravery on the battlefield. Or his command of troops, but because he was a true diplomat and statesman.

Marshall is most notably remembered for his leadership role during World War II and the Cold War that followed shortly thereafter. Marshall was chief of staff of the United States Army and chief military adviser under President Franklin D. Roosevelt, and served as secretary of state and then secretary of defense under President Harry S. Truman. He was hailed as the "organizer of victory" by Winston Churchill for his leadership of the Allied victory in World War II.

Marshall's honesty, integrity, and selfless service stand as shining examples for those who study the past and for those generations who will learn about him in the future. The Marshall Foundation is dedicated to celebrating his legacy. Marshall's career touched on many of the key events of the twentieth century—as a new Army officer following the Philippine insurrection; as a member of the staff of General of the Armies John J. Pershing during World War I; as U.S. Army chief of staff during World II; as secretary of state and the architect of European economic recovery following World War II; and as secretary of defense during the Korean War. He is the only person to have served in these three highest positions.

Marshall's name gave rise to the so-called Marshall Plan subsequent to a commencement address he presented as secretary of state at Harvard University in June 1947. The speech recommended that Europeans collectively create their own plan for rebuilding Europe after World War II. Marshall noted, "It is logical that the United States should do whatever it is able to do to assist in the return of normal economic health in the world."

Ultimately, the State Department developed most of the plan, which was aimed at the economic recovery of Western Europe after the war, and Truman was shrewd enough to let Marshall's name be attached to it. Unlike Truman, Marshall was widely admired by members of both political parties. He received the Nobel Peace Prize in 1953 for the Marshall Plan.

The Marshall Plan (officially the European Recovery Program, or ERP) was an American initiative in which the United States gave more than $12 billion (approximately $120 billion in dollar value as of June 2016) in economic support to help rebuild Western European economies after the end of the war. The plan was in operation for four years, beginning April 8, 1948. The goals of the United States were to rebuild war-devastated regions, remove trade barriers, modernize industry, make Europe prosperous again, and prevent the spread of communism. The Marshall Plan is considered the single most transformational act in the history of foreign relations and diplomacy. It literally rebuilt a war-torn Europe, forged NATO, and built alliances abroad that still serve us well to this day.

AMBASSADOR SHIRLEY TEMPLE BLACK[129]

"Nothing crushes freedom as substantially as a tank."
—Shirley Temple Black

A beloved child movie star of the 1930s, as an adult Shirley Temple Black became an equally beloved national diplomatic figure, serving under four U.S. presidents. An unlikely diplomat, Black was beloved because she knew how to connect with people—and not just her fellow Americans, but all people and nations.

Long before she grew up, left movies, and got into politics, Temple Black was a part of political conversation. President Franklin D. Roosevelt once famously declared: "As long as our country has Shirley Temple, we will be all right. . . . When the spirit of the people is lower than at any other time during this Depression, it is a splendid thing that, for just 15 cents, an American can go to a movie and look at the smiling face of a baby and forget his troubles."

Black's diplomatic career really got off the ground in 1974, when President Ford dispatched her as America's ambassador to Ghana. Black's early government appointments were controversial, with critics accusing the White House of awarding plum jobs to a valued GOP fund-raiser with little diplomatic experience. Even Henry Kissinger, her colleague, initially doubted her qualifications. The former secretary of state once heard her discussing Namibia at a party and was "surprised that I even knew the word," according to Black's telling. "Dr. Kissinger was a former child. Jerry Ford was a former child. Even F.D.R. was a former child. I retired from the movies in 1949, and I'm still a former child," she remarked pointedly in 1975. Kissinger, for what it's worth, eventually came around, calling her "very intelligent, very tough-minded, very disciplined."[130]

Black's experiences with men of power were common for a woman serving abroad as a diplomat. She was chided all her life for being the cute child movie star. But make no mistake: Black was an intellectual and diplomatic heavyweight, and considered by many to be a great statesman abroad. Some of her notable achievements:

1. Served in three ambassadorships. Her first diplomatic post was as U.S. delegate to the United Nations, appointed by President Richard Nixon in 1969; she was the ambassador to Ghana from 1974 to 1976, appointed by President Gerald Ford; and she was the ambassador to Czechoslovakia from 1989 to 1992, appointed by President George H. W. Bush.
2. First female U.S. chief of protocol at the State Department from 1976 to 1977, under Ford.
3. Worked for the Department of State as a foreign affairs officer and expert from 1981 to 1989, under President Ronald Reagan.

The greatest tribute to her service came in 1998, at the Kennedy Center Honors ceremony, when President Bill Clinton praised Black's service. "Shirley Temple had the greatest short career in movie history and then gracefully retired to, as we all know, the far less strenuous life of public service," Clinton said. "She did a masterful job as ambassador, from Ghana to Czechoslovakia, where she made common cause with Vaclav Havel in the final, decisive days of the Cold War. In fact, she has to be the only person who both saved an entire movie studio from failure and contributed to the fall of communism. From her childhood to the present day, Shirley has always been an ambassador for what is best about America."[131]

* * * * * * * * * * * * * * *

Key Leadership Code Points

As Ronald Reagan once said, "America is a shining city on a hill." It has always been that since the day of our founding. My prayer is that it will always be so. Our leadership abroad starts with our principles and values here at home. We have covered two key facets of American leadership in the world: diplomacy and statesmanship.

Here are some takeaways from this important Code on what we should understand as our leaders seek to undertake diplomacy in the twenty-first century:

1. **Diplomacy has changed,** because the way the world is interconnected has changed. Bad global actors, rogue nations, and terrorists no longer declare war by dropping bombs on our naval fleet, as they did at Pearl Harbor during World War II. Now they drive airplanes into buildings, explode themselves in airports with bombs, walk into nightclubs, or attack Americans at work. These are not state-sponsored acts in many cases. They are rogue factions who have gained power and act independently, making it difficult, if not impossible, to use anything other than military force to eradicate them.

2. **The intersection of public and private** sectors has now blurred the lines in diplomacy. Today, our diplomats are beginning to understand that public-private partnerships can get the most out of available resources, technology, knowledge, and networks. In fact, these partnerships might be the most effective foreign policy tool America has at its disposal today.

3. **Understand history.** No nation can conduct international affairs without knowing history. History provides us the hindsight to know better and to do better. It is the laboratory in which our most basic theories of how to engage others successfully and not so successfully are tested. History also shapes the narratives different people tell themselves about how they came to their present circumstances as a nation, for better or worse. History is a lens. And we must use it wisely when engaging in diplomacy and statesmanship.

★　★　★　★　★　★　★　★　★　★　★　★　★

"Equal laws protecting equal rights . . .

the best guarantee of loyalty

and love of country."

—JAMES MADISON

EQUAL PROTECTION AND
ENFORCEMENT OF THE LAWS

What did the Founding Fathers really think about equality? And, further than that, what did they really think about equality under the law? To answer these questions, we need to look beyond their obvious contradictions (slavery and the treatment of women) and once again look back to the Declaration of Independence.

The Declaration begins with an appeal to "natural law," and maintains that the proposition "all men are created equal" is a self-evident truth. What they meant was that it is an obvious fact that men are born equal in the sight of God. They went on to say that "all men are endowed by their Creator with certain unalienable rights, among these Life, Liberty and the pursuit of Happiness." Once again they were declaring for all the world to see that their rebellion and ultimate revolution against Great Britain was an honorable one that would result in the formation of the most non-oppressive, free form of governance ever known to man. Yet, I cannot help but ask, as many scholars and citizens before me have asked, how could the Founders speak and declare so fervently that all men were equal while denying enslaved men and women equality?

It is a fair question and one that I posed at the outset of this book. Let's start with a few truths that I think will help us better understand, and perhaps forgive our Founders the great transgression of slavery and inequality for women.

Let's start with the fact that in eighteenth-century America, women and Africans were chattel, property to be owned and commanded by their husbands, fathers, and masters. This was true in most of the world at that time. In some nations around the world it still is to this day. This paradox—and dare I say hypocrisy—was not lost on many colonists of the day, and certainly not on the outspoken Abigail Adams, who once famously wrote to her husband, John, who was then a delegate to the Continental Congress[132]:

> [R]emember the ladies, and be more generous and favorable to them than your ancestors. Do not put such unlimited power into the hands of the Husbands. Remember all Men would be tyrants if they could. If particular care and attention is not paid to the Ladies we are determined to foment a Rebellion, and will not hold ourselves bound by any Laws in which we have no voice, or Representation.

On the issue of Africans and slavery, it was a bit more complicated for the Founding Fathers. The revolution was a turning point in the national attitude against slavery—and several of the Founders contributed greatly to that change. In fact, one of the reasons given by Thomas Jefferson for the separation from Great Britain was a desire to rid America of the evil of slavery imposed on them by the British. It is true, however, that not all the Founders from the South opposed slavery. According to the testimony of Thomas Jefferson, John Rutledge, and James Madison, those from North Carolina, South Carolina, and Georgia favored slavery, whereas we know that Benjamin Franklin, John Adams, and Thomas Jefferson advocated for the abolition of slavery both in the original drafts of the Declaration and in the constitutional debates that followed.[133]

Nevertheless, despite the support in those states for slavery, the clear majority of the Founders was opposed to slavery—and their support went beyond words. For example, in 1774, Benjamin Franklin and Benjamin Rush founded America's first antislavery society; John Jay was president of a similar society in New York. When Constitution signer William Livingston heard of the New York society, he, as governor of New Jersey, wrote them, offering:

> I would most ardently wish to become a member of it [the society in New York] and . . . I can safely promise them that neither my tongue, nor my pen, nor purse shall be wanting to promote the abolition of what to me appears so inconsistent with humanity and Christianity. . . . May the great and the equal Father of the human race, who has expressly declared His abhorrence of oppression, and

that He is no respecter of persons, succeed a design so laudably calculated to undo the heavy burdens, to let the oppressed go free, and to break every yoke.

Other prominent Founding Fathers who were members of societies for ending slavery included Richard Bassett, James Madison, James Monroe, Bushrod Washington, Charles Carroll, William Few, John Marshall, Richard Stockton, Zephaniah Swift, and many more. This is not in any way, shape, or form an excuse for slavery or for the Founders not ending it. What is important when we deal with history, however, is that we deal in context. Otherwise, our birth as a nation founded on the principles of equality makes no sense in the twenty-first century.

In my humble opinion, and based on my study of the Constitution as a law student and as a young lawyer working under the umbrella of the Constitution as a committee counsel in the House of Representatives, what the Founding Fathers likely meant by "all men being created equal" goes something like this: All men share a common human *nature*. A right to exist. We are born equal in the eyes of God. We are born with certain "unalienable rights," which we cannot give back. Thomas Jefferson's wording "that all men are created equal" means that all persons are the *same* in *some* respect; it does not mean that all men are identical, or equally talented, wise, prudent, intelligent, or virtuous; rather, it means that all persons *possess* the inherent capacity to reason.

In his fine work *Religion and Capitalism: Allies, Not Enemies*, Edmund Opitz explains that "the writers of our

Declaration believed it axiomatic that 'all men are created equal.' They did not say '*are* equal' or '*born* equal,' which would deny the obvious; they said '*created* equal.' Equality before the law appeared to follow from this premise: the idea of one law for all men because all men are one in their essential humanness."

In this Code we are going to discuss two core principles that make America great. And that make her free: equal enforcement of the laws, and the equal protection clause.

Equal Protections and Enforcement of the Law

When they drafted the Constitution, our Founders believed that the document they drafted would stand the test of time. But there were concerns among the Federalists that the powers not expressly reserved to the states in the Constitution could be usurped by the government. What followed was the Bill of Rights in 1791, which included ten amendments or rights that preserved and expanded the people's liberties.

The Ten Original Amendments: The Bill of Rights. Passed by Congress September 25, 1789. Ratified December 15, 1791.

1. Congress shall make no law respecting an establishment of religion, or prohibiting the free exercise thereof; or abridging the freedom of speech, or of the press; or the right of the people peaceably to assemble, and to petition the government for a redress of grievances.

2. A well-regulated Militia, being necessary to the security of a free State, the right of the people to keep and bear Arms, shall not be infringed.

3. No Soldier shall, in time of peace be quartered in any house, without the consent of the Owner, nor in time of war, but in a manner to be prescribed by law.

4. The right of the people to be secure in their persons, houses, papers, and effects, against unreasonable searches and seizures, shall not be violated, and no Warrants shall issue, but upon probable cause, supported by Oath or affirmation, and particularly describing the place to be searched, and the persons or things to be seized.

5. No person shall be held to answer for a capital, or otherwise infamous crime, unless on a presentment or indictment of a Grand Jury, except in cases arising in the land or naval forces, or in the Militia, when in actual service in time of War or public danger; nor shall any person be subject for the same offence to be twice put in jeopardy of life or limb; nor shall be compelled in any criminal case to be a witness against himself, nor be deprived of life, liberty, or property, *without due process of law;* [Emphasis Mine] nor shall private property be taken for public use, without just compensation.

6. In all criminal prosecutions, the accused shall enjoy the right to a speedy and public trial, by an impartial jury of the State and district wherein the crime shall have been committed, which district shall have been previously ascertained by law, and to be informed of the nature and cause of the accusation; to be confronted with the witnesses against him; to have compulsory process for obtaining witnesses in his favor, and to have the Assistance of Counsel for his defense.

7. In Suits at common law, where the value in controversy shall exceed twenty dollars, the right of trial by jury shall be preserved, and no fact tried by a jury, shall be otherwise re-examined in any Court of the United States, then according to the rules of the common law.

8. Excessive bail shall not be required, nor excessive fines imposed, nor cruel and unusual punishments inflicted.

9. The enumeration in the Constitution, of certain rights, shall not be construed to deny or disparage others retained by the people.

10. The powers not delegated to the United States by the Constitution, nor prohibited by it to the States, are reserved to the States respectively, or to the people.

The Equal Protection Clause, however, was not part of the Bill of Rights, and was added after the Civil War as the Fourteenth Amendment to the Constitution. The clause, which took effect in 1868, provides that no state shall deny to any person within its jurisdiction "the equal protection of the laws." It is important when considering this amendment to once again focus on context. This amendment is a direct result of the post–Civil War, Reconstruction era. It also goes hand in hand with the Thirteenth Amendment, which abolished slavery and was ratified by the Congress in December 1865. And, of course, the Fifteenth Amendment, which prohibits the federal and state governments from denying a citizen the right to vote based on that citizen's "race, color, or previous condition of servitude," was ratified on February 3, 1870, as the third and last of the Reconstruction amendments. That amendment in essence gave black men the right to vote, but not black women, who, although formerly enslaved and of color, were not considered to be covered by the amendment.

Equal enforcement of the laws is the duty of the courts. It is the duty of federal agencies (like the Department of Justice) and law enforcement (at all levels). Prior to the Fourteenth Amendment in 1868, there was little case law by the U. S. Supreme Court on this issue of "equal protections." Before that, the Fifth Amendment and the "due process clause" in the Bill of Rights were what people relied on to preserve their rights. To truly understand the notion of "equal protections" and "equal enforcement" of the laws, we have to look at two distinct periods in our nation's history and those who were game-changers in the continuing effort to preserve liberty and justice for all men, and all women.

THADDEUS STEVENS AND THE RADICAL REPUBLICAN CONGRESS OF THE 1860S[134]

"No government can be free that does not allow all its citizens to participate in the formation and execution of her laws." —Thaddeus Stevens

The Radical Republicans were a wing of the Republican Party organized around an uncompromising opposition to slavery before and during the Civil War. They were called "radical" because they were a spirited and devoted group of leaders elected to Congress who undertook a vigorous campaign to secure rights for slaves before Lincoln's death and for the newly freed slaves during Reconstruction. In the late 1840s, before the

Republican Party was created, a small group of antislavery radicals in Congress (including Salmon Chase and Charles Sumner in the Senate, and Joshua Giddings, George Julian, and Thaddeus Stevens in the House) formed an unofficial alliance. They were ostracized at first, but as time wore on and the Fugitive Slave Law (1850), the Kansas-Nebraska Act (1854), and the *Dred Scott* decision (1857) seemed to prove to many northerners that the South was in fact conspiring against farmers and workers, their political fortunes improved. Radicals had already staked out the position to which moderates increasingly felt driven.

Congressman Thaddeus Stevens (April 4, 1792–August 11, 1868) was a member of the Radical Republicans. He was elected to the House from Pennsylvania and he was one of the leaders of the Radical Republican faction during the 1860s. A fierce opponent of slavery and discrimination against black people now freed from slavery, Stevens sought to secure their rights both before and during Reconstruction. In the first instance, he worked with President Lincoln to pass the Thirteenth Amendment, and then, after Lincoln's death, in opposition to President Andrew Johnson. As chairman of the House Ways and Means Committee during the Civil War, he played a major part in the war's financing, and he possessed the political clout to push through the series of amendments that would ultimately accrue to the benefit of former slaves.

During Reconstruction the Radicals urged the full extension of rights, and especially the franchise, to blacks. But Johnson imposed an extremely mild plan for Reconstruction that did not guarantee legal equality for freed slaves, and a majority of

Republicans supported him at first. The southern states, however, exploited the leniency by using strict "black codes" to reduce former slaves to de facto servitude once again. Republican moderates again felt driven to the position already occupied by the Radicals, and Congress overrode presidential vetoes of the Freedmen's Bureau and the Civil Rights Act of 1866, and passed the Fourteenth Amendment (guaranteeing equality before the law), thus beginning the period of congressional, or radical, Reconstruction.

I highlight the actions of the Republicans of the 1860s because they exemplified courage and, frankly, a moral indignation that is badly missing from our public life today. They led with their souls. They understood the Founders' vision for America. They worked to make our union more perfect. They worked to make us better. More whole. More free. And they held more closely to those "natural rights" given not by man, but by God himself.

CHIEF JUSTICE EARL WARREN AND THE U.S. SUPREME COURT, 1953–1969[135]

"The success of any legal system is measured by its fidelity to the universal ideal of justice." —Earl Warren

"When the rights of any individual or group are chipped away, the freedom of all erodes." —Earl Warren

In 1953, President Dwight D. Eisenhower appointed former California governor Earl Warren as the fourteenth chief justice of the United States. Warren was seen as a safe conservative choice for the Court and was easily confirmed. Yet history had a different fate in store for Warren. He would lead one of the most historic and influential courts in American history in the area of equal rights, civil rights, and liberty rights (such as the historic *Loving v. Virginia* case, which struck down anti-integrated-marriage laws in 1967). What made the Warren Court legend, however, was the historic *Brown v. Board of Education* ruling in 1954. It was among the Warren Court's most important decisions, as it was the ruling that made racial segregation in public schools unconstitutional. Another was the "one-man, one-vote" ruling that caused a major shift in legislative power from rural areas to cities.

One of the primary factors in Warren's leadership style as a chief justice was his political background, having served two and a half terms as governor of California (1943–53) and his experience as the Republican candidate for vice president in 1948, as the running mate of Thomas E. Dewey.

What's critical for the purposes of this Code is Warren's strong belief in the remedial power of law. According to historian Bernard Schwartz, Warren's view of the law was pragmatic, seeing it as an instrument for obtaining equity and fairness. Schwartz argues that Warren's approach was most effective "when the political institutions had defaulted on their responsibility to try to address problems such as segregation and reapportionment and cases where the constitutional rights of defendants were abused."[136]

More powerful, in my opinion, was a corollary component of Warren's leadership, which was his focus on broad ethical principles, rather than narrower interpretative structures (which is what most strict constructionists adhere to). Describing the latter as "conventional reasoning patterns," Mark Tushnet suggests Warren often disregarded these in groundbreaking cases such as *Brown*, *Reynolds v. Sims*, and *Miranda v. Arizona*, where such traditional sources of precedent were stacked against him. Tushnet suggests Warren's principles "were philosophical, political, and intuitive, not legal in the conventional technical sense."[137]

Whatever Warren's political leanings or philosophies, he and his Court changed American jurisprudence when it came to equal rights and living up to the American ideals of liberty, justice, and fundamental fairness for all. They brought to life the meaning of the Equal Protection Clause of the Fourteenth Amendment and gave birth to a new generation of legal thought and enforcement of equality under the law.

Key Leadership Code Points

Equality before the law is one of the most fundamental principles of our founding as a great nation. We never guarantee "equal outcomes." We only guarantee that before God "all men are created equal" and that, here in the United States of America, we incorporate into our laws, and our enforcement of those laws, equal treatment for all of our citizens.

Here are some key principles and values that leaders in our twenty-first century world would do well to remember:

1. We are all equal in the eyes of our Constitution and our laws. Man may not execute them in an "equal" manner, but we must always strive toward that perfect equality envisioned by our Founders when they liberated America from Great Britain's oppressive laws.

2. Our Constitution has proven itself to be expansive. It lives and it breathes. This is not to diminish those of our brethren who are strict constructionists of the Constitution. Our Founders' vision that the people's liberty must be protected was best modeled in the Bill of Rights. It is what has brought us this far as a great nation of many different people trying to become "one." Their vision still lives 240 years later.

3. Our leaders must ever keep before them the notion of *E Pluribus Unum*, out of many we are one nation. When they do that, they honor our essential liberty and our equality before God and before the laws of this land.

"To be prepared for war is one of the most effectual means of preserving peace."

—GEORGE WASHINGTON

"Even when there is a necessity of military power, within the land, a wise and prudent people will always have a watchful and jealous eye over it."

—SAMUEL ADAMS

CODE 5

PROVIDE FOR THE COMMON DEFENSE: KEEP THE NATION STRONG

We live in perilous times, some might say the most perilous the world has ever seen. Ever since President Harry S. Truman unleashed the first nuclear weapon on the world in 1945, man has possessed the ability to destroy himself and all mankind with nuclear weapons. America has faced and seen it all: Communism. Fascism. Nazism. Despotism. Two world wars. The Cold War. And many other international conflicts, such as Vietnam and the Persian Gulf War. America has fought in, negotiated through, and survived it all.

Our nation was born in revolution. Providing for the national defense is something that we Americans take very seriously. We have done it since Concord and Lexington. We protected the homeland from British invasion in the War of 1812. Yet our world today is very different. We are far more connected and interconnected as nations. After 9/11, providing for the common defense now includes a Department of Homeland Security; a larger federal law enforcement agency than our Founders could ever imagine; a CIA; an NSA; and many more agencies that work hand in hand with our allies' law enforcement, their military, and their intelligence agencies throughout the world.

Our leaders now have to lead an America in a global community of superpowers; the European Union (which Great Britain defected from by vote of their citizens in June 2016); NATO; the Arab states; China; Russia; and global threats of terrorism unlike the world has ever known. Yet our Founders understood that in order for us to remain free, our leaders must make provisions to protect us (and our interests) both at home and abroad. They eventually would create a navy and an army. America's armed forces are the safeguard of our nation's liberties and the instruments of freedom and security, providing for the common defense of the United States by protecting the homeland and securing America's interests abroad.

The U.S. Constitution creates a government of the people to "establish Justice, insure domestic Tranquility, provide for the common defense, promote the general Welfare, and secure the Blessings of Liberty to ourselves and our Posterity." It is one of our most sacred founding Codes and it is the one place where the Founders gave the federal government great power and latitude. (Whether they intended it to be as powerful as it is today is doubtful, but they learned from their relationship with Great Britain that having a powerful army or common defense was essential to preserving liberty in their new nation.)

In this Code we are going to consider two questions and then try to answer them:

1. Why did the Founding Fathers believe that the federal government must provide for the common defense?
2. Does today's military and national defense model fit the vision of the "common defense" that the Founders had for America? Or does it overreach?

Provide for the Common Defense

The Founders understood that under the Articles of Confederation,[138] written before they wrote and adopted the Constitution, America would need to create a stronger central government that could protect the individual states in time of war or invasion. This concerned them because they feared an executive (central) power in Washington that would be too strong. As you can imagine, this set off great conversation, debate, and angst among the members of the Congress. The Founders were careful to grant the federal government only the few, limited powers that were necessary for it to carry out its aims. Under the Constitution, most powers are reserved to the states, or to the people.

When the Articles of Confederation[139] were first written, the country still depended on a volunteer militia for defending the states and the country. The Continental Army, led by George Washington, was not at that time meant to be permanent. It was a provisional army, set up to defend against the British. So "to provide for the common defense" applied to defense of the various states, as one unit, as one core, as one united nation. The United States did not refer to itself as such until 1776.[140] Before that it was referred to as "united colonies." The states were bound together in a loose federation and many years and a lot of debate passed before we saw ourselves as a nation first and as independent states second. The Civil War was a war over states' rights, and only morphed into one over slavery for political reasons. Lincoln was described as believing that [i]f he could save the union by freeing the slaves he would do that, if he could do it by freeing some slaves and leaving the rest in bondage he would do that, if he could save the union by not freeing any, he would do that as well. Hence, he used the issue of freeing the slaves as a trump card to keep Britain and France out of the war.[141]

As the Founders saw it, the federal government was to be concerned only with issues that affected the welfare of the entire nation. It was thus given the exclusive power, for example, to create an army, to declare war, and to make treaties. As James Madison wrote in *The Federalist Papers,* "the operations of the federal government will be most extensive and important in times of war and danger."[142] For the Founders, a central job of the federal government was to "provide for the common defense." The Founders realized that only an organized and professional military could respond to both domestic and foreign threats. That is why they authorized the building of forts, the creation of the U.S. Navy, and the founding of the U.S. Military Academy at West Point.[143]

Our Founders had learned powerful lessons from their own taskmaster, Great Britain. They learned what was good, and what was not so good, meaning they grasped the power of having a powerful military force and navy. Yet they rightly feared the overuse and overreach of that power against citizens. In times of peace, the United States has often been tempted to believe that it need not grow our military or even to become isolationist. And when we have walked that path, as in World War I or World War II, we ultimately ended up in the conflicts abroad. The point is this: Our Founders were convinced that no peace was so secure that it could be taken for granted. They understood that no nation was so safe that it did not need to maintain sound and reliable defenses. A paradox of sorts for sure, but modern history teaches us that a strong national defense—a strong military and superior military preparedness—is the right way to go.

Be clear, however, that the Founders were suspicious of standing armies. They knew that in Europe such armies had been used by monarchies to oppress the people. In order to avoid this danger, while providing for the nation's security, the Founders made the common defense a shared responsibility of Congress and the president, the elected (and separate) branches of government. This ensured the American military would serve the interests of the nation, but not subvert the rule and will of the people.[144]

Does Today's Military Fulfill the Founders' Vision?

As mentioned many times at the beginning of this book and throughout, the Founders feared a large and powerful federal government. At the beginnings of the republic, then, our Founders had to set some parameters for how they would protect individual liberties, while ensuring domestic tranquility. They learned the power of alliances and diplomacy with nations such as France and Spain during the American Revolution. And they learned that no nation could long remain free without being able to properly defend herself or at times go on the offensive against nations threatening her sovereignty and peace.

There are several key principles that the Founders had to balance when considering how to create a national military or defense based on their own caveat that civilians, or we the people, needed to keep control of the military. Here is a recap of those balancing tests that the Founders had to consider:

1. A large federal military force would be viewed as a threat to liberty, a legacy of British history, and the British Army's occupation in the colonial period.
2. A large military force threatened American democracy. This notion was linked to the ideal of the citizen-soldier and fears of establishing an aristocratic or autocratic military class.
3. A large military force threatened economic prosperity. Maintaining large standing armies represented an enormous burden on the fledgling economy of a new nation, and on future generations, likely requiring more taxes.
4. A large military force threatened peace. The Founders accepted the liberal proposition that arms races led to war. But, George Washington believed, through keeping a large military force, we could prevent the prospect of war. Thus civilian control of the military arose from a set of historical circumstances and became embedded over time in American political thought through tradition, custom, and belief.

The issue we face today is whether or not we have slowly crept beyond these four balancing tests, and I think we can all agree that we have—out of necessity and out of the changing nature of technology, global connectivity, and interdependency. This takes us once again back to Code #3: equal enforcement and protection under the law. The Founders' original vision led to the expansion of those rights, over time, for women and blacks. It is the same premise here: We still have a civilian-led military (for example, you can't be both president of the United States and a general at the same time), the elected president is commander in chief, and the military answers to Congress for its funding and war-declaring authority. But our military and provision for the common defense has grown beyond what the Founders could have ever imagined. Our national defense spending is 16 percent of our federal budget each year—which has declined over the past two decades. Only health and Social Security claim bigger shares of the federal budget. In real dollars, in 2016, defense spending exceeded $829 billion.[145]

In the pages that follow, we will look at four Americans who helped to lead us down the pathway of becoming the greatest military power and force on the face of the earth. It started with the cry of the great Patrick Henry, in Virginia in 1775: "Give me liberty or give me death." And it came full circle in 1980, when President Ronald Reagan in 1980 likened America to a "Shining City on a Hill," paraphrasing Puritan colonist John Winthrop.[146] America has emerged over two and a half centuries as a great defender of other nations, and as a great protector of her own freedoms. As with every Code in this book, however, the Founders' ideals work only when citizens and elected leaders live them out for all to see.

GOVERNOR PATRICK HENRY[147]

"Give me liberty or give me death." —Patrick Henry

Patrick Henry was a Founding Father in every sense of the word. He was also one of the earliest proponents of common defense in the Virginia legislature and later on behalf of America through the Bill of Rights, of which he was a great advocate. Henry was considered a brilliant orator in his day and was a major figure in the American Revolution. He is, perhaps, best known for his words "Give me liberty or give me death," spoken at the Virginia Convention in 1775. Delegate Henry presented resolutions to raise a militia, and to put Virginia in a posture of defense prior to the American Revolution. Henry's opponents urged caution and patience until the Crown replied to Congress's final petition for reconciliation. Henry presented a proposal to organize a volunteer company of cavalry or infantry in every Virginia county. Interestingly, he declined to be a delegate to the Continental Congress, opting instead to raise his voice in his beloved Virginia as a legislator.

Born on May 29, 1736, in Studley, Virginia, Henry was an influential leader in the radical opposition to the British government, but accepted the new federal government only after the passage of the Bill of Rights, for which he was in great measure responsible. With his persuasive and passionate speeches, patriot Patrick Henry helped kick-start the American Revolution and is considered the "voice" of the revolution. He stood for the individual liberties of his fellow colonists and used his powerful oratory skills to move colonial leaders to action against state-sponsored tyranny. The Patrick Henry Center for Individual Rights in Virginia offers a great statement on Henry's impact on America for us to consider: "Our children know that George Washington was the first president of our nation, Thomas Jefferson was the writer of the Declaration of Independence, and Benjamin Franklin was a great statesman and inventor, but do they know how important Patrick Henry was to the American Cause? When Henry proclaimed, 'Give me liberty, or give me death!' he called an emerging nation into action!"[148]

PRESIDENT THEODORE ROOSEVELT[149]

"Do what you can, with what you have, where you are."
—*Theodore Roosevelt*

Teddy Roosevelt is my favorite president because he represented our resilient and tough American spirit. A great populist, he exemplifies Code #1 of this section: noblesse oblige, the obligation to serve from one's station in life. Teddy Roosevelt was from a wealthy upper-class New York family and was the elder cousin of President Franklin Roosevelt. One of our most famous presidents, Teddy Roosevelt is notably remembered for his tough talk, whether it was his famous "Man in the Arena" speech in Paris in 1910, or his views on American strength and leadership in the world: "Speak softly and carry a big stick; you will go far."[150]

Roosevelt didn't just talk about strength and exceptionalism. President Roosevelt is the only American president to have been awarded the Medal of Honor.[151] Lieutenant Colonel Theodore Roosevelt distinguished himself by acts of bravery on July 1, 1898, near Santiago de Cuba, in the Republic of Cuba, while leading a daring charge up San Juan Hill. Roosevelt is the stuff legends are made of: He was a man who lost his first wife and mother on the same day to typhoid fever. He was a man of strength, passion, and resilience. He believed that America should carry a big stick. He also put an end to the business monopoly of John D. Rockefeller and others.

Among his achievements and contributions to America's national defense was his service as assistant secretary of the Navy. He was among his era's most influential naval strategists, who thought about the overall planning for the U.S. Navy, its use as a military and diplomatic force, and the movement and disposition of the Navy's assets. For decades he strove tirelessly to transform the Navy into a highly capable instrument for turning the United States into a great power. He made his first contribution as a young amateur historian in the early 1880s and continued to influence U.S. naval strategy right up to his death in 1919.[152] As an undergraduate at Harvard University, Roosevelt started a serious study of the naval aspects of the War of 1812. He tirelessly pursued primary sources, including official papers and other original documents. He completed two chapters of what became *The Naval War of 1812* while still at Harvard, and finished the book in 1882 at age twenty-four—in time for the seventieth anniversary of the then-obscure war's start. (He was also said to read one book a day.) Prior to Roosevelt's work, serious studies had pegged the cause of the conflict as the failed U.S. foreign policy designed to avoid war, particularly war with Great Britain. Jefferson's isolationist foreign policy had been lauded, and historians tended to ignore the naval operations and focus on the land war.

In the annals of history, Theodore Roosevelt and trust busting is synonymous. Even though he had been born into a family of privilege and power, he was raised to respect hard work and "fair play." During his rise in political office, he witnessed the massive, exponential growth of industry superpowers such as J. P. Morgan and John D. Rockefeller. Disgusted by such unchecked power and wealth, Teddy decided he would fight to change the system. . His first major attack against monopolistic corporations, using the largely ignored Sherman Act, was aimed at none other than Morgan himself, head of the Northern Securities Company (NSC), a colossal railroad trust that threatened any chance of competition. In 1902, Roosevelt ordered his attorney general, Philander C. Knox, to file suit against Morgan for restricting trade by limiting traffic between Chicago and the Northwest. Morgan pleaded with Teddy, along with Mark Hanna (a former political colleague and advisor to Roosevelt), but their requests fell on deaf ears.

Long tired of the corporate stranglehold on the country, Teddy was determined to make progress. In 1904, the U.S. Supreme Court voted 5–4 in favor of the government, ordering the NSC to be dismantled. This victory served to redefine the highest court's view of trusts, stopped an impending national railroad consolidation in its tracks, curtailed public interest in holding companies, and made Teddy more popular than ever among the average citizenry.[153]

Teddy Roosevelt was a man of action, and preferred to lead from the front. He had stunned the country when he resigned his post as assistant secretary of the Navy to instead establish and lead the famous "Rough Riders" in the Spanish-American War. He achieved international fame for his bravery, for which he was awarded the nation's highest military honor, the Medal of Honor.

He was also a great diplomat and statesman, winning the Nobel Peace Prize for having negotiated peace in the Russo-Japanese War in 1904–1905. He also resolved a dispute with Mexico by resorting to arbitration, as recommended by the peace movement.

PRESIDENT HARRY S. TRUMAN[154]

"America was not built on fear. America was built on courage, on imagination and an unbeatable determination to do the job at hand." —Harry S. Truman

Sworn in as the thirty-third president after popular president Franklin Delano Roosevelt's sudden death in April 1945, former senator and then vice president Harry S. Truman presided over the end of World War II by making a decision that would forever change American warfare: He unleashed the new weapon of nuclear power on the world, and, in doing so, devastated two cities in Japan, forcing them to surrender. With no prior experience in foreign policy, Truman was thrust into the role of commander in chief and charged with ending a world war. In the first six months of his term, he announced the Germans' surrender, dropped atomic bombs on Hiroshima and Nagasaki—ending World War II—and signed the charter ratifying the United Nations.

Truman was famously known for his slogan "The buck stops here," meaning, with the American president. Truman was a former military man who started everything late in his life. When World War I erupted, Truman volunteered for duty. Though he was thirty-three years old—two years over the age limit for the draft—and eligible for exemption as a farmer, he helped organize his National Guard regiment, which was ultimately called into service in the 129th Field Artillery. Truman was promoted to captain in France and assigned Battery D, which was known for being the unruliest battery in the regiment. In spite of a generally shy and modest temperament, Truman captured the respect and admiration of his men and led them successfully through heavy fighting during the Meuse-Argonne campaign.[155]

Once he returned home from World War I, Truman ran for office and eventually landed in the U.S. Senate from Missouri. In his second term, he chaired a special committee to investigate the National Defense Program, to prevent war profiteering and wasteful spending in defense industries. He gained public support and recognition for his straightforward reports and practical recommendations, and he won the respect of his colleagues and the populace alike. Truman fits well into this Code because he was truly a man of humble beginnings in Missouri, and rose to become the most powerful man in the world, and America's first civilian president to drop a nuclear weapon on our adversaries in order to protect American military lives and secure the peace.

PRESIDENT RONALD WILSON REAGAN[156]

*"If we ever forget that we are One Nation Under God,
then we will be a nation gone under." —Ronald Reagan*

Known as "the Great Communicator," Ronald Wilson Reagan was, ironically, first a member of the Democratic Party and campaigned for Democratic candidates; however, his views grew more conservative over time, and in the early 1960s he officially became a Republican.[157]

In 1964, Reagan stepped into the national political spotlight when he gave a well-received televised speech for Republican presidential candidate Barry Goldwater, a prominent conservative. Two years later, in his first race for public office, Reagan defeated Democratic incumbent Edmund "Pat" Brown, Sr., by almost 1 million votes to win the governorship of California. Reagan was reelected to a second term in 1970. After making unsuccessful bids for the Republican presidential nomination in 1968 and 1976, Reagan received his Party's nod in 1980. In that year's general election, he and running mate, George H. W. Bush, faced off against President Jimmy Carter and Vice President Walter Mondale. Reagan won the election by an electoral margin of 489–49 and captured almost 51 percent of the popular vote. At age sixty-nine, he was the oldest person elected to the U.S. presidency.

What we remember President Reagan for is returning America to her greatness around the world. When Reagan took office after the 1980 election, Americans were dispirited and angry. We had been humiliated around the world with the capture of fifty-two Americans who had been held hostage in Iran for more than 440 days. I remember the yellow ribbons, and the general sense of dis-ease the nation felt under President Carter when it came to national security, and the security of Americans here at home during the Cold War.

The American military expanded greatly under President Reagan, to much criticism on the left and to great relief on the right. After America closed her doors to an expensive war in Vietnam, the nation was in need of an overhaul of the economy, the military, and the public morale. Ronald Reagan's 1980 presidential campaign and his ultimate victory signaled what many believed the country needed to get back on its superpower footing again: He lifted the American people with lofty, soaring rhetoric and an unapologetic love for America.

As a result of the Carter administration policies, the American military was plagued by low morale, low pay, outdated equipment, and practically zero maintenance on existing equipment. Important U.S. military personnel were not reenlisting; it just wasn't worth it to them. In fact, thousands of enlisted men's families survived on food stamps. One of Reagan's controversial proposals was the Strategic Defense Initiative (SDI), a system intended to make the United States invulnerable to nuclear missile attacks by the Soviet Union. By stationing those defenses in outer space, the United States was able to circumvent the U.S.-Soviet Anti-Ballistic Treaty.[158]

Reagan's American restoration delivered patriotism, prosperity, and peace. American pride revived as the economy soared and the Soviet domination of Eastern Europe collapsed. As Reagan challenged Mikhail Gorbachev in Berlin in 1987, "Mr. Gorbachev, tear down this wall." "All in all," Reagan said in his 1989 farewell address, "not bad, not bad at all."

★ ★ ★ ★ ★ ★ ★ ★ ★ ★ ★ ★ ★ ★ ★ ★

Key Leadership Code Points

In the twenty-first century, the most likely problem for the United States is not that the professional military will ignore or in any way oppose civilian control as our Founders commanded. Rather, the issue is whether civilian leaders will have the technical expertise by background and experience to deal with the complex and dangerous problems of the twenty-first century. The challenge is for the civilian leadership to work effectively with military professionals to ensure that the president and his staff have access to necessary technical expertise and information that is required for effective decision-making on a global economic and military playing field.

There is only one key takeaway from this Code: Our leaders must understand and respect the notion of civilian control over the military. According to military historian Michael Cairo, there are two important principles that are critical in our democratic republic to ensure that the military is always kept under the watchful eye of the citizenry.

First, the U.S. Constitution divides military power between the legislative and the executive branches, a division aimed to preventing abuses of power. Also, the Constitution clearly establishes the president—a popularly elected civilian leader—as commander in chief of the armed forces. The crucial element here is that the president's powers are defined and limited as a whole, and Congress, the U.S. courts, and the electorate have substantial power. Thus the president's command of the military does not lead to command of other sectors. The president's primarily civilian status has been borne out through the country's history. Only four presidents—Washington, Jackson, Grant, and Eisenhower—had significant careers in the military prior to becoming president. Each of them understood the need to keep military and political functions separate and distinct. General Dwight Eisenhower carried this principle so far while he was commanding Allied forces in Europe during World War II that he did not vote.

The second key principle requires that the military serves in an administrative, not a policy-making, role. Eisenhower's refusal to vote while in the Army is representative of his belief that military decisions must not be clouded by political decisions. Generals should not be involved in the political decision-making process. Instead they should only concern themselves with offering advice regarding the use of the military to achieve policy-makers' goals. Further, Eisenhower honored a time-tested principle that political decisions should be left to politicians, and not to military men and women.

★ ★ ★ ★ ★ ★ ★ ★ ★ ★ ★ ★ ★ ★ ★

"The people in general ought to have regard to the moral character of those whom they invest with authority either in the legislative, executive, or judicial branches."

—SAMUEL ADAMS

"Look well to the characters and qualifications of those you elect and raise to office and places of trust."

—WILLIAM PATTERSON

CODE
6

MORAL AND VIRTUOUS LEADERSHIP

Today, perhaps, more than at any other time in our nation's history, we find ourselves disappointed in our leaders. Our nation has just come through a difficult national election cycle. The top two presidential candidates both had the highest unfavorability ratings ever measured in the history of political polling.[159] The country did not feel inspired. The country seemed resigned. Disinterested. Restless. It was the first election cycle in my lifetime where we had two primary candidates, Democratic senator Bernie Sanders of Vermont (an avowed socialist/independent turned Democrat) and Republican businessman Donald Trump, of New York, surge in the primaries and capture historic numbers of new and disenfranchised voters. In the general election, we had two wealthy, older candidates, one a woman, former secretary of state Hillary Clinton, and the other billionaire real estate mogul Donald Trump.

I believe the 2016 election cycle was a national wake-up call for our leaders as well as for we the people, to take a long, hard look at who we have become as a nation when it comes to our founding principles. First among those principles is our Founders' strong belief that the republic could stand only if it were led by virtuous and moral leaders. What makes the Founders' vision so bold is that they placed the trust of virtues and morals in the hands of the people (see Code #2 of the Citizens' Codes). They believed that virtuous people would select virtuous leaders, that moral people would elect moral leaders. In theory that is good practice. It makes sense. They also believed that, by encouraging freedom of religion, men would use their faith and belief in God as a standard of good moral conduct. Of course, they were both right and wrong. As we have discovered many times throughout American politics—as well as throughout world history—the men and women we elect to both high office and local office are often not what and who they appear to be while campaigning. Some will say anything to get elected. Some will surprise us for the better. And some, like our nation's sixteenth president, Abraham Lincoln, will rise up to meet the challenges of the nation at just the right moment, regardless of their personal shortcomings or frailties.

Regrettably, Americans have become used to political scandal. We have endured rumors of presidential adultery and sexual exploits dating back to Thomas Jefferson. We have witnessed bribery of our elected officials, misuse of power in office, the resignation of an American president in the 1970s, allegations of the illegal smuggling of weapons and guns to armed rebels in other nations. And, in the case of one recent president, we witnessed an impeachment due to allegations of lying under oath and having inappropriate relations with a young woman working under him in the White House.

And let's not forget the House of Representatives banking scandal of the early 1990s, in which nearly two dozen congressional representatives embroiled themselves in writing checks they knew they could not cover, and stuck the American people with the tab. The way the thievery played out is that the House bank allowed members to overdraw their accounts with impunity and without repercussions. When members overdrew their accounts, the clearinghouse simply covered the overdrafts, essentially funneling free money to House members. More than four hundred members overdrew accounts at one time or another, and one member, Representative Tommy Robinson, Republican of Arkansas, wrote well over nine hundred "bounced checks."[160] When the scandal leaked, it played into the common belief among the public that Congress was a corrupt, broken institution, and that helped to lead to the 1994 Republican takeover via their "Contract with America."[161]

The issue of virtue in American leadership must be viewed in light of the Founders' belief in "natural law."[162] As we discovered in Code #2 of the Citizens' Codes, the Founding Fathers placed a premium on human nature. In their opinion, the question of the best form of government cannot be separated from natural and unalienable rights, for it is from our Creator that we have such rights, and from which government has its origin and purpose. They stressed that these rights came from our Creator, because they were reasonably certain, given human history, that some human beings would try to usurp such rights from other human beings.

In short, in order to understand the proper relation of virtue or moral leadership to governance, one must first understand human nature as the foundation upon which our system of representative democracy was built. This is the only Code of our founding Codes in this book that comes up for *both* for citizens and leaders. I include this Code in both sections because it helps to better define the principles so familiar to us Americans: the separation of powers; checks and balances; a bicameral legislature; and so forth. All these were institutionalized in our form of government within the context of moral and virtuous leadership.

In this Code, we are going to define once again the meaning of virtue and morals. Different from the responsibility the Founders placed on us as the citizens of this great nation is their belief that remaining a great nation rested in a virtuous and moral leadership. However, as with many of the Codes we have considered, the Founders' reality and our present-day reality are quite different. That is why it is so important that, when we evaluate the Founders' values and guiding principles, we take time to study context, history, and the meaning of certain virtues of their day.

What Is Virtue in a Leader?

Let's start with a premise: All of us are a mixture of good and bad, light and darkness. We all have in our power this thing called "free will." The Founding Fathers understood this and they feared the darkness of men who might be elected to power in this republic. Thomas Jefferson was most vocal among the Founding Fathers on this point.

In a letter to Colonel Edward Carrington of Virginia, Thomas Jefferson wrote: "The natural progress of things is for liberty to yield and government to gain ground." He noted that "one of the most profound preferences in human nature is for satisfying one's needs and desires with the least possible exertion; for appropriating wealth produced by the labor of others, rather than producing it by one's own labor. . . . [T]he stronger and more centralized the government, the safer would be the guarantee of such monopolies; in other words, the stronger the government, the weaker the producer, the less consideration need be given him and the more might be taken away from him."[163]

It is important to take Jefferson's concerns and put them into context. Jefferson was an original proponent of Republican virtues (the Jeffersonian Republican Party). Abraham Lincoln is later credited with the resurgence of a form of that party. Republicanism is the guiding political philosophy of the United States. It has been a major part of American civic thought since its founding.

Republicanism stresses *liberty* and *unalienable individual rights* as central values, making people sovereign as a whole. Rejecting monarchy, aristocracy, and inherited political power, republicanism expects citizens to be independent in their performance of civic duties, and vilifies corruption. American republicanism was founded and first practiced by the Founding Fathers in the eighteenth century. For them, according to one team of historians, "republicanism represented more than a particular form of government. It was a way of life, a core ideology, an uncompromising commitment to liberty, and a total rejection of aristocracy."

The term *republicanism* is derived from the term *republic,* of course, but the two words have different meanings. A republic is a form of government (one without a hereditary ruling class); republicanism involves the values of the citizens in a republic.[164]

For our Founders there was an unbreakable link between their desires to preserve individual liberty and to safeguard the liberty of the republic. They believed (as is evidenced in many of their writings, letters, and public speeches) that virtue came from God to man, and that man passed them on to governments. Virtue, then, is a set of principles and actions that must be exhibited by a leader and by a nation. We define virtue with words like *honesty, integrity,* and *humility.* But true virtue is not what we know—it's what we do. A few virtues we would do well to require from our leaders are:

1. A leader walks his talk. He lives his credo. He is willing to stand on principle and, if needed in governance of a nation, die for the principles of his nation.
2. A leader inspires his countrymen with hope, vision, and character.
3. A leader protects and defends his nation.
4. A leader is a good and open communicator.
5. A leader sets an example for young people to follow. He is a model citizen first before he can lead other citizens.

Virtues are building blocks. They allow us to extend ourselves to others, to serve others, to honor others as we ourselves want to be honored. Virtue is how America came to be. Our

Founders understood that it was wrong for one man, even though he be a king, to rule with impunity. They understood that vices and virtues often walk hand in hand. So they sought to build a government of free men and free individuals who could control their own destiny by the virtues they held dear.

Do Morals Still Matter in Our Leaders?

Does morality in our leaders still matter? History warns us that many forms of government have started with good intentions, only to fail as human weaknesses and vices become apparent. In most cases, the failure of great civilizations, like Rome (a republic), came down in part due to the moral downfall of the leaders and of the general populace. Often, of course, the leader was a reflection of the people—and vice versa.

The truth is, morally speaking, America seems to be drifting dangerously out of control. There are no more absolutes. Truth is an absolute. Honesty is an absolute. Integrity and character are absolutes. In the past months, years, and decades, however, one poll after another has shown that morality and virtue are no longer American values.

Time after time, Americans have watched television commentators, legal analysts, and people on the street assure us that it's nobody's business what elected officials do in private; the only thing that matters is how they do their job. We have become brainwashed and numb to what is right and wrong. We seem to believe that what our leaders do with their private lives is, well, private—that it's nobody's business, or it's just between him and his wife. We have been told to forget what our Founders told us was the cornerstone of our nation: morals and virtue. Political correctness rules us all. Our leaders do not lead—they take polls first, then decide what they think.

The worst part is that we the people tolerate and accept it all. Our instincts have degenerated to the point where we can only react emotionally to what is right under our noses, rather than understand how much our country's freedom and well-being depend on actually demanding that our leaders act like leaders. There has been a gradual acceptance of moral relativism: that moral absolutes do not exist. Such sentiments ignore a leader's fundamental responsibility to properly lead and model virtue to his people.

You see, public office is a public trust. It is the citizens placing trust in a fellow citizen to guard and further their liberty. In 1888, President Grover Cleveland coined the saying "Public office is a public trust." Written into our code of federal regulations is a whole list of what the public trust means—each federal employee has a responsibility to the United States government and its citizens to place loyalty to the Constitution, laws, and ethical principles above private gain.

I'll ask the question again: Does moral leadership matter? Can lack of moral values and exemplary leadership coexist? What are the consequences of strong political power without a moral foundation? The four Americans we will rediscover in this Code all exemplified moral courage. Values. And strong political power with an even stronger moral foundation.

PRESIDENT ABRAHAM LINCOLN[165]

*"Nearly all men can stand adversity, but if you want to test
a man's character, give him power."* —*Abraham Lincoln*

What do you say about the greatest president America
has ever known? The man who saved the Union. The
man who kept the United States united. The man who freed the
slaves. The man who presided over the Civil War and who, after
the last great battle was fought, showed mercy, grace, and charity toward the defeated South in his second inaugural address at
Gettysburg as he called us back to be one united people:

> Four score and seven years ago our fathers brought forth
> on this continent, a new nation, conceived in Liberty,
> and dedicated to the proposition that all men are created
> equal. Now we are engaged in a great civil war, testing
> whether that nation, or any nation so conceived and so
> dedicated, can long endure. We are met on a great battle-
> field of that war. We have come to dedicate a portion of
> that field, as a final resting place for those who here gave
> their lives that that nation might live. It is altogether fit-
> ting and proper that we should do this. But, in a larger
> sense, we cannot dedicate—we cannot consecrate—we
> cannot hallow—this ground. The brave men, living and
> dead, who struggled here, have consecrated it, far above
> our poor power to add or detract. The world will little
> note, nor long remember what we say here, but it can
> never forget what they did here. It is for us the living,

rather, to be dedicated here to the unfinished work which they who fought here have thus far so nobly advanced. It is rather for us to be here dedicated to the great task remaining before us—that from these honored dead we take increased devotion to that cause for which they gave the last full measure of devotion—that we here highly resolve that these dead shall not have died in vain—*that this nation, under God, shall have a new birth of freedom—and that government of the people, by the people, for the people, shall not perish from the earth.*[166] [Emphasis Mine]

The only thing you can say about a man like this is that he was appointed to serve our nation at the perfect time. He was a man born of humble roots, in a one-room cabin in Kentucky. He had very little formal education, but he read voraciously when he was not working on his father's farm. He was truly a self-made man. A self-described "prairie lawyer," Lincoln would rise through politics starting in 1832, when he ran for the Illinois legislature, and he enlisted in the Illinois Militia to fight in the Black Hawk War.[167] Lincoln lost his race for the assembly in 1832, but would win in 1834. He would go on to lose more elections for the House of Representatives, then the U.S. Senate. He would go on to suffer many losses, personal, financial (his store), and emotional (his children). At times considered by friends and foes alike as "sullen," "depressed," even "mad," Lincoln is hardly the man we would have picked to one day be the great emancipator of the slaves, and the great healer of a badly torn and tattered nation.

On November 6, 1860, Lincoln won the presidential election without the support of a single southern state. Talk of secession, bandied about since the 1830s, took on a serious new tone. The Civil War was not entirely caused by Lincoln's election, but the election was one of the primary reasons the war broke out the following year, in 1861. Lincoln's decision to fight, rather than to let the southern states secede, was not based on his feelings toward slavery. Rather, he felt it was his sacred duty as president of the United States to preserve the Union at all costs. His first inaugural address was an appeal to the rebellious states, seven of which had already seceded, to rejoin the nation. According to historian Harold Holzer, Lincoln's original text for the speech reveals the influence of William Henry Seward, Lincoln's former rival for the nomination and his secretary of state. Originally, Lincoln was going to end the speech with the bellicose statement, "Shall it be peace or sword." But Seward convinced Lincoln to substitute a more conciliatory and elegiac ending, Holzer says.

"We are not enemies, but friends," Lincoln said in the closing passage of his first inaugural speech in 1861. "We must not be enemies. Though passion may have strained, it must not break our bonds of affection. The mystic chords of memory, stretching from every battlefield and patriot's grave, to every living heart and hearthstone, all over this broad land, will yet swell the chorus of the Union, when touched again, as surely they will be, by the better angels of our nature."[168] In short, Lincoln understood that he had to preserve the nation, just as our founders understood that the original thirteen colonies had to remain "one" union.

President Lincoln is beloved in our nation's history because he was considered a leader who led with virtue, though clearly a flawed and frail man at times. But I believe, as do many historians, that Lincoln was the right man to preside over the nation at a time when we had to be held to the vision of our Founding Fathers. The Founders were wrong to allow slavery to remain legal at the beginning of our nation's birth, and it came back to haunt us in the form of the Civil War, the bloodiest war in our nation's history.

President Lincoln personifies the virtuous and moral man entrusted with leading a great nation. He was just a man, but he has become mythical and godlike to us when we see him enshrined at the Lincoln Memorial in Washington, D.C., larger than life, even in death. Lincoln's mere presence calls us higher as Americans, for, at the foot of his great memorial, the greatest speeches and movements have taken place. Dr. Martin Luther King, Jr., gave his "I Have a Dream" speech there. The March on Washington was held there. Protests against the Vietnam War, the fight for women's rights, and every kind of moral cause always take place under the watchful eye of the Great Emancipator.

Lincoln was a great leader because he was a great man. He did not separate public and private conduct. He was authentic. He was "Honest Abe." Aside from political reasons, Lincoln understood that it was immoral to allow slavery to continue in a nation founded upon the principles of "liberty, equality, and freedom." And he understood that it was immoral to allow the South to break apart from the United States. I think he summed it up best in his December 1862 address to Congress:

Fellow-citizens, we cannot escape history. We of this Congress and this administration, will be remembered in spite of ourselves. No personal significance, or insignificance, can spare one or another of us. The fiery trial through which we pass, will light us down, in honor or dishonor, to the latest generation. We say we are for the Union. The world will not forget that we say this. We know how to save the Union. The world knows we do know how to save it. We—even we here—hold the power, and bear the responsibility. In giving freedom to the slave, we assure freedom to the free—honorable alike in what we give, and what we preserve. We shall nobly save, or meanly lose, the last best hope of earth.[169]

Lincoln understood that morals and virtue mattered greatly in political leadership. A less virtuous man in his place would have not been able to preserve the union. Thank God for Lincoln, because it was his virtue and moral leadership that kept this nation whole and as "one" united republic.

ELEANOR ROOSEVELT[170]

> "Do what you feel in your heart to be right—for you'll be criticized anyway." —Eleanor Roosevelt

The niece of President Teddy Roosevelt, and the wife of our nation's longest-serving president, Franklin D. Roosevelt, Eleanor Roosevelt may have come from a famous lineage of men, but she was her own woman at a time when being an outspoken woman leader was not the norm. For more than thirty years, she was the most powerful woman in America. She was at the center of much of the twentieth century's history—a charismatic woman of charm and of contradictions. Aristocratic in voice and manner, she was also "tough as nails," says historian Geoffrey Ward. "In fact, she was one of the best politicians of the 20th century."[171]

Eleanor Roosevelt was born in 1884, into a well-established and wealthy New York family, the daughter of society belle Anna Hall and the charming and affluent Elliott Roosevelt, the younger brother of Teddy Roosevelt. Eleanor was a shy and awkward girl, who married her fifth cousin once removed, Franklin Roosevelt, in 1905. They had five children together (with one dying in infancy). Eleanor blossomed into a confident political helpmate to her husband during his various campaigns, and ultimately became the most popular and influential woman in America during his presidency.

But what makes Eleanor worthy of mention in a book about Americans who exemplified and modeled the charge of our great motto, *E Pluribus Unum*, is that she was a change agent for her time. Though just the president's wife (which is how all first ladies before her had been viewed), she used her platform as first lady to help set in motion the process that would help integrate the U.S. military. She spoke out and up for the rights of women to participate in industry, public life, and educational advancement.

Eleanor had played a huge role in her husband's life and career success after he suffered a polio attack in 1921. She was the mastermind behind his comeback into public life and she stepped forward to help Franklin with his political career. When

FDR became president in 1933, Eleanor dramatically changed the role of the first lady. Not content to stay in the background and handle domestic matters, she showed the world that the first lady was an important part of American politics. She gave press conferences and spoke out for human rights, children's causes, and women's issues, working on behalf of the League of Women Voters. She even had her own newspaper column, "My Day." She also focused on helping the country's poor, stood against racial discrimination, and, during World War II, traveled abroad to visit U.S. troops.[172]

Like Lincoln, Eleanor Roosevelt led from a place of right and wrong, of moral absolutes, whether it was speaking out for rights for women, or against racial segregation in America. One example of her boldness and virtue happened in March 1941, when as first lady Eleanor hopped in the back of pilot C. Alfred "Chief" Anderson's plane at the Tuskegee Army Air Field in Alabama and went for a flight. The significance of the event was that Anderson was one of the black pilots being trained for combat missions in World War II. Yet, because these were "colored" troops, they were not being assigned to combat overseas. Her bold move to showcase the "Tuskegee Flyers" resulted in them being sent on combat missions in Morocco and Berlin as the 332nd Fighter Group, and the 477th Bombardment Group of the Army Air Force.[173]

Though Eleanor was recognized eleven consecutive times in Gallup polls as the most admired woman in the world, few people were neutral about her.[174] To admirers she was a woman with immense moral courage; through her newspaper columns, radio broadcasts, and public appearances, she was cast as the nation's familiar friend. Her detractors saw her as a dangerous meddler, a dilettante, and a traitor to her class, while political cartoonists had a field day with her physical profile. Whatever the criticism, she never shrank back. She was determined to live life on her own terms, and she did. Eleanor Roosevelt traveled far from her sheltered upper-class beginnings to become one of America's most admired and moral figures of all time.

SENATOR MARGARET CHASE SMITH[175]

> *"The right way is not always the popular and easy way. Standing for right when it is unpopular is a true test of moral character."* —Margaret Chase Smith

For more than three decades, Margaret Chase Smith served as a role model for women aspiring to national politics. As the first woman to win election to both the U.S. House and the U.S. Senate, Smith cultivated a career as an independent and courageous legislator.

She was born in Skowhegan, Maine, on December 14, 1897. Her entry into politics came through the career of her late husband, Clyde Smith. Clyde had been elected to the United States House of Representatives in 1936, and she served as his secretary. When Clyde died in 1940, she succeeded her husband. After four terms in the House, she won election to the United States Senate in 1948. In so doing, she became the first woman elected to both houses of Congress.

Though she believed firmly that women had a political role to assume, Smith refused to make an issue of her gender in seeking higher office. "If we are to claim and win our rightful place in the sun on an equal basis with men," she once noted, "then we must not insist upon those privileges and prerogatives identified in the past as exclusively feminine." As a member of the Armed Services Committee, Smith passed her landmark legislative achievement in the House: the Women's Armed Forces Integration Act. With a wartime peak enrollment of about 350,000, women were still considered volunteers for the armed services and did not receive any benefits. In April 1947, while chairing the Armed Services Subcommittee on Hospitalization and Medicine, Smith authored a bill giving regular status to Navy and Army nurses, which was passed by her House colleagues because it covered women in traditional "angel of mercy" roles.

Margaret Chase Smith's defining moment in the U.S. Senate came on June 1, 1950, when she took the floor to denounce the investigatory tactics of the red-baiting Wisconsin senator, Joseph R. McCarthy. She bravely denounced McCarthyism at a time when others feared speaking out would ruin their careers. In a speech she later called a "Declaration of Conscience," Smith charged that her Republican colleague had "debased" Senate deliberations "through the selfish political exploitation of fear, bigotry, ignorance and intolerance." She said, "The American people are sick and tired of being afraid to speak their minds lest they be politically smeared as 'Communists' or 'Fascists' by their opponents. Freedom of speech is not what it used to be in America. It has been so abused by some that it is not exercised by others."

Margaret Chase Smith was awarded the Presidential Medal of Freedom by President George H. W. Bush in 1989.

REPRESENTATIVE JACK F. KEMP[176]

"Democracy without morality is impossible." —*Jack Kemp*

Jack Kemp was more than an MVP quarterback in the NFL who happened to get elected to Congress, eventually becoming the vice presidential nominee of his party. Jack Kemp was a different kind of "freedom fighter." Kemp took the lessons he learned on the football field (playing at a time when football was still segregated)—lessons like the value of leadership, teamwork, equality, and competition—and brought them to bear in his public service.

His later politics were informed by his witnessing racism up close in what was then the American Football League. During a 1960 visit to Houston, for a game when he was the quarterback for the Los Angeles Chargers, Kemp and his team were forced to stay in dorms at the University of Houston because hotels wouldn't admit black guests. In January 1965, he supported a boycott of New Orleans and helped move the AFL all-star game out of the city because it barred African Americans from taxis and nightclubs.

A staunch conservative, Kemp was once dubbed by the *Wall Street Journal* as a "happy warrior."[177] He was a leader in Congress who both understood and could powerfully communicate the power of ideas, human capital, and opportunity for all Americans. Kemp was secretary of the Department of Housing and Urban Development during the Rodney King riots in Los Angeles in 1992. Unlike others in the GOP, who had no clue what to say or do in response, Kemp went to Los Angeles, rolled up his sleeves, and tossed a football around in the streets while assuring residents that there was a way out of racism and poverty. That way was Kemp's way—economic empowerment, home ownership, enterprise zones. He believed passionately in equality of opportunity.

Before heading to Congress, in 1967 Kemp served as a special assistant to California governor Ronald Reagan. A few years later, as a congressman from the Buffalo, New York, area in 1970, Kemp's commitment to racial equality was firm. The GOP was increasingly—and successfully—appealing to southern white Democratic voters through code words such as "states' rights," and through opposing school-integration busing programs. Faced with the GOP's vocal opposition to government programs that seemed to benefit minorities, Kemp tried to find market-based answers to the problems of poverty and race.[178] He was a bright light in a Republican Party growing dim. Fast-forward to our present day GOP: It is in disarray. There is no Jack Kemp. No moral conscience. No virtuous voice demanding that the GOP live up to its great history and founding ideals.

I knew Jack Kemp, who passed away in 2009, and I admired him greatly. He is the reason I became interested in "Republican" politics in college in 1988. I miss his sunny optimism and passion in national politics. Kemp stood for inclusiveness, engagement, and encouragement. He drew the support and earned the respect of Americans from all walks of life because he lived by a philosophy of principled pragmatism, brotherly love, political collaboration, bold ideas, and economic freedom, empowering those without power and especially reaching out to those who had not yet attained the American Dream.

I will end with some words from an article I wrote about my political mentor after his death[179]:

> Jack Kemp was everybody's favorite Republican/Conservative. The GOP leadership would do well to model itself after him in class, temperament, and substance. In my tribute to Kemp titled, "Jack Kemp: Why I Became a Republican," published in Monday's *Washington Post*, I spoke about Kemp's unique ability to combine fiscal conservatism and a strong military defense with urban policy and meaningful outreach to the less fortunate among us. No other conservative that I am aware of has been able to walk successfully across such different pastures, and be well liked by both sides for doing so.

Jack Kemp, Margaret Chase Smith, Eleanor Roosevelt, and Abraham Lincoln all played a central role in our nation becoming a more perfect and unified union. They all shared two leadership traits: virtue and morality. They were beloved not just in their own times, but forever through the ages because they were courageous, honorable, bold, and, most of all, brave. They well understood that this great nation can remain so only when our leaders lead from the soul, the soul of a nation founded like no other. The soul of a diverse and talented people always striving to become one.

★ ★ ★ ★ ★ ★ ★ ★ ★ ★ ★ ★ ★ ★ ★

Key Leadership Code Points

The key takeaway from this Code is that leadership and character are inseparable. In their book the *Ten Virtues of Outstanding Leaders*, authors Al Gini and Ronald Green ask: What is good leadership? They insist that "ethics, character, and virtue are essential to real leadership" and anything else is *mis-leadership*. They suggest that leadership is not just a set of learned skills, a series of outcomes, a career, a profession, or a title. Leadership, at its core, is about character: specifically, a character attuned to its ethical responsibilities to others. It is the kind of character that, in regard to others, always tries to do the right thing, for the right reason, on purpose.

The ten virtues put forth by Gini and Green:

1. Deep honesty

2. Moral courage

3. Moral vision

4. Compassion and care

5. Fairness

6. Intellectual excellence

7. Creative thinking

8. Aesthetic sensitivity

9. Good timing

10. Deep selflessness[180]

★ ★ ★ ★ ★ ★ ★ ★ ★ ★ ★ ★ ★ ★ ★

"How little do my countrymen know what precious blessings they are in possession of, and which no other people on earth enjoy!"

—THOMAS JEFFERSON

CODE
7

VISIONARY AND EXPANSIVE LEADERSHIP

Two hundred and forty years ago, a small group of brave and audacious merchants, planters, and lawyers assembled in Philadelphia to declare their independence from King George and Mother England. They did so for two distinct reasons. First, they were tired of being oppressed by a tyrannical king. Overtaxed. Fearful of the occupying force of soldiers from the Crown. They had no liberty. They had no property. They had no religious sanctity that was beyond the reach of the king or his agents whenever they felt compelled to take from these men all they held dear. And second, they had a vision of what life was supposed to be about in the new world.

That vision began with a simple premise, written by Thomas Jefferson: "We hold these truths to be self-evident, that all men are created equal, that they are endowed by their Creator with certain unalienable Rights, that among these are Life, Liberty and the pursuit of Happiness." Jefferson believed that human beings possess the ability to do remarkable and good things, and that a government could be created that could tap into this good, and so see men thrive with liberty and freedom. The power of America is a combination of compelling aspirations and ideals that prevailed against all odds. Great men like Thomas Jefferson understood that this new nation would require a powerful vision to prevail over the great sacrifice and price they had all paid during the American Revolution.

Visionary leadership is what has made America great. A visionary is one who sees beyond his present reality or circumstance and paves the way for others who come after him to get to where he himself would like to be. America has moved ever steadily and gradually according to Jefferson's great words in the Declaration of Independence. We did not start out honoring the words "all men are created equal." But eventually we got there. We became more inclusive. More united. More equal. And more free. Of course there is still more work to do.

Expansive leaders like Jefferson are those who reach out to others who may not agree with them, to get them to buy into their vision. They are people who inspire, who offer hope. They also know how to be pragmatic managers. They get it done. President Lyndon B. Johnson was a master at this skill. He knew how to move legislation. He knew how to get it done. President Franklin Roosevelt was another man of great vision who helped to lead a depressed nation out of the darkness and into a great "New Deal."[181]

Great leaders transform the people and the times in which they live. Major visionary leaders live more in the future, and they often use a vision of the future as a way to mobilize followers. *Sometimes, vision in leadership is more of a journey than the destination. This was the case with the men we will consider in this Code. Great leaders must also construct the means toward their vision.*

One of the great hints that our Founders left for us about their vision for America can be found in our founding symbols. It is found on every dollar bill, which displays the reverse of the Great Seal of the United States. There is the All-Seeing Eye of God, or Spirit, placed above a pyramid, a symbol representing "spiritual vision" that is found in many secret societies, such as the Freemasons. The pyramid was used by some ancient cultures, such as the Egyptians and the Mayans, as an initiation chamber. The All-Seeing Eye seems to be placed as a capstone at the top of the pyramid. If you stand at the base of the pyramid, there are many different viewpoints, depending on which of the four sides you are standing on and looking out from. But, at the top, all the viewpoints unite, because there we see with the Eye of Spirit.

Metaphorically speaking, various religious and political groups stand at the base of the pyramid, fighting for their limited view, when they need to climb higher to see the more inclusive, higher vision from the top: the radiant Eye of Spirit. Several intriguing Latin phrases can also be found on the Great Seal and the dollar bill: *Annuit Coeptus* (indicating God "Favors our Undertakings") and *Novus Ordo Seclorum* ("The New Order of the Ages"). You can see that our Founding Fathers were visionaries planning for a new age. *E Pluribus Unum* ("Out of many, one") reflects not only the unity of the original thirteen states, but also, on a deeper level, the One Life, the Divine Presence, which pervades all life and creates unity in diversity.

In this final Code, the end of this book, I want to talk about vision, because that is what America is all about—vision. And that vision has expanded time and time again to make us a more perfect union. But I will not, as I did in the other Codes, give an exposition on the values of vision and expansion. They are in and of themselves self-explanatory. The men who follow embodied both. They were visionaries. They understood operating in the time and context in which they lived, but each one of them knew that the generations following them needed guideposts. A road map. America is an ideal that has grown in increments, as I mentioned before, by and through great men and women of vision, courage, and optimism for better things to come.

Three Men Whose Vision Changed America by Expanding Liberty

PRESIDENT THOMAS JEFFERSON[182]

> *"I hold it, that a little rebellion, now and then, is a good thing, and as necessary in the political world as storms in the physical."* —*Thomas Jefferson*

> *"A people who mean to be their own governors must arm themselves with the power that knowledge gives."*
> —*Thomas Jefferson*

Thomas Jefferson embodied American optimism, the promise of a bright future for such a new and hopeful country.

He was the father of the Declaration of Independence and the Statute of Virginia for Religious Freedom; he was governor of Virginia, ambassador to France, secretary of state, third president of the United States, and founder of the University of Virginia. Through his gifted pen he voiced the aspirations of a new nation as no other individual of his generation. As a public official, historian, philosopher, and plantation owner, he served his country for more than five decades.

The great irony of Jefferson was that, while he declared "independence" for himself and his fellow colonists in 1776, there were more than 540,000 enslaved people, unrecognized as Americans at the time.[183] That fact is indeed the great sin of our Founders. They made a choice not to do what they knew was right and instead chose what was in their own best economic interests. They delayed the promise of liberty for all men in exchange for an immediate convenience of free labor to build the nation that they had fought so hard to liberate from tyranny.

Jefferson was a complex and sentimental man. A deep thinker. A true Renaissance man. From all accounts, he was a quiet, somewhat sullen, and gentle man. He suffered great losses in his life. The loss of his beloved wife, Martha, took something from him. He pledged on her deathbed never to marry again, and he did not. He lost all but one of his children. He turned to his books, writings, and his beloved Monticello for solace. At some point during or after his return from Paris as ambassador, Jefferson began a complicated and scandalous relationship with his young mulatto slave Sally Hemings (who was said to be the half-sister of his late wife sired by her father and his slave, Elizabeth Hemings—Sally's mother). The relationship between Jefferson and Hemings was the subject of more than two hundred years of allegations and newspaper articles. Finally, DNA tests in the late 1990s confirmed that Jefferson was indeed the father of at least one of Sally's offspring, and quite likely the father of them all.[184]

Jefferson personifies the sad paradox of American history—greatness riddled with personal failure. Was he a man who fell in love with his slave and fathered six children but was unable to marry or legitimize her as his wife? Or was he simply a hypocrite, like so many other slave owners of his day, who spoke with a forked tongue about equality? We will never know who Thomas Jefferson really was behind closed doors, in his private world. But we do know that there are great inconsistencies between his life as a man and his vision for America.

Yet, it is not that Jefferson who interests me. Jefferson is chronicled in this Code because he presided over the greatest expansion of America in her history, with the Louisiana Purchase and commissioning the famous Lewis and Clark expeditions, which also expanded America westward. In May 1804, Meriwether Lewis and William Clark, two young military officers, set out on an amazing expedition across the Louisiana Territory at the behest of then-president Jefferson.

These two American heroes faced unknown people, harsh conditions, and unexplored lands to secure a place in history as two of the world's greatest explorers. One of the expedition's stops along the way was near present-day Yankton, South

Dakota. The Yankton Area Chamber of Commerce along with the *Yankton Daily Press and Dakotan* has put together an historical site, part of the National Park Service, to celebrate Yankton's place in history, as well as sites along the rest of the Lewis and Clark Trail. But their most famous encounter was with a woman named Sacagawea, who, according to Wikipedia, helped the Lewis and Clark Expedition.[185]

But Jefferson the visionary was also Jefferson the statesman. He was savvy about Europe and European power. By purchasing Louisiana from France, he effectively removed Britain, Spain, Russia, and France as threats to American sovereignty. He protected and established this continent and its territory as American lands. Jefferson was an explorer by nature—a great thinker. His enlightened program challenged Americans to explore and discover untapped resources. The Louisiana Purchase was the largest land deal in history. It cost the United States $15 million in 1803,[186] twice the size at that time of the federal budget. Jefferson loved the notion of discovery. He relished the idea of America being a treasure trove of the undiscovered. Even before it was purchased he had already engaged Lewis and Clark to begin exploring the great territory.

His vision for America during 1801–08, while he was president, radically changed the expansion and power of American lands. He also was a great proponent of public education and learning, and sold his 6,700-volume collection of books to the U.S. government for $24,000 in 1815. They formed the core of the Library of Congress.

PRESIDENT FRANKLIN DELANO ROOSEVELT[187]

"The only thing we have to fear is fear itself."
—*President Franklin Delano Roosevelt*

Franklin Delano Roosevelt assumed the American presidency height of the Great Depression. A man born of great wealth and social privilege, Roosevelt had served as governor of New York and assistant secretary of the Navy. He was married to his fifth cousin once removed, Eleanor Roosevelt, profiled in Code #6 of this section. He was a handsome and virile man who was struck with polio early in his life, which left him crippled from the waist down.

It is often said that from great tragedy, great men are born. I believe, as do many historians, that Roosevelt's experience with physical disability changed and shaped his life. Much like President Lincoln, his personal challenges prepared him to be a better leader. He became more caring, more attuned to people's sufferings. And more connected to the everyday plight of everyday people. With Eleanor always at his side, lifting and encouraging him, Roosevelt beat back depression, defeat, and despair in his own life, to stand up and inspire the nation from its own depression, defeat, and despair.

As if the Great Depression he inherited were not enough, Roosevelt also presided over the start of World War II, during which he helped my grandparents' generation, the "Greatest Generation," believe they could win. He brought hope to a nation in a state of depression.

FDR would leave a lasting legacy in the power of the federal government. He expanded the authority and power of government in ways never before seen in American politics. He called it the New Deal. Under his leadership Social Security was born, as was what was formerly called Aid to Families with Dependent Children. He created the Securities and Exchange Commission and the Federal Deposit Insurance Corporation (FDIC). During his tenure unemployment fell from 25 percent to 2 percent.[188]

Born in 1882 at Hyde Park, New York—now a national historic site—Roosevelt attended Harvard University and Columbia Law School. He is the longest-serving president in U.S. history. Unlike Washington, who could have served as long as he wanted and left after two terms in office, President Roosevelt was beloved and could have served as long as he wanted had he not taken ill and died in 1945.

PRESIDENT LYNDON B. JOHNSON[189]

"Yesterday is not ours to recover, but tomorrow is ours to win or lose." —President Lyndon B. Johnson

Imagine being the vice president to a charismatic and beloved president, a president who was the youngest man ever elected to the office and who had a wife who was the epitome of grace, beauty, and class. Senator John F. Kennedy (covered in Code #1 of this section) was the antithesis of Senate Majority Leader Lyndon B. Johnson.

On the issue of civil rights, Kennedy was much more of a pragmatist. He walked carefully around southern Democrats, whom he needed to help pass other critical legislation important to his administration, such as tax cuts. Kennedy, a wealthy New Englander, attended prep schools and graduated from Harvard University. Johnson was raised poor in Texas.

Johnson transformed from a staunch southern leader to a great southern visionary for civil rights. After the president's assassination in 1963, the task to enact civil rights legislation fell to Johnson. The no-nonsense, six-foot-four Texan had his work cut out for him. Johnson inherited an America in deep turmoil, much like the one that Abraham Lincoln inherited in 1861. But he saw the future by seizing the moment. One of the greatest moments of LBJ's presidency came just days after President Kennedy's burial, when he addressed a joint session of Congress. He seized the moment that was so tragically handed to him and called on the Congress to pass the Civil Rights Act in memory of President Kennedy, who had first introduced it.[190] Greatness comes when men seize the right moments. Johnson knew how to build coalitions and pass legislation. He reached out to Dr. Martin Luther King, Jr., immediately after the death of Kennedy and he assured King that the cause of civil rights would be his great cause, too. And Johnson delivered. In 1965, the Voting Rights Act was passed, again with Johnson's support and heavy hand after the march from Selma to Montgomery, Alabama, was televised and millions of Americans watched on live TV as their fellow citizens were being beaten, some to death, simply for being black.

LBJ, much like FDR, expanded government's reach to help the less fortunate. He dubbed it the "Great Society." Some may argue that this was not such a good thing, because government gained more power over people's lives and their personal liberty. Some say Johnson's administration created a dependency on the federal government.

Johnson summoned the courage to go against his mentor, the powerful, avowed segregationist Richard Russell., Jr., U.S. senator from Georgia. He hired a young black woman named Gerri Whittington to be his personal secretary, the first African American ever to serve a president of the United States in that capacity. Johnson also was the first president to nominate an African-American justice to the Supreme Court, famed civil rights attorney Thurgood Marshall, profiled in Code #4 in Section I.

President Johnson declared a "War on Poverty" in response to the 19 percent of Americans at that time who were living in poverty.[191] The War on Poverty became the unofficial name for legislation first introduced by Johnson during his State of the Union address on January 8, 1964. The speech led Congress to pass the Economic Opportunity Act, which established the Office of Economic Opportunity to administer the local application of federal funds targeted against poverty.

Many of the programs Johnson introduced—including Medicare and Head Start—made a lasting impact in the areas of health, education, urban renewal, conservation, and civil rights. Despite his impressive domestic achievements, however, Johnson's legacy was equally defined by his failure to lead the nation out of the quagmire of the Vietnam War (1954–75). He declined to run for a second full term in office, and retired to his Texas ranch after leaving the White House in January 1969.

Three presidents. Three great leaders. Three men living at very different times in our nation's history. Three great visionaries who changed the course of history in America. Jefferson expanded the American frontier. Roosevelt created Social Security and modern welfare programs, expanded federal public works projects, and built up our military during World War II. Johnson did something quite different. He expanded civil liberties and civil rights. He restored basic human decency to millions of black citizens in the South and impoverished citizens in America by passing powerful legislation to aid them during his two terms in office. All of them understood well our great motto: *E Pluribus Unum—Out of many, one.*

★ ★ ★ ★ ★ ★ ★ ★ ★ ★ ★ ★ ★ ★ ★ ★

Key Leadership Code Points

In this final Code I wanted to end with three Americans who left an indelible mark on the American character and American life. Thomas Jefferson, the greatest of visionaries. Franklin Roosevelt, the great healer during the Great Depression. And Lyndon Johnson, the big and tall Texan with a heart of compassion that brought this nation once and for all back to Jefferson's credo: *All men are created equal.*

The key takeaway from these great men is that, regardless of party affiliation or political persuasion, each loved his country. And each of them expanded the depth and breadth of our nation's promise. One of them, Jefferson, was a staunch Republican who believed in small government. The other two believed in the power of the federal government to do good and expand rights to those who had been wrongfully denied them.

These men ascended to the nation's highest leadership position through a combination of personal gifts, luck, social privilege, education, and hard work. But what each of them shared was a vision of America and her greatness beyond what she was at the time each of them took high office. Jefferson failed to lead on slavery as he wanted to. But he led on our great westward expansion. Roosevelt led our country out of a Great Depression by using the tool of the government to help the people. And Johnson fulfilled the promise of equality for all men one hundred years after the Civil War by signing into law the Civil Rights Act and Voting Right.

★ ★ ★ ★ ★ ★ ★ ★ ★ ★ ★ ★ ★ ★ ★ ★

EPILOGUE

The Culmination of the Founders' Vision

The Founders had a vision. And it was bold. They left us the DNA of a superpowerful and brave America that has for centuries been a beacon of light, liberty, ingenuity, innovation, industry, strength, virtue, exceptionalism, military might, generosity, and compassion to the world. The Founders were not perfect men. In fact, they were imperfect men. They oppressed women and enslaved Africans. They marginalized Native Americans by entering into treaties that kept them as a separate group of nations (tribes) and took this land called "North America" and claimed it as their own. They often put profit over virtue. They did what they felt they had to do to build America and did so with the free labor of slaves and indentured servants, which went against the very ideals they espoused. And by so doing, they set in 1776 a course of disharmony and disunity for our nation that would have to be fought and settled in the great Civil War of 1861.

But we should be clear: America's Founders were men of their time. Men of vision, and yet men of limitation by what they understood as custom and privilege. Perhaps, even by Providence. Women had no rights. And nor did anyone else, except for Anglo-Saxon men. Yet, whatever you believe about the men who forged this great nation in rebellion, and revolted against a king, be clear that they were men who understood that liberty and freedom are at the very core of human happiness. They understood that no man should be held to answer to a tyrannical king or overbearing government. They understood that a man's faith must be his own. And that a great country must be founded on certain virtues and rights that only God himself can give. They got it right, my fellow Americans. They simply got it right!

And the irony of their genius is that despite their own limitations and the constraints and norms of their time, they set in motion a process of American gradualism by which the vision will eventually catch up with itself. When Thomas Jefferson penned the words "We hold these truths to be self-evident," he was making one of the most powerful and purposeful statements in the history of mankind. He was saying that there is in fact, truth. And that one of man's greatest truths is that "all men are created equal" and endowed by their "Creator" with certain "inalienable rights," that among them are the rights of life, liberty, and the pursuit of happiness. Jefferson was a complicated man. Brilliant, eloquent, a patriot. But he like many of our Founders was a slaveholder. Slavery was an institution he personally abhorred, yet he benefited from it. He is alleged to have had a longtime intimate relationship with one of his slaves, Sally Hemings, which resulted in at least five or more children that we know of. Should we throw Jefferson away? Should we consider him an evil man who did not have a conscience, and wish he had made better choices? I think not.

I have heard a lot of commentary as of late on the racism of our Founders and of our founding. And that because America had slaves and denied women basic rights to vote, own property, and the like, somehow there should be no celebration of our Founders. I respectfully disagree. America is bigger than the fifty-five men who signed the Declaration of Independence. America, as I said at the outset of this book, is the story of "us," of all of "us," of "we the people." America eventually righted her wrongs against African Americans and women, as we saw in the various Codes of our founding. And the great men and women who forced this nation to live up to its best and greatest ideals. The men and women profiled in this book had great courage, conviction, character, and a common belief that despite her flaws America could be the greatest nation ever on the face of the earth.

Yet, in order to accurately understand America and who we are in 2017, you must look back to how we began in 1776. The rancor and division that we have all experienced over the past year or more in our great nation is a symptom that we have traveled too far from our Code. Our unique and amazing American Code. Our values. Our core. Our pride. And our love of freedom and liberty for all.

PRESIDENT BARACK H. OBAMA[192]

"Change will not come if we wait for some other
person or some other time. We are the ones we've been
waiting for. We are the change that we seek."
—*President Barack H. Obama*

As I write this, the current president of the United States is still a man named Barack H. Obama. He is by birth part African and part American. Barack Obama is the forty-fourth president of the United States. His story is the American story— raised with the values of the heartland, a middle-class upbringing in a strong family, hard work overcoming life's obstacles and stumbling blocks, as well as a good education that allowed him to get ahead, and the conviction that he needed to enter into public service to help others.

His father, Barack Obama, Sr., hailed from Kenya and his mother, Ann Dunham, from Kansas. Barack Obama, Jr., was born in Hawaii on August 4, 1961. He was raised with help from his grandfather, who had served in World War II in Patton's army, and from his grandmother, who worked her way up from the secretarial pool to middle management at a bank. After working his way through college with the help of scholarships and student loans, Obama moved to Chicago, where he worked with a group of churches to help rebuild communities devastated by the closure of local steel plants. He went on to attend law school, where he became the first African-American president of the *Harvard Law Review*. Upon graduation, he returned to Chicago to help lead a voter registration drive, teach constitutional law at the University of Chicago, and remain active in his community.

President Obama is married to First Lady Michelle Obama and is the father of two teenage daughters. He was elected to the United States Senate in 2004 from the great state of Illinois. And he was elected to the presidency in November 2008. His two most notable achievements while commander in chief and president is the raid carried out by Navy SEALs on the Pakistan compound of 9/11 mastermind terrorist Osama bin Laden, which led to bin Laden's killing, and the passage of Obamacare, which is America's version of universal health care.

Whether you like President Obama or not, agree with his policies or not, he is the culmination of what our Founders set in motion more than 240 years ago. It took more than 230 years for America to elect an African-American president, but the point is that we elected a man of such background because our Constitution and our Code works. It always works. Also worth noting is that in the late summer of 2016, Hillary Rodham Clinton became the first woman to ever win a major political party nomination for president of the United States. And although she didn't win the election, she has made it possible for a woman to become the president of our nation in the future. Once again, the great vision of our founding and the amazing documents drafted around our national virtues paved the way for these two people, these two Americans, to make history.

Where We Go from Here

My hope is that this book inspires us to love our great country in a deeper and richer way. And that we all come to agree and embrace that we are in fact always stronger and better together. That we are always better when our diversity is viewed as our strength. The men and women profiled in this book are a microcosm of the talent and contributions put forth for this country by Americans just like them. We still have great men and women walking among us. We must dare to start a national conversation about who we are as Americans and what we want from America. It is time to move forward. It is time to move to our next great American century.

I encourage you to take the last section of each of the sixteen Codes and use them as a discussion guide in your book clubs and classrooms. This book is a reminder of how we started and of the many great men and women who came before us to keep us on course to fulfilling the promise of the great words penned by Thomas Jefferson, "We hold these truths to be self-evident, that all men are created equal, that they are endowed by their Creator with certain unalienable Rights, that among these are Life, Liberty and the pursuit of Happiness." America started out with some major imperfections for sure. But gradually we got it right. The men and women profiled in this book made us live up to the promise of our founding through their faith and devotion to the greatest and highest good for all Americans. America is not perfect. But America is always striving to become a more perfect union. Thank you for reading this book. God bless you and God bless the United States of America.

ACKNOWLEDGMENTS

It is by God's grace that I have finished and published my third nonfiction book in a five-year period. I am thankful to God for His grace and mercy, His providence over America the beautiful, and His continual provision over and for me.

My first two books were about and for women, and I acknowledged all the women in my life who have helped me in each work. This time I want to acknowledge the men in my life who have helped to support, encourage, mentor, and lift me when life was challenging. First to the men in my family who wore the uniform of the United States Army: Staff Sergeant Samuel E. Smith, maternal grandfather (World War II, Korea, Vietnam, Purple Heart and Bronze Star recipient); Sergeant Ronald Nelson, Sr., father (Vietnam, decorated); Sgt. Douglass A. Ward, Sr. maternal uncle (Vietnam, decorated); and Lieutenant (promoted to Captain) Ronald Nelson, Jr., brother (post-911 Middle East, Signal Corps). Thank you for your service to your nation. And the model you set for me about service, honor, and valor.

A big shout-out to all of my big brothers, who really helped me get through the manuscript with prayers, support, and encouragement during a very challenging season for my family; as well as to those who have supported me in general throughout my life with great encouragement, prayer, counsel, friendship, and mentorship: Senator Joe Kyrillos (R-NJ), my longtime friend and mentor. Bishop T. D. Jakes, Bishop Clifford Johnson, Pastor John K. Jenkins, Pastor Charlie Whitlow, Minister Mark Thompson, Brothers James Redic and Joseph Tucker. My security detail and big brother Reginald Williams. Little/big brother Devon Franklin. My two newer big brothers, actor Dondre Whitfield and Walgreens executive/author Steve Pemberton. Roland Martin. Mark Wilson, MD. Colonel Angelo Haygood (USAF, retired), Colonel Darold Hamlin (USA, retired), Raoul Davis (Ascendant Group), the best IP attorney in the world Robert Labate, Esq. (Holland & Knight LLP), Ron Nelson, Jr. (my brother), Dr. Floyd Hayes, Greg Campbell, Jeff Riner, Uncle Eddie Daniels, Dan Agatino, Esq., Jeff Armstrong, Mike Woodsmall, John Mitchell, Dan Cooper, Max Lancaster, Dr. Fred Steinberg, and Mike Spokony. Also my new neighbors Clifford and John.

Thank you to Dupree Miller for taking me on as a literary client, and taking my writing career to the next level. To my publisher Hachette/Center Street division for making this book a reality in such a short time frame. Kate Hartson, Grace Tweedy, and to my longtime former literary agent, second mom, and now editorial manager, Claudia Menza; it was a wild ride but we did it!! A special thanks to Ralph Lauren (Tyson's Corner, Virginia), Glam Squad (Tina, Summer, Kandi, in Dallas, Texas), Jas. Townsend and Sons Historic & Reproduction Clothing, and

Jessi Zhou/Arthur Christine Editorial Refinement Photography & Videography.

As in every book, I give a great shout-out to my mom, Sandria A. Nelson. She is my ride-or-die chick. And she always gives me great feedback on my books before they go to print. Thanks, Mom. I love you. And big hugs to my only living grandparent, my maternal grandmother Evelyn M. Smith, who will be eighty-six this January 15, and who got to see me speak and sign my last book in 2016. To all my maternal aunts: Debbie, Belinda, Brenda, Sharon, and Regina. Thanks for being my biggest cheerleaders all of my life. I want to list the names of some key members of my vast "girl tribe," whom I love so very much. These women pray for me, love me, check me, push me, support me, cry with me, and celebrate me. I could not have done this without you. Thank you.

Sorors Serita A. Jakes, Madame Supreme Dorothy Buchanan Wilson, Pastor Renee Hornbuckle, TJ, Haygood (BFF), Chelle Wilson (2nd BFF), Trish L. Smith, Monica Wood, Kayla Tucker Adams, Zakia Larry, Angela Pitcher, Deidre Fontaine, Lesleigh Robertson, Adrienne Gibson, Kay Broady, Lisa Riley and Mary Ann Jackson, Adrienne, Roz, PRO sorors, Barbara Sutton, Dawn Baskerville, Lisa Bennett, and to all of my pink and green ladies all over the United States who have bought out all of my books so faithfully and hosted amazing events. Lady Trina Jenkins, Lady Alethia Ramsey, Talaya Simpson (my biggest champion), Michel Wright, Andrea Morris (sisters forever), Carla Farmer (what a blessing to know you), Shenita Muse (so grateful for you, girl) Patricia Tichenor (what would

I do without you sister), PJ, Lauren, Tina Moore, Cheryl Williams (my favorite Delta), Carla Shellis (my sister from another mother), Amy Griffiths (friends for over twenty-five years), Carmen Studer, Shonny Young, Anna McCoy, Donna Joyner, Tanyai Cato and Angel Williams, Towanna Freeman, Dishan Winters, Dr. Sabrina Jackson, Chandra Cooper, Vanessa Maddox, Mira Lowe, Michel Wright, Barbara Holt Streeter, Lauren Zingraff, Val Meekins, Shawn Meekins, Sweet Melani Ismail, Crystal Smith, Kimmie Woodsmall, Monique Pressley, and Mikki Taylor! To my Philly posse Andrea Agnew, Kim S. Reed, Terri Dean, Barb, Tina, got nothing but love for you. To Cousins Brittani and Shanitra, proud of you both. To Angie Harmon, Garcelle, Lorraine Bracco, Karen Horne, Traci Blackwell (girl, you and Diana kept me straight when it got crazy!!!), Holly Carter, Keesha and Dana Sims at ICM, I love my Hollywood girl posse!

Last, but not least, Terrell A. Fletcher. You already know what you mean to me. How rare that two people get to share such a special relationship and acknowledge each other in their respective books within four months of publication. I will never forget 2015, when both our parents (my mom and your dad) took ill and we were there for each other ride or die just as I was starting to outline this book. Thank you for being the nerd, renaissance man, to my nerd, renaissance woman. I will forever treasure our amazing courageous conversations (some were hard but we always got through them wiser), our purposeful and powerful prayers, the trust and the tears, the marathon phone calls, challenging one another to be our best all-around selves, the crazy laughter, the discussions about America, the church, your ordination service as a bishop in the church, the Woman Code LA event (where you were brave enough to be the only guy in the room supporting me), and our priceless walks and talks in La Jolla Cove, Mission Beach, Coronado, and San Diego. Most of all I will never forget touring the Lincoln and MLK, Jr., Memorials at night in Washington, D.C. in the dead of winter. And spending all day at Arlington National Cemetery paying our respects to our national heroes. These are priceless times forever treasured by me. I am very proud of all you've accomplished this past year: a new author, a new Bishop, and a PhD candidate. Know that no matter where life takes us, I will always be here cheering you on.

Love you all. Very much. I have an amazing life front row!!

ENDNOTES

1 Quoting Lincoln's acceptance of the Republican nomination address of June 15, 1858, Old State Capitol Springfield Illinois.

2 *The Eclipse of White Christian America*, Robert P. Jones. The Atlantic Magazine. July 12, 2016.

3 Ibid.

4 See CharlesThompson.com; Philadelphia Historical Society, Greatseal.com: "Although few people today have heard of Charles Thomson (1729–1824), he was one of America's most significant and influential Founding Fathers—a man very well qualified to translate the idea and ideals of America into symbolic imagery." John Jay, who became the first Chief Justice of the U.S. Supreme Court in 1789, wrote in a letter to Thomson six years earlier: "I consider that no Person in the World is so perfectly acquainted with the Rise, Conduct, and Conclusion of the American Revolution, as yourself." As the only secretary of the Continental Congress for its entire fifteen years, Thomson was a tremendous unifying factor. He kept the minutes of all sessions of Congress, including special minutes of all the secret affairs. His journals and files became the archives of our nation.

5 The Atlantic Slave Trade. Digital America. 2016.

6 Slavery in the Colonies: Stats on Slavery, Weber State University; slave population of the U.S. 1790–1860 (U.S. Census returns), and University of Delaware, Center for Teachers' Education, Slavery Statistics in the Colonies and Post-Revolutionary War.

7 *Washington Times*, March 28, 2008.

8 Millennials are totally mixed up about what they believe in, *New York Post*, September 3, 2016, Kyle Smith.

9 Gallup Polling Data via CBS News: http://www.cbsnews.com/news/poll-congress-approval-rating-drops-to-11-percent/.

10 Howard J. Gold, "Americans' attitudes toward political parties and the party system," *Oxford Journal*, 2015.

11 America's Electoral Future: How Changing Demographics Could Impact Presidential Elections from 2016–2032, February 2016. *Politico* exit polls 2008. http://www.politico.com/story/2008/11/exit-polls-how-obama-won-015297, and NBC News reporting http://firstread.nbcnews.com/_news/2012/11/19/15282553-obama-performance-with-white-voters-on-par-with-other-democrats?lite.

12 Ibid.

13 Bishop T. D. Jakes commissioned two studies. The April 2016 study was the second of two that he commissioned between 2015 and 2016.

14 Declaration of Independence, July 4, 1776, Philadelphia.

15 James Madison, *The Federalist Papers*, No. 10 (1787).

16 This quote is often misquoted as Thomas Jefferson but accurately sums up his beliefs. It first appears in an online article. This quotation seems to have originated in an article of the same title on PicktheBusiness.com. It is an accurate paraphrase of Jefferson's views on education, but the exact phrasing seems to belong to the author of the article, and not Jefferson. The article title appears to have been mistaken by others as a direct quotation from Jefferson's 1816 letter to Charles Yancey, which is mentioned in the article, but the exact quotation does not appear in that letter or in any other known Jefferson writings. Source: Monticello.org.

17 Source of Paul Revere's biographical sketch compiled by Paul Revere Heritage Project, Biography.com, History.com, Massachusetts Historical Society.

18 Paul Revere's most famous quote, "The British are coming," is actually a misquote. He never said it. Historians point out that at the time of the English invasion, most colonists still considered themselves British, so the phrase would have been meaningless to them. If Revere said anything at all, which many historians question because shouting could have drawn unwanted attention from English soldiers, it would have been to the effect of the "Regulars." *Regulars* was the term colonists used to refer to British soldiers. Contrary to popular belief, Paul Revere did not ride alone on the journey during which he supposedly uttered his most famous words. At least two other men rode with him.

19 Paul Revere's military service from *Encyclopaedia Britannica*, https://www.britannica.com/biography/Paul-Revere.

20 Sources used to compile biography of Elizabeth Cady Stanton: History.net Elizabeth Cady Stanton page, Wikipedia, and the National Park Service.

21 Declaration of Sentiments, document outlining the rights that American women should be entitled to as citizens, which emerged from the Seneca Falls Convention in New York in July 1848. "Resolved, therefore, That, being invested by the Creator with the same capabilities, and the same consciousness of responsibility for their exercise, it is demonstrably the right and duty of woman, equally with man, to promote every righteous cause, by every righteous means; and especially in regard to the great subjects of morals and religion, it is self-evidently her right to participate with her brother in teaching them, both in private and in public, by writing and by speaking,

by any instrumentalities proper to be used, and in any assemblies proper to be held; and this being a self-evident truth, growing out of the divinely implanted principles of human nature, any custom or authority adverse to it, whether modern or wearing the hoary sanction of antiquity, is to be regarded as self-evident falsehood, and at war with the interests of mankind."

22 Wikipedia.

23 History.net, Elizabeth Cady Stanton profile.

24 Sir Edmund Burke quotations from GoodReads. See also *Bartlett's Quotations.*

25 *The Autobiography of Ben Franklin* was published in 1793, three years after Franklin's death.

26 Sources used for Ben Franklin biographical sketch include Wikipedia, Biography.com, History.com.

27 Thirteenvirtues.com, dedicated to these virtuous principles of Ben Franklin.

28 Walter Isaacson, *Benjamin Franklin: An American Life* (New York: Simon & Schuster, 2003).

29 Sources used for Harriett Beecher Stowe biographical sketch include Biography.com, History.com, and Wikipedia.

30 Wikipedia.

31 Harriet Beecher Stowe letters and personal archives, as well as the Fugitive Slave Act of 1850.

32 In 1832, twenty-one-year-old Harriet Beecher moved with her family to Cincinnati, where her father, Lyman, became president of Lane Theological Seminary. There she met and married Calvin Stowe, a theology professor she described as "rich in Greek & Hebrew, Latin & Arabic, and alas rich in nothing else." Six of Stowe's seven children were born in Cincinnati, and in the summer of 1849, Stowe experienced for the first time the sorrow many nineteenth-century parents knew when her eighteen-month-old son, Samuel Charles Stowe, died of cholera. Stowe later credited that crushing pain as one of the inspirations for *Uncle Tom's Cabin* because it helped her understand the pain enslaved mothers felt when their children were taken from them to be sold.

33 See Wikipedia, https://en.wikipedia.org/wiki/Harriet_Beecher_Stowe.

34 United States Constitution, Bill of Rights.

35 See website dedicated to Ralph Waldo Emerson, EmersonCentral.com, Essay II on "Self-Reliance," 1841.

36 Sources used for Jackie Robinson biographical sketch include Jackie Robinson Foundation, Wikipedia, Biography.com, and History.com.

37 Jackie Robinson Foundation and Biography.com.

38 Sources for Amelia Earhart biographical sketch include Biography.com, History.com, and Wikipedia.

39 Wikipedia.

40 The actual quote is: "I disapprove of what you say, but I will defend to the death your right to say it." It was written by English author Evelyn Beatrice Hall in 1903, writing about Voltaire. Pseudonym is S. G. Tallentyre.

41 "What Kind of Nation Did the Founders Aim to Create," *National Review*, July 3, 2015.

42 Ibid.

43 Library of Congress, Primary Documents in American History. The Continental Congress adopted the Articles of Confederation, the first constitution of the United States, on November 15, 1777. However, ratification of the Articles by all thirteen states did not occur until March 1, 1781. The Articles created a loose confederation of sovereign states and a weak central government, leaving most of the power with the state governments. The need for a stronger Federal government soon became apparent and eventually led to the Constitutional Convention in 1787. The present United States Constitution replaced the Articles of Confederation on March 4, 1789.

44 Bill Clinton Speech declaring "The era of big government is over," State of the Union address, January 23, 1996, Joint Address to 104th Congress.

45 Sources used to compile biographical sketches for Bob Woodward and Carl Bernstein include *Washington Post* archives, Biography.com, Wikipedia.

46 Sources used for Thurgood Marshall biographical sketch include NAACP, Biography.com, History.com, and United States Supreme Court archives.

47 Biography.com and NAACP archives.

48 Wikipedia.

49 Thomas Jefferson, First Inaugural Address, March 1, 1804.

50 See Foundation for Economic Education article by John Majewski, July 1, 1986, "The Industrial Revolution: Working Class Poverty or Prosperity." See also Wikipedia and History.com.

51 History Channel's *The Men Who Built America* (also known as *The Innovators: The Men Who Built America* in some international markets) is a six-hour, four-part miniseries docudrama broadcast in fall 2012. The series focuses on Cornelius Vanderbilt, John D. Rockefeller, Andrew Carnegie, J. P. Morgan, and Henry Ford and how their industrial innovations and business empires revolutionized modern society. Their names are synonymous with innovation

and big business in America. They all built empires and created advances in technology. They helped shape the country in its early days by doing things such as developing the models for modern railroads, creating the modern financial system, and making cars accessible to the masses. The men came from meager beginnings to build their respective empires, which helped formulate the concept of the American Dream.

52 Ibid.

53 Laurel King, "Trust Buster Theodore Roosevelt," AboutTheodoreRoosevelt. com, November 6, 2013.

54 Ibid.

55 Theodore Roosevelt State of the Union address, December 2, 1902, cited in Stephen D. Foster, Jr., "What the Founding Fathers Thought About Corporations," AddictingInfo.com, June 9, 2013.

56 In *United States v. Lopez* (1995), the Supreme Court ruled that Congress had exceeded its constitutional authority under the commerce clause when it passed a law prohibiting gun possession in local school zones.

57 Sources used for Richard Sears biographical sketch include Sears archives, Wikipedia, and Britannica.com.

58 Edward Stegerson is mentioned in the Sears biography on Wikipedia as being the changing event in his young life as a merchant. Stegerson rejecting the watches turned into Sears's fortune.

59 Wikipedia.

60 Ibid.

61 Ibid.

62 Quote from The Official Madam C. J. Walker website: Madamcjwalker.com

63 Permission granted by A'Lelia Bundles, author of *On Her Own Ground: The Life and Times of Madam C. J. Walker* (New York: Scribner, 2001). The official website used to develop the biographical sketch on Madam C. J. Walker is www.madamcjwalker.com.

64 Thomas Jefferson took the phrase "pursuit of happiness" from Locke and incorporated it into his famous statement of a peoples' inalienable right to "life, liberty, and the pursuit of happiness" in the Declaration of Independence. Locke coined the phrase "pursuit of happiness" in his book *An Essay Concerning Human Understanding,* 1689 and 1690.

65 James Madison, Federalist Papers 51, February 6, 1788, speech to New York *Independent Journal.*

66 "Woman Who Rejected Marriage Offer Burnt to Death," BBC World News, http://www.bbc.com/news/world-asia-36425946, June 1, 2016.

67 Francis Hutcheson, 1725 treatise, *An Inquiry into the Origin of Our Ideas of Beauty and Virtue.*

68 "Lexical Investigations: Happiness," Dictionary.com/blog, October 1, 2013.

69 Justice Anthony Kennedy, 2005 speech to National Conference on Citizenship, as quoted in ibid.

70 Sources used for Tecumseh biographical sketch include Ohiocentralhistory. com, Biography.com, and Wikipedia.

71 1813 Tecumseh speech at Fort Malden, historical marker preserves the text of the speech. Adapted part of that speech for this Code to show that native Americans wanted to preserve their land as much as the Colonists did from the British.

72 Source used to compile Alice Paul biographical sketch include Wikipedia. com, AlicePaul.com, and History.com.

73 Sources used for Rosa Parks biographical sketch include Biography.com, History.com, and her autobiography *Quiet Strength: The Faith, the Hope, and the Heart of a Woman Who Changed a Nation* (Grand Rapids, MI: Zondervan, 1994); Library of Congress archives.

74 *Montgomery Advertiser,* December 1, 1955, through December 6, 1955.

75 Sources used for Martin Luther King biographical sketch include Wikipedia, History.com, Biography.com, and primary newspaper articles, speeches, and writings.

76 This quote comes from Dr. King's first speech as the NAACP president on the night Rosa Parks was arrested, December 1, 1955, in Montgomery, Alabama.

77 Martin Luther King, Jr., speech, August 28, 1963. (Permission in process from the King Center in Atlanta.)

78 Ibid.

79 Scott E. Yenor, "The True Origin of Society: The American Founders on Marriage and Family," Heritage Foundation, October 16, 2013.

80 Ryan T. Anderson, "Marriage as Purposeful Institution," Heritage Foundation, April 23, 2013.

81 See note 1, also National Center for Constitutional Studies, "Marriage and Family: The Stabilizing Foundation of Civilizations," July 1, 2014.

82 United States Census Bureau. As of summer 2016 the population is 324.6 million Americans.

83 Thomas Jefferson, letter to James Monroe from Paris, June 17, 1785; Monticello website and archives.

84 Sources used for the Lovings' biographical sketch include ACLU.org, U.S.

Supreme Court Archives, Encyclopedia Virginia, and Biography.com.

85 Sources used for Caser Chavez biographical sketch include Biography.com, History.com, and ufw.org (United Farm Workers).

86 Sources used to compile the biographical sketch of Alex Haley include Biography.com, Britannica.com, and History.com.

87 John Madison in his speech to the Virginia General Assembly, June 20, 1785, Federalist Papers No. 8.

88 Fundamental Orders of Connecticut. The Fundamental Orders, inspired by Thomas Hooker's sermon of May 31, 1638, provided the framework for the government of Connecticut colony from 1639 to 1662. For two years before the adoption of the Fundamental Orders, Windsor, Hartford, and Wethersfield cooperated under a simple form of government composed of magistrates and representatives from each town, but the towns had no formal instrument of government. Roger Ludlow of Windsor, the only trained lawyer in the colony, probably drafted the Fundamental Orders, although he may have been assisted by Hartford residents John Haynes (a former governor of the Massachusetts Bay Colony), Edward Hopkins, and John Steel. The document consisted of a preamble and eleven orders or laws. The preamble was a covenant that bound the three towns to be governed in all civil matters by the orders. The preamble, then, was a civil equivalent of a church covenant. (The model of the biblical covenant served as the foundation for all Puritan organizations.) The Connecticut General Court adopted the Fundamental Orders on January 14, 1639. (The colonists did not follow current conventions for marking a year and, thus, the date on the document itself is listed as 1638.) See http://connecticuthistory.org/the-fundamental-orders-of-connecticut.

89 Frank Lambert, *The Founding Fathers and the Place of Religion in America*, March 19, 2006.

90 See religioustolerance.org.

91 First U.S. Congress convened on June 8, 1789. http://teachingamericanhistory.org/bor/madison_17890608/.

92 Sources for Muhammad Ali biographical sketch include *Sports Illustrated*, Biography.com, and Wikipedia.

93 Sources for Sojourner Truth biographical sketch include Wikipedia, Biography.com, and National Park Service website biography on Truth.

94 *Anti-Slavery Bugle*, October 1856.

95 Sabbath School Convention, Battle Creek, Michigan, June 1863.

96 *Anti-Slavery Bugle*, June 1851.

97 Joyce Lee Malcolm, "*The Rights of the People to Keep and Bear Arms: The*

Common Law Foundation," *Hastings Constitutional Law Quarterly* (1983): 285–314, Constitution.org.

98 U.S. Constitution, Article I. Sec. 8.

99 The Militia Act of 1792, passed May 8, 1792, providing federal standards for the organization of the militia. "An ACT more effectually to provide for the National Defence, by establishing a Uniform Militia throughout the United States."

100 Ibid.

101 "Guns and America," *Saturday Evening Post*, October 24, 2011, http://www.saturdayeveningpost.com/2011/10/24/in-the-magazine/trends-and-opinions/guns-and-america.html; Encylopedia.com.

102 Tim Brown, "The British Banned Guns on Our Founding Fathers—It Brought About a Revolution," Freedomoutpost.com, January 22, 2013, http://freedomoutpost.com/the-british-banned-guns-on-our-fathers-it-brought-about-a-revolution/.

103 Wikipedia, History.com, American Revolutionary War facts website: http://www.american-revolutionary-war-facts.com/Events-Leading-To-American-Revolution/Quartering-Act-Facts.html.

104 At the outbreak of the American Revolution, Lancaster riflemen were among the first to march to Boston. It was the largest and wealthiest inland town in the American colonies. Lancaster and its patriots had a great impact on the Revolutionary War and the growth of the nation after the war.

105 Richard Henry Lee, *Federal Farmer No. 18*, January 25, 1788; James Madison Research Library and Information Center.

106 Thomas B. McAffee and Michael J. Quinlan Jr., "Bringing Forward the Right to Keep and Bear Arms: Do Text, History, or Precedent Stand in the Way?," 1997, Scholarly Works, Paper 512; Jack N. Rakove, *Original Meanings: Politics and Ideas in the Making of the Constitution* (New York: Knopf, 1996).

107 William Blackstone, "Right of Revolution," *Commentaries* 1:119–23, 157, 237–38, 243–44.

108 *District of Columbia v. Heller*, 554 U.S. 570 (2008), was a landmark case in which the Supreme Court of the United States held in a 5–4 decision that the Second Amendment to the United States Constitution applies to federal enclaves and protects an individual's right to possess a firearm for traditionally lawful purposes, such as self-defense within the home. The decision did not address the question of whether the Second Amendment extends beyond federal enclaves to the states, which was addressed later by *McDonald v. Chicago* (2010). It was the first

Supreme Court case to decide whether the Second Amendment protects an individual's right to keep and bear arms for self-defense. On June 26, 2008, the Supreme Court affirmed the Court of Appeals for the D.C. Circuit in *Heller v. District of Columbia*. The Supreme Court struck down provisions of the Firearms Control Regulations Act of 1975 as unconstitutional, determined that handguns are "arms" for the purposes of the Second Amendment, found that the Regulations Act was an unconstitutional ban, and struck down the portion of the Regulations Act that requires all firearms including rifles and shotguns be kept "unloaded and disassembled or bound by a trigger lock." Prior to this decision the Firearms Control Regulation Act of 1975 also restricted residents from owning handguns except for those registered prior to 1975.

109 Thomas Jefferson, *Commonplace Book*, quoting eighteenth-century criminologist Cesare Beccaria, 1774–76.

110 Pennsylvania Constitution of 1776, Declaration of Rights, art. 13. XIII. "That the people have a right to bear arms for the defence of themselves and the state; and as standing armies in the time of peace are dangerous to liberty, they ought not to be kept up; And that the military should be kept under strict subordination to, and governed by, the civil power."

111 Ibid.

112 See note 98.

113 Gordon S. Wood, *Revolutionary Characters: What Made the Founders Different* (New York: Penguin, 2006).

114 Tensions started between colonists and the Crown over a series of taxing edicts from 1768 to 1770. There are three major things that led to the Boston Massacre: First was the growing mistrust among the British soldiers and Americans. There were a number of other incidents where the British clashed with the patriots and their supporters. Individual soldiers were beaten on street corners and soldiers abused unarmed civilians. The Americans in Boston made it clear that the British soldiers were unwanted. The second reason is somewhat odd. The removal of two out of four regiments meant there were inadequate numbers of soldiers to keep the peace. There were enough on the other hand to remind the patriots of the great British military. The last reason would be the revolt of the Townshend Acts. The patriots and Americans did not agree and strife with the British soldiers over it. The Act built tension between the two. On March 5, 1770 the dreadful day came. A mob of people went in front of the Customs Office in Boston and started to throw things and insult the soldiers. As a result, to this so-called harassment the soldiers fired on the crowd. The first to die was an African-American man named Crispus

Attucks. He was a native of Framingham, Massachusetts. He escaped
from slavery in 1750 and had become a sailor. Crispus Attucks is considered
the first martyr of the American independence. The four others who
died were Samuel Gray, a rope maker; James Caldwell, a sailor; Samuel
Maverick, a seventeen-year-old apprentice; and Patrick Carr, a leather
worker and Irish immigrant. All were unarmed and brutally murdered.
The soldiers provoked the citizens countless times. "British soldiers and
citizens fought and clashed during the winter of 1769." The soldiers even
fired in the streets, endangering a great number of lives. The soldiers
also frequently wounded people with their bayonets and cutlasses. "The
numerous instances of bad behavior in the soldiery, made us early sensible
that the troops were not sent here for any benefit to the town or province,
and that no good to expect from such conservators of the peace." http://
www.bostonmassacre.net/academic/essay2.htm.

115 Sources for President Kennedy biographical sketch include Official White
House website, John F. Kennedy Presidential Library, Biography.com, and
History.com.

116 Sources for Jacqueline Bouvier Kennedy Onassis biographical sketch
include Official White House website, Biography.com, and John F.
Kennedy Presidential Library.

117 Ibid.

118 Alexander Marriott, "Republic, Democracy. What's the Difference?,"
Capitalism Magazine, January 4, 2003.

119 James Madison, Federalist Papers No. 51.

120 James D. Best, "The Founder's Fears," September 14, 2011. James D. Best
is the author of *Tempest at Dawn*, a novel about the 1787 Constitutional
Convention, and *Principled Action, Lessons from the Origins of the American
Republic*.

121 Sources for Sam Adams biographical sketch include Massachusetts
Historical Society, Wikipedia, and Biography.com.

122 The Sons of Liberty started out as a secret Boston association known
as The Loyal Nine, composed of elite gentlemen, mainly law men and
artisans, who met discreetly to organize ways to begin to effectively oppose
the actions of the Crown. The Loyal Nine were responsible for putting
boundaries on the rampant violence of Boston, and setting limits on how
far the demonstrations should progress. They actively stood against British
policies they found to be immoral and unlawful, and had their hands in
projects such as The Boston Tea Party.

123 Intentionally deleted.

124 Sources used for Shirley Chisholm biographical sketch include Biography. com, History.com, and the *Congressional Record*.

125 *New York Times*, quotes by History.House.gov/ShirleyChisholm.

126 Wikipedia, France's Role in the U.S. Revolutionary War.

127 http://www.naturalawakeningsmag.com/Natural-Awakenings/October-2012/The-Four-Qualities-of-a-True-Statesman/.

128 Sources for biographical sketch for General George C. Marshall compiled from the George C. Marshall Foundation (marshallfoundation.org), Wikipedia, History.com.

129 Sources for Shirley Temple Black biographical sketch include Biography. com, History.com., Britannica.com, and Wikipedia.

130 Uri Friedman, "Shirley Temple: Actress, Ambassador, Honorary African Chief," Atlantic, February 11, 2014.

131 *Politico*, "Shirley Temple: 10 Political Facts," 2014.

132 Abigail Adams, *The Letters of John and Abigail Adams*.

133 Don Fehrenbacher, *The Slaveholding Republic* (New York: Oxford University Press, 2001), 36–38, 218, 244; cf. D. L. Robinson, *Slavery in the Structure of American Politics* (New York: Norton, 1979), 23–24 and Ch. 5.

134 Sources used to compile this section on the Radical Republicans of the 1860s and Representative Thaddeus Stevens include Wikipedia, Britannica.com, Steve Moyer, "Remarkable Radical—Thaddeus Stevens," *Humanities* 33, no. 6 (November/December 2012).

135 Sources used to compile biographical sketch of Justice Earl Warren include U.S. Supreme Court archives, Wikipedia, Biography.com, PBS, and Britannica.com. See also University of California, San Diego archives: https://warren.ucsd.edu/about/biography.html; Warren College.

136 Bernard Schwartz, *Super Chief: Earl Warren and His Supreme Court* (New York: New York University Press, 1983).

137 Mark Tushnet, The Warren Court in Historical and Political Perspective (Charlottesville: University Press of Virginia, 1993), p. 40.

138 The Articles of Confederation was the first written constitution of the United States. Stemming from wartime urgency, its progress was slowed by fears of central authority and extensive land claims by states before it was ratified on March 1, 1781. Under these articles, the states remained sovereign and independent, with Congress serving as the last resort on appeal of disputes. Congress was also given the authority to make treaties and alliances, maintain armed forces, and coin money. However, the central government lacked the ability to levy taxes and regulate commerce,

issues that led to the Constitutional Convention in 1787 for the creation of new federal laws.

139 Ibid.

140 Up until September 9, 1776, the colonists called themselves the United Colonies. After we declared independence on July 4, it took about three months before the Congress declared the nation as the "United States." In the congressional declaration dated September 9, 1776, the delegates wrote, "That in all continental commissions, and other instruments, where, heretofore, the words 'United Colonies' have been used, the stile be altered for the future to the 'United States.' Source: History.com.

141 Lincoln used the Emancipation Proclamation strategically to keep foreign powers from getting into the Civil War. Both Britain and France had considered supporting the Confederacy in order to expand their influence in the Western Hemisphere. However, many Europeans were against slavery. Although some in the United Kingdom saw the Emancipation Proclamation as overly limited and reckless, Lincoln's directive reinforced the shift of the international political mood against intervention while the Union victory at Antietam further disturbed those who didn't want to intervene on the side of a lost cause. Source: CivilWar.org, "10 Facts About the Emancipation Proclamation."

142 James Madison, *The Federalist Papers.*

143 On March 16, 1802, the United States Congress authorized President Thomas Jefferson to organize a Corps of Engineers, which "shall be stationed at West Point . . . and shall constitute a military academy." The chief engineer of the Corps would be the superintendent of the academy, and the secretary of war would purchase books, implements, and apparatus for the institution. The idea of an American military academy had developed during the American Revolution and was supported by many of the Founding Fathers, but it had a difficult journey to becoming reality. Americans were suspicious of military power because of their very unpleasant experiences under the British Empire. The Declaration of Independence had listed many grievances against George III, two of which were: "He has kept among us, in Times of Peace, Standing Armies, without the consent of our Legislatures," and "He has affected to render the Military independent of, and superior to the Civil Power." During the revolution itself, the revolt of the Pennsylvania Line and the Newburgh plot added to the uneasiness over "standing armies." Nevertheless, the contacts between Continental Army officers and the European officers who had come to aid the American cause convinced

the Americans that they must have a trained officer corps, especially in the scientific fields of artillery and engineering. Key to this was the alliance with France, many of whose officers had been trained at the excellent Ecole Militaire. Even before the French arrived, however, Colonel Henry Knox of the artillery, Washington's future secretary of war, was proposing a military academy. Knox, who had been the proprietor of the London Book Store in Boston before the revolution, educated himself in military affairs not only by reading his stock of books, but also by talking with British officers who were stationed in the city. He eventually joined a local militia company, the crack Boston Grenadier Corps. Source: Schiller Institute.

144 Mackenzie Eaglen, "Why Provide for the Common Defense," Heritage Foundation, January 19, 2011, http://www.heritage.org/research/reports/2011/01/why-provide-for-the-common-defense.

145 Michael F. Cairo, "Civilian Control of the Military," Democracy Papers, https://www.ait.org.tw/infousa/zhtw/DOCS/Demopaper/dmpaper12.html. U.S. Defense Spending 2016, Congressional Research Office, GAO Reports, Congressional Record. Department of Defense Annual Budget and Spending Reports.

146 "Standing on the tiny deck of the *Arbella* in 1630 off the Massachusetts coast, John Winthrop said, 'We will be as a city upon a hill. The eyes of all people are upon us, so that if we deal falsely with our God in this work we have undertaken and so cause Him to withdraw His present help from us, we shall be made a story and a byword throughout the world.'"

147 Sources for the biographical sketch of Patrick Henry include Wikipedia, Britannica.com, History.com, and the Patrick Henry Center for Individual Liberty, Centerville, VA.

148 Source: Patrick Henry Center for Individual Liberty website.

149 Sources for the biographical sketch of Teddy Roosevelt include Biography.com, History.com, and official White House website.

150 The first known use of the phrase occurs in a private letter from Roosevelt (then governor of New York) to Henry L. Sprague, dated January 26, 1900. Roosevelt wrote, in a bout of happiness after forcing New York's Republican committee to pull support away from a corrupt financial adviser: "I have always been fond of the West African proverb: 'Speak softly and carry a big stick; you will go far.'" In an article about an interview with Governor Roosevelt, published in the *Brooklyn Daily Eagle* on April 1, 1900, a reporter noted, "His motto, he says, he has taken from the South African people: 'Speak softly—carry a big stick—and you

will go far.'" Roosevelt would go on to be elected vice president later that year, and subsequently used the aphorism publicly in an address to the Minnesota State Fair, titled "National Duties," on September 2, 1901: "A good many of you are probably acquainted with the old proverb: Speak softly and carry a big stick—you will go far." Source: Wikipedia.

151 U.S. Medal of Honor Winners. See http://www.history.army.mil/moh/. Theodore Roosevelt is the only U.S. president to have received the Medal of Honor, which he was awarded posthumously. When the Spanish-American War broke out, Assistant Secretary of the Navy Theodore Roosevelt famously quit his job to lead a volunteer regiment known as the Rough Riders.

152 See Theodore Roosevelt Library, Naval History.

153 Theodore Roosevelt Center, Dickinson State University; Gilder Lerhman Institute of American History.

154 Sources used for Harry S. Truman biographical sketch include official White House website, Wikipedia, Biography.com, and Harry S. Truman Library.

155 Ibid.

156 Sources used for Ronald Reagan's biographical sketch include the official White House website, Biography.com, Wikipedia, Brittanica.com, The Reagan Presidential Library and history.com.

157 Wikipedia.com Ronald Wilson Reagan political history from democrat to conservative.

158 The Gilder Lehman Institute and USHistory.com.

159 Gallup tracked both Clinton and Trump since the 2016 primaries and well into the general election, as did other news agencies. These two sources were the most current at the time this book was completed: *Politico*, http://www.politico.com/story/2016/07/gallup-favorability-clinton-trump-226295; and *Newsweek*, http://www.newsweek.com/false-equivalence-clinton-trump-negatives-472818.

160 The House banking scandal broke in early 1992, when it was revealed that the United States House of Representatives allowed members to overdraw their House checking accounts without risk of being penalized by the House bank (actually a clearinghouse). This is also sometimes known as Rubber Gate (from "rubber check" (bounced check) and "Watergate"). The term is misleading because House checks did not bounce; they were honored because the House Bank provided overdraft protection to its account holders; the Office of the Sergeant at Arms covered the House Bank with no penalties. It was also sometimes known as the "check-kiting scandal." Representative Tommy Robinson (R-AR) was the worst

offender with over 996 bounced checks and Representative Robert Mrazek (D-NY), wrote well over 920 bounced checks, making him the second-worst abuser of the scam. Source: Wikipedia.

161 The GOP Contract with America was the conservative promise of more than three hundred Republican congressional candidates who signed it. Led by then Speaker of the House Newt Gingrich, the contract was presented at a September 27, 1994, national press conference.

162 Natural law is a philosophy that certain rights or values are inherent by virtue of human nature and universally cognizable through human reason. Historically, natural law refers to the use of reason to analyze both social and personal human nature to deduce binding rules of moral behavior. The law of nature, being determined by nature, is universal.

163 Article on the 1976 Bicentennial, https://fee.org/articles/a-theme-for-the-bicentennial-the-founding-fathers-fear-of-power/.

164 Wikipedia "Republicanism."

165 Sources for Abraham Lincoln biographical sketch include official White House website, Abraham Lincoln Presidential Library, History.com, and Britannica.com.

166 Gettysburg Address, President Abraham Lincoln.

167 Abraham Lincoln Presidential Library, Wikipedia on Abraham Lincoln military service. See https://en.wikipedia.org/wiki/Abraham_Lincoln_in_the_Black_Hawk_War.

168 NPR *All Things Considered*, interview with historian and author Harold Holzer, February 12, 2009.

169 Lincoln used the December 1, 1862, address to present a moderate message concerning his policy toward slavery. Just ten weeks before, he had issued his Emancipation Proclamation, which declared that slaves in territories still in rebellion as of January 1, 1863, would be free. The measure was not welcomed by everyone in the North—it met with considerable resistance from conservative Democrats who did not want to fight a war to free slaves.

170 Sources used for biographical sketch of Eleanor Roosevelt include Biography.com, official White House website, History.com, and Franklin D. Roosevelt Library.

171 Historian Geoffrey Ward in the PBS series *Eleanor Roosevelt* talked about her strength of character and her political savvy. Source: PBS.org.

172 Biography.com on Eleanor Roosevelt.

173 FDR Library, "Eleanor Roosevelt and the Tuskegee Airmen," and NPR, Mito Habe-Evans, "Eleanor Roosevelt and the First Black Aviators,"

March 25, 2011.

174 Gallup polling data beginning in 1948–98 tracked the most admired men and women in America. See http://www.gallup.com/poll/3415/most-admired-men-women-19481998.aspx.

175 Sources used for the biographical sketch on Margaret Chase Smith include Margaret Chase Smith Library, Biography.com, and History.com.

176 Sources used for the biographical sketch of Jack Kemp include Wikipedia, Biography.com, *Washington Post, New York Times, and Atlantic.*

177 Mort Kondracke and Fred Barnes, "The Jack Kemp Model for Republicans," *Wall Street Journal,* September 27, 2015.

178 Matthew Dallek, "Donald Trump is the Ultimate Republican Repudiation of Jack Kemp's Legacy," *Washington Post,* May 12, 2016, https://www.washingtonpost.com/posteverything/wp/2016/05/12/donald-trump-is-the-ultimate-republican-repudiation-of-jack-kemps-legacy/.

179 "Inclusion Matters or the Party of Lincoln Will Perish," *Huffington Post,* June 8, 2009; "The Reason I Became a Republican," *Root Magazine,* May 4, 2009.

180 Al Gini and Ronald M. Green, *Ten Virtues of Outstanding Leaders: Leadership and Character* (New York: Wiley, 2013).

181 The New Deal was a series of programs enacted in the United States between 1933 and 1938, and a few that came later. They included both laws passed by Congress as well as presidential executive orders during the first term (1933–37) of President Franklin D. Roosevelt. The programs were in response to the Great Depression, and focused on what historians refer to as the "Three R's": Relief, Recovery, and Reform: relief for the unemployed and poor, recovery of the economy to normal levels, and reform of the financial system to prevent a repeat depression.

182 Sources used for the biographical sketch of Thomas Jefferson include PBS, History.com, Biography.com, the official White House website, University of Virginia, and Monticello.

183 Ken Burns, PBS series, *The Roosevelts: An Intimate History.*

184 "Thomas Jefferson and Sally Hemings: A Brief Account," Monticello.org; Report of Research Committee on Thomas Jefferson and Sally Hemings done by the Thomas Jefferson Foundation. January 2000.

185 Lewis and Clark Expedition. Yankton, South Dakota, *National Geographic,* http://www.nationalgeographic.com/lewisandclark/record_tribes_019_2_8.html, and Lewis Clark Trail website. http://lewisandclarktrail.com/section2/sdcities/yankton/index.htm. Sacagawea helped the Lewis and Clark Expedition achieve each of its

chartered mission objectives exploring the Louisiana Purchase. With the expedition, between 1804 and 1806, she traveled thousands of miles from North Dakota to the Pacific Ocean, established cultural contacts with Native American populations, and researched natural history.

186 The Louisiana Purchase cost the U.S. $15 million in 1803. Sources: Library of Congress, Monticello, Wikipedia. There were thirteen states in that purchase.

187 Sources used for the biographical sketch of Franklin Roosevelt include the official White House website, Biography.com, and History.com.

188 The national unemployment rate fell from 25 percent to 2 percent under FDR's leadership. Sources: FDR Library, Wikipedia, History.com.

189 Sources for biographical sketch of Lyndon B. Johnson include LBJ Presidential Library, History.com, Biography.com, and official White House website.

190 Address to a Joint Session of Congress. November 27, 1963. This address was delivered by LBJ after the tragic death of President John F. Kennedy. In this speech Johnson calls for unity and to enact the civil rights legislation in memory of President Kennedy.

191 Source: Wikipedia. "The War on Poverty is the unofficial name for legislation first introduced by United States President Lyndon B. Johnson during his State of the Union address on January 8, 1964. This legislation was proposed by Johnson in response to a national poverty rate of around nineteen percent. The speech led the United States Congress to pass the Economic Opportunity Act, which established the Office of Economic Opportunity (OEO) to administer the local application of federal funds targeted against poverty. As a part of the Great Society, Johnson believed in expanding the federal government's roles in education and health care as poverty reduction strategies. These policies can also be seen as a continuation of Franklin D. Roosevelt's New Deal, which ran from 1933 to 1935, and the Four Freedoms of 1941. Johnson stated 'Our aim is not only to relieve the symptom of poverty, but to cure it and, above all, to prevent it.' The legacy of the War on Poverty policy initiative remains in the continued existence of such federal programs as Head Start, Volunteers in Service to America (VISTA), TRiO, and Job Corps."

192 Sources for the biographical sketch for President Barack H. Obama include the official White House website, various news reports, Biography. com, and History.com.

★ ★ ★ ★ ★ ★ ★ ★ ★ ★ ★ ★ ★ ★ ★ ★ ★

ABOUT THE AUTHOR

SOPHIA A. NELSON, ESQ.

B est known for her inspirational and self-help books for women around the globe, award-winning author and Washington, D.C., journalist Sophia A. Nelson, Esq., takes us on an inspirational and powerful journey through America's political soul.

Nelson covered the White House during the first term of the historic Obama administration for *Jet Magazine*. She has appeared on every major network around the world. She is a woman of deep principle and faith, who has written two best-selling (one award-winning) books. As a longtime Republican insider turned political journalist, Nelson's columns and her national TV and radio analyses speak to men and women from all walks of life. Her books are read by people of faith, corporate executives, people of color, women, leaders, and citizens around the world. She embodies the notion of "Oneness" and national unity in everything she does. Nelson lives in Virginia. Follow her on social media @iamsophianelson and on the book's website, Epluribus.one.

★ ★ ★ ★ ★ ★ ★ ★ ★ ★ ★ ★ ★ ★ ★ ★